AF696398

ECONOMICS AND THE WIND

ECONOMICS AND THE WIND

BRADLEY T. EWING
AND
JAMIE B. KRUSE
EDITORS

Nova Science Publishers, Inc.
New York

Copyright © 2005 by Nova Science Publishers, Inc.

All rights reserved. No part of this book may be reproduced, stored in a retrieval system or transmitted in any form or by any means: electronic, electrostatic, magnetic, tape, mechanical photocopying, recording or otherwise without the written permission of the Publisher.

For permission to use material from this book please contact us:
Telephone 631-231-7269; Fax 631-231-8175
Web Site: http://www.novapublishers.com

NOTICE TO THE READER
The Publisher has taken reasonable care in the preparation of this book, but makes no expressed or implied warranty of any kind and assumes no responsibility for any errors or omissions. No liability is assumed for incidental or consequential damages in connection with or arising out of information contained in this book. The Publisher shall not be liable for any special, consequential, or exemplary damages resulting, in whole or in part, from the readers' use of, or reliance upon, this material.

This publication is designed to provide accurate and authoritative information with regard to the subject matter covered herein. It is sold with the clear understanding that the Publisher is not engaged in rendering legal or any other professional services. If legal or any other expert assistance is required, the services of a competent person should be sought. FROM A DECLARATION OF PARTICIPANTS JOINTLY ADOPTED BY A COMMITTEE OF THE AMERICAN BAR ASSOCIATION AND A COMMITTEE OF PUBLISHERS.

LIBRARY OF CONGRESS CATALOGING-IN-PUBLICATION DATA:
Available Upon Request

ISBN: 1-59454-280-5.

Published by Nova Science Publishers, Inc. ✦ New York

CONTENTS

INTRODUCTION

This edited volume of papers addresses many of the economic issues surrounding wind-related disasters. The research and ideas expressed in this volume are necessarily multidisciplinary in nature. Wind events such as tornadoes, hurricanes, and cyclones affect regional economies, individual households and businesses, as well as entire industries. Consequently, it is important to understand the impact that wind has on the markets in which businesses and people interact. Moreover, households, firms and government policymakers may take steps to mitigate the losses and/or adverse effects associated with wind storms either before or after the event occurs. Thus, it is inevitable that the study of economics and wind would be intertwined.

Contributors include social scientists, economists, risk management and insurance specialists, and civil engineers from around the world. They include researchers from universities and private industry, many of whom are engaged in ongoing research programs funded by state and federal agencies. Several of the papers were presented at the 11th International Conference on Wind Engineering (ICWE) which was held in Lubbock, Texas in June 2003. This conference brought together some of the brightest individuals engaged in wind-related research and we are pleased to have these contributions in this volume. Other papers were first presented at the Wind Economics Session of the Southern Economic Association's annual meetings of 2002 and 2003. Additionally, we have invited several experts to contribute some of their work in this growing area of research.

The volume begins with a paper by one of the most distinguished experts on natural disasters. Professor Dennis Mileti addresses the multidisciplinary nature of wind-related research and the need for more research in this area. The remaining contributions can be grouped into four broad categories, which are not necessarily mutually exclusive. The first group of papers focuses on regional economic impacts of wind. The paper by Dakshina Desilva, Jamie Kruse, and Yongsheng Wang, as well as the paper by Bradley Ewing, Jamie Kruse and Mark Thompson looks at how local markets responded to tornadoes. The second group of papers addresses various insurance related aspects of wind. This group includes papers by George Walker; Siamak Daneshvaran and Robert Morden; and Bradley Ewing and Guillermo Covarrubias. Another set of papers looks specifically at behavioral microeconomic issues and decision-making toward risk. The papers by Jamie Kruse and Kevin Simmons; Ozlem Ozdemir; William Ridley, Daniel Sutter, and Kevin Simmons; and Robert Burrus, Christopher Dumas, and Edward Graham fall into this category. The fourth group of papers deals with cost-benefit analysis and value of life and included papers by John Whitehead;

John Crooker and Jamie Kruse; and Nicole Sadowski and Daniel Sutter. The paper by Chuck Howe and Hal Cochrane provides a set of guidelines for defining, identifying and measuring economic damages from natural hazards. The closing chapter of this volume is a paper by Kishor Mehta, an expert in wind engineering and a member of the National Academy of Engineering. In his paper, Professor Mehta discusses the multidisciplinary nature of wind science research and, in particular, the role that economics plays in this growing field.

Finally, we thank the fine people at Nova Science for their help in putting this volume of papers together. We also thank the contributors for all their hard work and for meeting deadlines on time.

Bradley T. Ewing and Jamie B. Kruse

In: Economics and the Wind
Editors: B. T. Ewing, et. al., pp. 1-12
ISBN: 1-59454-280-5
©2005 Nova Science Publishers, Inc.

Chapter 1

DISASTERS BY DESIGN

Dennis S. Mileti
Natural Hazards Center, University of Colorado, Boulder, CO

INTRODUCTION

A quarter-century ago geographer Gilbert F. White and sociologist J. Eugene Haas published a pioneering report on the United State's ability to withstand and respond to natural disasters (White and Haas, 1975). At that time, research on disasters was dominated by physical scientists and engineers. As White and Haas pointed out in their *Assessment of Research on Natural Hazards*, little attempt had been made to tap the social sciences to better understand the economic, social, and political dimensions of extreme natural events.

White and Haas attempted to fill this void. But they also advanced the critical notion that rather than simply picking up the pieces after disasters, the nation could employ better planning, land-use controls, and other preventive and mitigation measures to reduce the toll in the first place. Today, at long last, public and private programs and policies have begun to adopt mitigation as the cornerstone of the United State's approach to addressing natural and technological hazards.

The 1975 report also had a profound impact by paving the way for an interdisciplinary approach to research and management, giving birth to a "hazards community"-people from many fields and agencies that address the myriad aspects of natural disasters. Hazards research now encompasses disciplines such as climatology, economics, engineering, geography, geology, law, meteorology, planning, seismology, and sociology. Professionals in those and other fields have continued to investigate how engineering projects, warnings, land-use management, planning for response and recovery, insurance, and building codes can help individuals and groups adapt to natural hazards, as well as reduce the resulting deaths, injuries, costs, and social, environmental, and economic disruption. These people have improved our understanding during, and after disasters. Yet troubling questions remain about why more progress has not been made in reducing dollar losses.

One central problem is that many of the accepted methods for coping with hazards have been based on the idea that people can use technology to control nature to make themselves safe. What's more, most strategies for managing hazards have followed a traditional planning model: study the problem, implement one solution, and move on to the next problem. This approach casts hazards as static and mitigation as an upward, positive, linear trend.

But events during the past quarter-century have shown that natural disasters and the technological hazards that may accompany them are not linear problems that can be solved in isolation. Rather, they are symptoms of broader and more basic problems. Losses from hazards—and the fact that the United States cannot seem to reduce them—result from shortsighted and narrow conceptions of the human relationship to the natural environment.

To redress those shortcomings, a shift is needed to a policy of "sustainable hazard mitigation." This concept links wise management of natural resources with local economic and social resiliency, viewing hazard mitigation as an integral part of a much larger context. Many aspects of this strategy were implicit in the recommendations formulated by White and Haas a quarter-century ago. But to head off the continued rise in tolls from disasters, those principles must become more explicit.

This paper, and the report on which it is based (Mileti, 1999), reflect the efforts of over a hundred experts who have worked and debated since 1994 to take stock of Americans' relationship to hazards past, present, and—most importantly- future. Those contributions have been used to outline a comprehensive approach to enhancing society's ability to reduce the costs of disaster.

THE ROOTS OF THE PROBLEM

Many disaster losses—rather than stemming from unexpected events—are the predictable results of interactions among three major systems: the physical environment, which includes hazardous events; the social and demographic characteristics of the communities that experience them; and the buildings, roads, bridges, and other components of the constructed environment. Growing losses in the United States result partly from the fact that the nation's capital stock is expanding, but they also stem from the fact that all these systems—and their interactions—are becoming more complex with each passing year.

Three main influences are at work. First, the earth's physical systems are constantly changing—witness the current warming of the global climate. Scientists expect a warming climate to produce more dramatic meteorological events such as storms, floods, drought, and extreme temperatures. Second, recent and projected changes in the demographic composition and distribution of the U.S. population mean greater exposure to many hazards. The number of people residing in earthquake-prone regions and coastal counties subject to hurricanes, for example, is growing rapidly. Worsening inequality of wealth also makes many people more vulnerable to hazards and less able to recover from them. Third, the built environment—public utilities, transportation systems, communications, and homes and office buildings—is growing in density, making the potential losses from natural forces larger.

Settlement of hazardous areas has also destroyed local ecosystems that could have provided protection from natural perils. The draining of swamps in Florida and the bulldozing of steep hillsides for homes in California, for example, have disrupted natural runoff patterns and magnified flood hazards. And many mitigation efforts themselves degrade the environment and thus contribute to the next disaster. For example, levees built to provide flood protection can destroy riparian habitat and heighten downstream floods.

Another major problem has become clear over the past 20 years: some efforts to head off damages from natural hazards only postpone them. For example, communities below dams or behind levees may avoid losses from floods those structures were designed to prevent. But such communities often have more property to lose when those structures fail, because additional development occurred that counted on protection. Such a situation contributed to catastrophic damage from the 1993 floods in the Mississippi basin. And many of the U.S.'s dams, bridges, and other structures are approaching the end of their designed life revealing how little thought their backers and builders gave to events 50 years hence. Similarly, by providing advance warnings of severe storms, the U.S. may well have encouraged more people to build in fragile coastal areas. Such development, in turn, makes the areas more vulnerable by destroying dunes and other protective natural features.

WHO IS AT RISK

Research has shown that people are typically unaware of all the risks and choices they face. They plan only for the immediate future, overestimate their ability to cope when disaster strikes, and rely heavily on emergency relief.

Hazard researchers now also recognize that demographic differences play a large role in determining the risks people encounter, whether and how they prepare for disasters, and how they fare when disasters occur. For example, non-minorities and households with higher socioeconomic status fare better, while low-income households are at a greater risk mainly because they live in lower-quality housing, and because disasters exacerbate poverty.

The need for mitigation and response efforts that acknowledge the demographic differences among U.S. citizens will become even more critical as the U.S. population becomes more diverse. Research is also needed to shed further light on how mitigation programs ranging from public education to disaster relief can be rendered equitably.

DISASTER LOSSES ARE GROWING IN THE UNITED STATES

From 1975 to 1994, natural hazards killed over 24,000 people and injured some 100,000 in the United States and its territories. About one-quarter of the deaths and half the injuries resulted from events that society would label as disasters. The rest resulted from less dramatic but more frequent events such as lightning strikes, car crashes owing to fog, and localized landslides.

The United States has succeeded in saving lives and reducing injuries from some natural hazards such as hurricanes over the last two decades. However, casualties from floods—the nation's most frequent and injurious natural hazard—have failed to decline substantially. And deaths from lightning and tornadoes have remained constant. Meanwhile injuries and deaths from dust storms, extreme cold, wildfire, and tropical storms have grown.

The dollar losses associated with most types of natural hazards in the U.S. are rising. A conservative estimate of total dollar losses during the past two decades is $500 billion (in

1994 dollars). More than 80% of these costs stemmed from climatological events, while around 10% resulted from earthquakes and volcanoes. Only 17% were insured. Determining losses with a higher degree of accuracy is impossible because the United States has not established a systematic reporting method or a single repository for the data. Further, these numbers do not include indirect costs such as downtime for businesses, lost employment, environmental damage, or emotional effects on victims. Most of these losses result from events too small to qualify for federal assistance, and most are not insured, so victims must bear the costs.

Seven of the ten most costly disasters–based on dollar losses–in the U.S. history occurred between 1989 and 1994. In fact, since 1989 the nation has frequently entered periods in which losses from catastrophic natural disasters averaged about $1 billion per week. The dramatic increase in disaster losses is expected to continue.

Many of the harshest recent disasters could have been far worse: had Hurricane Andrew been slower and wetter or torn through downtown Miami, for example, it would have wreaked devastation even more profound than the damage it did inflict. And the most catastrophic likely events, including a great earthquake in the Los Angeles area, have not yet occurred. Such a disaster would cause up to 5,000 deaths, 15,000 serious injuries, and $250 billion in direct economic losses.

A New Approach to Hazards

Researchers and practitioners in the hazards community need to shift their strategy to cope with the complex factors that contribute to disasters in today's—and especially tomorrow's-world. Here are the main guidelines for improving our ability to mitigate hazards.

Adopt a Global Systems Perspective

Rather than resulting from surprise environmental events, disasters arise from the interactions among the earth's physical systems, its human systems, and its built infrastructure. A broad view that encompasses all three of these dynamic systems and interactions among them can enable us to find better solutions.

Accept Responsibility for Hazards and Disasters

Human beings—not nature—are the cause of disaster losses, which stem from choices about where and how human development will proceed. Nor is there a final solution to natural hazards, since technology cannot make the world safe from all the forces of nature.

Anticipate Ambiguity and Change

The view that hazards are relatively static has led to the false conclusion that any mitigation effort is desirable and will—in some vague way—reduce the grand total of future losses. In reality, change can occur quickly and nonlinearly. Human adaptation to hazards must become as dynamic as the problems presented by hazards themselves.

Reject Short-term Thinking

Mitigation as frequently conceived is too shortsighted. In general, people have a cultural and economic predisposition to think primarily in the short term. Sustainable mitigation will require a longer-term view that takes into account the overall effect of mitigation efforts on this and future generations.

Account for Social Forces

Societal factors, such as how people view both hazards and mitigation efforts or how the free market operates, play a critical role in determining which steps are actually taken, which are overlooked, and thus the extent of future disaster losses. Because such social forces are now known to be much more powerful than disaster specialists previously thought, growing understanding of physical systems and improved technology cannot suffice. To effectively address natural hazards, mitigation must become a basic social value.

Embrace Sustainable Development Principles

Disasters are more likely where unsustainable development occurs, and the converse is also true: disasters hinder movement toward sustainability because, for example, they degrade the environment and undercut the quality of life. Sustainable mitigation activities should strengthen a community's social, economic, and environmental resiliency, and vice versa.

FOSTERING LOCAL SUSTAINABILITY

Sustainability means that a locality can tolerate—and overcome—damage, diminished productivity, and reduced quality of life from an extreme event without significant outside assistance. To achieve sustainability, communities must take responsibility for choosing where and how development proceeds. Toward that end, each locality evaluates its environmental resources and hazards, chooses future losses that it is willing to bear, and ensures that development and other community actions and policies adhere to those goals.

Six objectives must simultaneously be reached to mitigate hazards in a sustainable way and stop the trend toward increasing catastrophic losses from natural disasters.

Maintain and Enhance Environmental Quality

Human activities to mitigate hazards should not reduce the carrying capacity of the ecosystem, for doing so increases losses from hazards in the longer term.

Maintain and Enhance People's Quality of Life

A population's quality of life includes, among other factors, access to income, education, health care, housing, and employment, as well as protection from disaster. To become sustainable, local communities must consciously define the quality of life they want and select only those mitigation strategies that do not detract from any aspect of that vision.

Foster Local Resiliency and Responsibility

Resiliency to disasters means a locale can withstand an extreme natural event with a tolerable level of losses. It takes mitigation actions consistent with achieving that level of protection.

Recognize that Vibrant Local Economies are Essential

Communities should take mitigation actions that foster a strong local economy rather than detract from one.

Ensure Inter- and Intra-generational Equity

A sustainable community selects mitigation activities that reduce hazards across all ethnic, racial, and income groups, and between genders equally, now and in the future. The costs of today's advances are not shifted onto later generations or less powerful groups.

Adopt Local Consensus Building

A sustainable community selects mitigation strategies that evolve from full participation among all public and private stakeholders. The participatory process itself may be as important as the outcome.

A long term, comprehensive plan for averting disaster losses and encouraging sustainability offers a locality the opportunity to coordinate its goals and policies. A community can best forge such a plan by tapping businesses and residents as well as experts and government officials. And while actual planning and follow-through must occur at the local level, a great deal of impetus must come from above. Nothing short of strong leadership from state and federal governments will ensure that planning for sustainable hazard mitigation and development occurs.

Mitigation Tools

Over the past few decades an array of techniques and practices has evolved to reduce and cope with losses from hazards and disasters. These and other tools will be vital in pursuing sustainable hazard mitigation.

Land Use

Wise land-use planning that limits expansion into sensitive areas is essential to sustainable hazard mitigation. Indeed, land-use planning, hazard mitigation, and sustainable communities are concepts with a shared vision in which people and property are kept out of the way of hazards, the mitigative qualities of the natural environment are maintained, and development is resilient in the face of natural forces.

Unfortunately, no overarching guidance informs development in hazard-prone areas of the United States. Instead, a patchwork of innumerable federal, state, and local regulations creates a confusing picture and often reduces short-term losses while allowing the potential for catastrophic losses to grow. This scattershot approach, as well as the federal and state trend to cut risk and assume liability, have undermined the responsibility of local governments for using land-use management techniques to reduce exposure to hazards.

Warnings

Since the first assessment was completed, significant improvements in short-term forecasts and warnings (hours to days ahead of a hazardous event) have dramatically reduced loss of life and injury in the United States. Yet many communities lag in their ability to provide citizens with effective warning messages. The nation needs to make local warning systems more uniform, develop a comprehensive model for how they work, and provide this information to local communities along with technical assistance. Better local management and decision-making are now more critical than most future advances in technology.

It's also important to remember that short-term warning systems do not significantly limit damage to the built environment, nor do they mitigate economic disruption from disasters. Long-range forecasts that help define the risks to local communities years to decades ahead of potential hazards could assist local decision makers in designing their communities to endure them.

Engineering and Building Codes

The ability of the built environment to withstand the impacts of natural forces plays a direct role in determining the casualties and dollar costs of disasters. Disaster-resistant construction of buildings and infrastructure is therefore an essential component of local resiliency. Engineering codes, standards, and practices have been promulgated for natural hazards. Local governments have also traditionally enacted building codes. However, investigations after disasters have revealed shortcomings in construction techniques and code enforcement. Codes, standards, and practices for all hazards must be reevaluated in light of the goal of sustainable mitigation, and communities must improve adherence to them.

Insurance

The public increasingly looks to insurance to compensate for losses from many types of risk-taking behavior. However, most property owners do not buy coverage against special perils, notably earthquakes, hurricanes, and floods. For example, nationwide only about 20 percent of the homes exposed to floods are insured for them. Many people assume that federal disaster assistance will function as a kind of hazard insurance, but such aid is almost always limited. And even when larger amounts are available, they are usually offered in the form of loans, not outright grants.

Insurance does help minimize some disruption by ensuring that people with coverage receive compensation for their losses as they begin to recover. The insurance industry could facilitate mitigation by providing information and education, helping to create model codes, offering financial incentives that encourage mitigation, and limiting the availability of insurance in high-hazard areas.

The industry already has problems providing insurance in areas subject to catastrophic losses because many insurers do not have the resources to pay for a worst case disaster. Furthermore, the current regulatory system makes it difficult for an insurance company to aggregate adequate capital to cover low-frequency but high-consequence events.

New Technology

Computer-mediated communication systems, geographic information systems (GIS), remote sensing, electronic decision-support systems, and risk-analysis techniques have developed substantially during the last two decades and show great promise for supporting sustainable hazard mitigation. For example, GIS models enable managers to consolidate information from a range of disciplines, including the natural and social sciences and engineering, and to formulate plans accordingly.

Remote sensing can be used to make land-use maps and show changes over time, feed information to GIS models, and gather information in the wake of disasters. Finally, decision-support systems can fill a gap in hazards management by analyzing information from core databases, including data on building inventories, infrastructure, demographics, and risk. The systems can then be used to ask "what-if" questions about future losses to inform today's decision making. Such systems are now constrained by the lack of comprehensive local data, but they will become more important as the process of evaluating and managing risk grows in complexity.

Emergency Preparedness and Recovery

Even if encouraged by more holistic state and federal policies, sustainable hazard mitigation will never eliminate the need for plans to address the destruction and human suffering imposed by disasters. In fact, one way to progress toward sustainable hazard mitigation is by creating policies for disaster preparedness, response, and recovery that support that goal.

A great deal of research has focused on pre-disaster planning and response since the 1975 assessment. Studies have found that pre-disaster planning can save lives and injuries, limit property damage, and minimize disruptions, enabling communities to recover more quickly.

Recovery was once viewed as a linear phenomenon, with discrete stages and end products. Today it is seen as a process that entails decision making and interaction among all stakeholders—households, businesses, and the community at large. Research has also shown that recovery is most effective when community-based organizations assume principal responsibility, supplemented by outside technical and financial assistance. An even further shift—away from an exclusive focus on restoring damaged structures toward effective decision making at all levels—may be needed. Outside technical assistance can help strengthen local organizational and decision-making capacity.

Local leaders too often fail to take advantage of the recovery period to reshape their devastated communities to withstand future events. Most local disaster plans need to be extended not only to explicitly address recovery and reconstruction but to identify opportunities for rebuilding in safer ways and in safer places.

Fortunately, revisions to disaster legislation in the last several years have allowed a greater percentage of federal relief monies to fund mitigation programs. Pre-disaster planning for post-disaster recovery is vital to communities' ability to become disaster resilient.

Essential Steps

The shift to a sustainable approach to hazard mitigation will require extraordinary actions. Here are several essential steps; many initial efforts are already under way in the United States.

Building Local Networks, Capability, and Consensus

Today hazard specialists, emergency planners, resource managers, community planners, and other local stakeholders seek to solve problems on their own. An approach is needed to forge local consensus on disaster resiliency and nurture it through the complex challenges of planning and implementation.

One potential approach is a "sustainable hazard mitigation network" in each of the nation's communities that would engage in collaborative problem solving. Each network would produce an integrated, comprehensive plan linking land-use, environmental, social, and economic goals. An effective plan would also identify hazards, estimate potential losses, and assess the region's environmental carrying capacity. The stakeholder network especially needs to determine the amount and kind of damage that those who experience disasters can bear. These plans would enable policymakers, businesses, and residents to understand the limitations of their region and work together to address them. Full consensus may never be reached, but the process is key because it can generate ideas and foster the sense of community required to mitigate hazards.

This kind of holistic approach will also situate mitigation in the context of other community goals that, historically, have worked against action to reduce hazards. Finally, the process will advance the idea that each locality controls the character of its disasters, forcing stakeholders to take responsibility for natural hazards and resources and realize that the decisions they make today will determine future losses.

Federal and state agencies could provide leadership in this process by sponsoring–through technical and financial support–a few prototype networks such as model communities or regional projects.

Establish a Holistic Government Framework

To facilitate sustainable mitigation, all policies and programs related to hazards and sustainability should be integrated and consistent. One possible approach toward this goal is a conference or series of conferences that enable federal, state, county, and city officials to reexamine the statutory and regulatory foundations of hazard mitigation and preparedness, in light of the principles of sustainable mitigation. Potential changes include limiting the subsidization of risk, making better use of incentives, setting a federal policy for guiding land use, and fostering collaborations among agencies, nongovernmental organizations, and the private sector.

Other efforts to foster a comprehensive government framework could include a joint congressional committee hearing, a congressional report, a conference by the American Planning Association to review experiences in sample communities, and a joint meeting of federal, state, and professional research organizations.

Conduct a Nationwide Hazard and Risk Assessment

Not enough is known about the changes in or interactions among the physical, social, and constructed systems that are reshaping the nation's hazardous future. A national risk assessment should meld information from those three systems so hazards can be estimated interactively and comprehensively, to support local efforts on sustainable mitigation.

Local planning will require multi-hazard, community-scale risk assessment maps that incorporate information ranging from global physical processes to local resources and buildings. This information is not now available, and will require federal investment in research on risk-analysis tools and dissemination to local governments.

Build National Databases

The nation must collect, analyze, and store standardized data on losses from past and current disasters, thereby establishing a baseline for comparison with future losses. This database should include information on the types of losses, their locations, their specific causes, and the actual dollar amounts, taking into account problems of double-counting, comparisons with gross domestic product, and the distinction between regional and national impacts. A second database is needed to collate information on mitigation efforts–what they are, where they occur, and how much they cost–to provide a baseline for local cost-benefit analysis. These archives are fundamental to informed decision making and should be accessible to the public.

A central repository for hazard-related social science data is also lacking. This third central archive would speed development of standards for collecting and analyzing information on the social aspects of hazards and disasters.

Provide Comprehensive Education and Training

Today hazard managers are being called upon to tackle problems they have never before confronted, such as understanding complex physical and social systems, conducting sophisticated cost-benefit analyses, and offering long-term solutions. Education in hazard mitigation and preparedness should therefore expand to include interdisciplinary and holistic degree programs. Members of the higher education community will have to invent university-based programs that move away from traditional disciplines toward interdisciplinary education that solves the real-world problems entailed in linking hazards and sustainability. This will require not only new degree programs but also changes in the way institutions of higher education reward faculty, who now are encouraged to do theoretical work.

Measure Progress

Baselines for measuring sustainability should be established now so the nation can gauge future progress. Interim goals for mitigation and other aspects of managing hazards should be set, and progress in reaching those goals regularly evaluated. This effort will require determining how to apply criteria such as disaster resiliency, environmental quality, intra- and inter-generational equity, quality of life, and economic vitality to the plans and programs of local communities.

Also important is evaluating hazard-mitigation efforts already in place before taking further steps in the same direction. For example, the National Flood Insurance Program, which combines insurance incentives, and land-use and building standards, has existed for 30 years, yet its effectiveness has never been thoroughly appraised.

Each disaster yields new knowledge relevant to hazard mitigation and disaster response and recovery, yet no entity collects this information systematically, synthesizes it into a coherent body of knowledge, and evaluates the nation's progress in putting knowledge into practice. Systematic post-disaster audits, called for in the 1975 assessment by White and Haas, are still needed.

Share Knowledge Internationally

The United States must share knowledge and technology related to sustainable hazard mitigation with other nations, and be willing to learn from those nations as well. In the U.S. and abroad, disaster experts also need to collaborate with development experts to address the root causes of vulnerability to hazards, including overgrazing, deforestation, poverty, and unplanned development. Disaster reduction should be an inherent part of everyday development processes, and international development projects must consider vulnerability to disaster.

THE KEY ROLE OF THE HAZARDS COMMUNITY

To support sustainable mitigation, researchers and practitioners need to ask new questions as well as continue to investigate traditional topics. Important efforts will include interdisciplinary research and education, and the development of local hazard assessments, computer-generated decision-making aids, and holistic government policies.

Future work must also focus on techniques for enlisting public and governmental support for making sustainable hazard mitigation a fundamental social value. Members of the hazards community will play a critical role in initiating the urgently needed national and global conversations on attaining that goal.

REFERENCES

Mileti, D S. (1999), *Disasters by Design: A Reassessment of Natural Hazards in the United States,* Joseph Henry Press, Washington D.C.

White, G F and Haas, J E. (1975) *Assessment of Research on Natural Hazards,* The Massachusetts Institute of Technology Press, Cambridge, Massachusetts

In: Economics and the Wind
Editors: B. T. Ewing, et. al., pp. 13-23
ISBN: 1-59454-280-5
©2005 Nova Science Publishers, Inc.

Chapter 2

FUJITA SCALE AND DOLLAR LOSSES: EVIDENCE FROM THE MAY 1999 OKLAHOMA CITY TORNADO

Dakshina G. De Silva
Department of Economics, Texas Tech University, Lubbock, TX
Jamie Brown Kruse
Wind Science and Engineering Research Center, Texas Tech University, Lubbock, TX, and Center for Natural Hazards Mitigation, East Carolina University, Greenville, NC
Yongsheng Wang
Department of Economics, Texas Tech University, Lubbock, TX

INTRODUCTION

The purpose of this study is to examine the relationship between two measures of damage caused by a tornado. We use the well known *F* scale, an engineering-based measure of tornado damage [Fujita, 1971]. We relate the *F* scale assignment to an economic measure of damage—more specifically, the estimate of the reduction in property market value assigned by the office of a county tax assessor. We use data from the May 3, 1999 tornado outbreak that damaged homes in Oklahoma County.

In the RAND Report entitled, "Assessing Federal Research and Development for Hazard Loss Reduction," Meade and Abbott (2003) identify the lack of accurate economic loss data as a severe constraint to measuring the effectiveness of national hazard loss Research and Development. The research reported in this paper contributes to the effort to fill the gap described by Meade and Abbott (2003) as the *missing metric.* Our dataset includes F-scale damage ratings that were assigned individually to damaged buildings by a damage survey team comprised of researchers from Texas Tech University and led by T. Marshall. (See Marshall (2002) for details). The Fujita Scale or *F*-scale [Fujita, 1971] has become the standard method for classifying tornado intensity. It has been used to rate tornadoes in the

U.S. since the mid 1970's.[McCarthy, 2003] Further, storms prior to 1971 were retroactively rated to create a national database that contains about 50,000 observations and spans over fifty years. [http://www.spc.noaa.gov/archive/tornadoes/] The Fujita scale infers information about wind speeds from damage characteristics [Blong, 2003]. The estimated wind speeds reported for the Fujita Scale are much debated and, to date, have not been scientifically verified. The original scale had twelve levels roughly related to the Beaufort scale and Mach number 1 [McDonald, 2000]. The damage associated with each F-scale rating is described as follows: light (*F0*), moderate (*F1*), considerable (*F2*), severe (*F3*), devastating (*F4*), incredible (*F5*), and finally, inconceivable (*F6-F12*). Although popularly accepted, the limitations of F-scale are widely recognized by the engineering and meteorological scientific community [McDonald and Mehta, 2002]. The precision of the damage assessment can suffer due to regional variation, personal variation and expertise of the assessment team, as well as the construction quality of the structures that are rated [Mani, McDonald, and Mehta, 2003]. Although alternatives to the original (eg. Modified F-Scale, Enhanced F-Scale) have been proposed, none have replaced the Fujita standard [McDonald and Mehta, 2002]. The incidence of tornadoes (which is usually reported as the return period, i.e., reciprocal of the annual probability) and their F-scale ratings are used to identify regions of the U.S. that are vulnerable to extreme winds. In addition, special-purpose engineered buildings such as nuclear power plants and corporate facilities use estimates of tornadic wind loads in their design requirements. The F-scale gives a measure of the ferocity of the tornado in physical damage terms. Table 1 gives the estimated wind speeds and description of damage for each F-scale rating.

Monetizing the losses gives a measure of the economic harm done by a tornado. Severe and especially devastating windstorms are accompanied with estimates of economic losses in the public storm reports. There have been relatively few studies that have used disaggregate data to examine the relationship between severe wind storms and direct economic losses. Scholarly research that relates monetary losses to wind storm characteristics has been reported by Sparks et al (1994), Huang et al (2001), Sparks (2003). This work has focused on insured losses that relate to tropical storms and hurricanes. In order to estimate direct economic damage values to human-made capital assets Howe and Cochrane (1993) state that the *depreciated replacement value* is the appropriate economic value measure. One potential bias in using insured losses is that they often reflect a "replacement plus upgrade" value. For example, Sparks (2003) assumes that the insured value of the property was 150% of the value of the structure. There have been relatively few studies that have used micro level data to examine the relationship between severe wind storms and direct economic losses. Kruse, Simmons, and Tiglioglu (1999), using limited data from the April 6, 1998, Nashville Tornado, explored the relationship between monetary losses as determined by the county tax assessor and the damaged structure's distance from the tornado's path. Individual F-scale damage ratings were not available and therefore not used in this analysis. Shaw et al (2001) examined the relationship between radar images of the May 3, 1999 Oklahoma City Tornado and economic damage using the OKC Tax assessor's data base. Kruse et al (2001) provides a summary of the information collected from the OKC Tax Assessor, Insurance claims paid out, and the Texas Tech Damage Assessment reports. Neither of these papers provides a statistical analysis of the relationship between the damage measures.

Table 1. The Fujita Scale

F-Scale Number	Intensity Phrase	Wind Speed	Type of Damage Done
F0	Gale tornado	40-72 mph	Some damage to chimneys; breaks branches off trees; pushes over shallow-rooted trees; damages sign boards.
F1	Moderate tornado	73-112 mph	The lower limit is the beginning of hurricane wind speed; peels surface off roofs; mobile homes pushed off foundations or overturned; moving autos pushed off the roads; attached garages may be destroyed.
F2	Significant tornado	113-157 mph	Considerable damage. Roofs torn off frame houses; mobile homes demolished; boxcars pushed over; large trees snapped or uprooted; light object missiles generated.
F3	Severe tornado	158-206 mph	Roof and some walls torn off well constructed houses; trains overturned; most trees in fores uprooted
F4	Devastating tornado	207-260 mph	Well-constructed houses leveled; structures with weak foundations blown off some distance; cars thrown and large missiles generated.
F5	Incredible tornado	261-318 mph	Strong frame houses lifted off foundations and carried considerable distances to disintegrate; automobile sized missiles fly through the air in excess of 100 meters; trees debarked; steel re-enforced concrete structures badly damaged.
F6	Inconceivable tornado	319-379 mph	These winds are very unlikely. The small area of damage they might produce would probably not be recognizable along with the mess produced by F4 and F5 wind that would surround the F6 winds. Missiles, such as cars and refrigerators would do serious secondary damage that could not be directly identified as F6 damage. If this level is ever achieved, evidence for it might only be found in some manner of ground swirl pattern, for it may never be identifiable through engineering studies

Source: http://www.tornadoproject.com/fscale/fscale.htm

In order to evaluate the effectiveness of hazard mitigation investment we need an adequate description of the monetary losses associated with tornadoes of different intensities and their associated probabilities. Although it is imprecise, the large national database of tornado damage ratings provides the necessary basis for statistical loss modeling. A better understanding of the relationship between F-scale ratings and monetary losses is useful for public officials charged with cost effective mitigation planning decisions. This research should also help in projecting the impact of a tornado on school, county and municipal budgets that are funded through property tax revenue on the one hand and serve as the funding source for emergency response and recovery on the other hand. In addition, our results should be useful for insurance companies by providing an alternative to insured losses that is calibrated in dollar terms. Since insured loss information is proprietary, the estimated market value of real property (public information) can serve as a basis to evaluate relative loss exposure.

DATA

In this study, we examine the impact of the Oklahoma City May 3, 1999 tornado using data from the Oklahoma County Tax Assessor (OKCTA) and the Texas Tech Damage Assessment (Marshall, 2002). From the OKCTA, we obtained information about the assessed value of real property before and after the tornado and other characteristics of homes such as year built, parcel ID, area in square feet, roof type, number of floors, location, and zip code. The tax assessor's office also provided their assessment of percent damage due to the May 3, 1999 tornado. The assessed value is the OKCTA's estimate of the current market value of a property. The properties each have a parcel identification number. When a property is damaged by a tornado, even if the structure is totally destroyed, the lot remains. However, the cost of cleaning up and salvaging the lot would also reduce the market price at which the lot would change hands. The OKCTA estimate of loss in market value reflects the cost of salvage operation as well as the destruction of the structure.

The Texas Tech damage assessment included individual F-scale damage assignments on hand-drawn maps on several hundred homes that were in the path of the tornado that passed through Moore, OK and continued into Del City in Oklahoma County. The fact that the F-scale rating was assigned on a house-by-house basis provides the opportunity to construct a unique data set. The structural integrity of each building was taken into consideration when damage ratings were assigned as suggested by Fujita (1992). The Texas Tech F-Scale damage assessment took the quality of construction into consideration, and was performed by the same team of trained professionals in the same region and therefore should not be subject to some of the previous mentioned sources of inconsistency. After putting the information in digital form, this data set includes all the information available from OKCTA by parcel ID and corresponding F-scales for the May 3, 1999 OKC tornado in the Del City Area. From these data sources, we were able to cross match and identify 89 residential houses damaged by the tornado near the Del Air, Del Brook, and Frolich Heights subdivisions in Del City.

Table 2 provides descriptive statistics for the houses before and after the tornado. Figure 1 illustrates the relationship between dollar loss (where dollar losses are calculated as follows: $value_{98}$ - $value_{99}$) and F-scale. This figure shows considerable dispersion in dollar losses, especially for the *F-0* damage rating, which ranges from \$7,000 to \$83,000. Since ratio scales of damage are considered to be more potentially useful we construct a ratio scale for the sample [Blong, 2003]. Note that relative dollar losses are calculated as follows: $\{(value_{98} - value_{99})/ value_{98}\}$. The relationship between the loss ratio and the F-scale assignment is shown in Figure 2. Casual observation of this figure indicates that the modal loss ratio for all F-scales is 80-90%. For the damage rating of *F-0*, the loss ratio is still quite dispersed as it ranges from 12% and 91%. The *F-0* damage rating was originally intended to reflect the case where winds are less than hurricane force. A tropical storm becomes a named hurricane of Category 1 on the Saffir-Simpson Scale when the sustained wind speed reaches 70 miles per hour. The original Fujita Scale estimate of wind speed in an *F-0* tornado was 40-70 miles per hour. Wind speeds associated with *F0*, *F1* and *F2* generally match current residential damage descriptions according to Minor et al. (1977). The International Building Code (2000) indicates that in the Midwest, buildings should be able to withstand a three-second 90-miles-per-hour gust of wind. It is noteworthy that, an interpretation of Figure 1 and Figure 2 must be tempered by the fact that we have not *statistically* controlled for building or wind damage characteristics. Therefore a more careful analysis using standard methods of ordinary least squares (OLS) is reported in the next section.

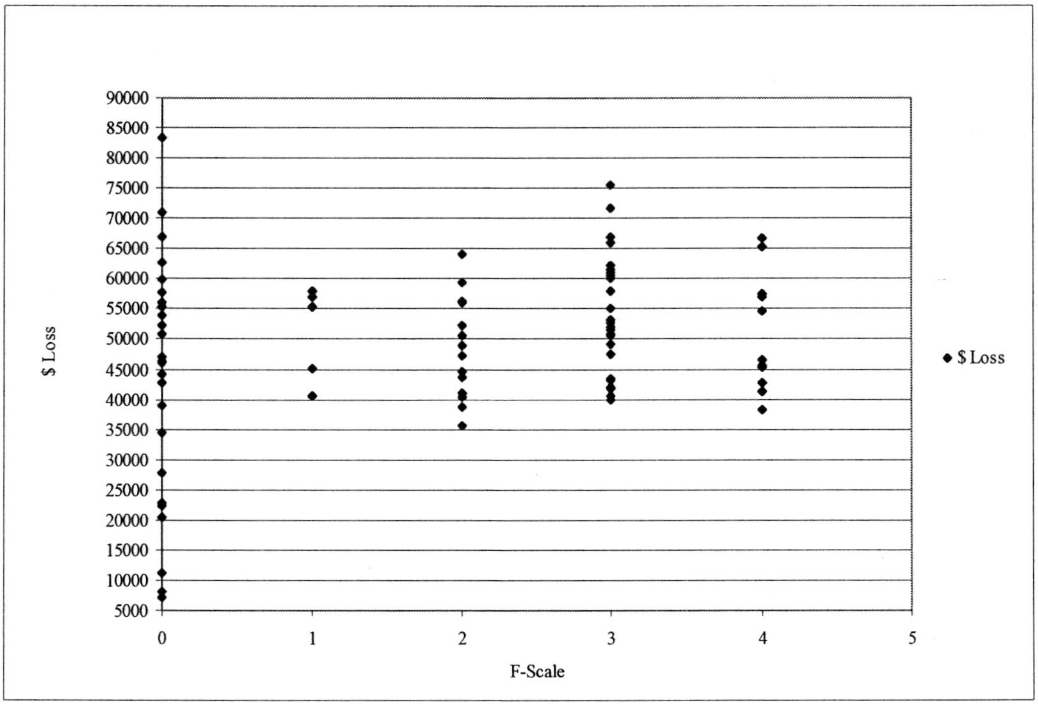

Figure 1. F-Scale and Dollar Loss .

Table 2. Descriptive Statistics of Damaged Houses

	Damaged Houses	
Variable	**Before Tornado**	**After Tornado**
Number of Units		
Value	59823.65	11205.67
	(9529.79)	(14126.26)
Number of Square Feet	1327.25	—
	(295.856)	
Number of Floors	1.034	—
	(0.146)	

Note: Standard errors are in parentheses.

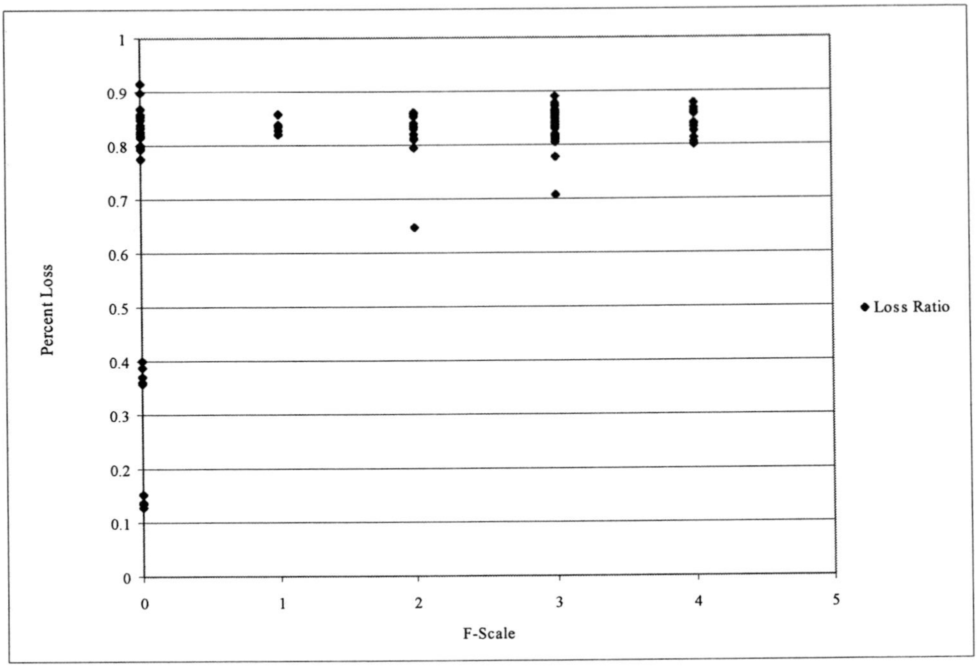

Figure 2. F-Scale and Percent Loss

Empirical Analysis

In this section we empirically model the impact of wind damage on the market value of residential houses. The basic structure of the regression model is as follows:

$$y_i = W\mathrm{B} + H\Gamma + \varepsilon_i$$

Our regressions use either total dollar losses per parcel or the dollar loss ratio as the dependent variable, y. Dollar losses and the loss ratio are measured as described earlier in the discussion of Figures 1 and 2 and taken from the OKCTA data. The independent variables include two sets of controls where W controls for wind characteristics and H controls for building characteristics.

In modeling wind damage characteristics, we have created four dummy variables, *F-1, F-2, F-3,* and *F-4*, to identify wind storm intensity. The omitted group is *F-0*. These variables should capture the variation in losses that can be attributed to wind storm intensity as indicated by the observed physical damage.

To describe building characteristics, we included the following variables taken from the OKCTA data. In order to control for the size of the house, we included two variables, *Number of Stories* and the area in *Number of Square Feet*. The variable, *Year Built*, captures the variation in losses due to building age. There are three roof types in the sample (hip, gable and flat). We included dummy variables to capture the variation in losses due to roof types.

The roof type dummy variables are *Roof Type-Hip* and *Roof Type-Gable* leaving flat roof types as the omitted group.

When investigating dollar losses, we used the OLS technique to investigate the loss in market value of 89 residential dwellings that were damaged in the May 3, 1999 Oklahoma City Tornado. Table 3 provides summary statistics on the regression variables. From this table we see that the mean dollar loss was $48,618. We see that 6% of the sample had an *F-1* damage rating, 16% were *F-2*, 36% were *F-3*, 12% were *F-4* with the remaining 30% at an *F-0* damage rating. By today's standards the homes in the sample were relatively small with an average area of 1378 square feet. As for roof types, 33% were hip, 54% were gable , and 13% were flat.

Table 3. Summary Statistics of Regression Variables

Variable	Sample
Loss	48617.98
	(14126.26)
Loss Ratio	0.776
	(0.178)
F-1	0.06
	(0.23)
F-2	0.16
	(0.37)
F-3	0.36
	(0.48)
F-4	0.12
	(0.33)
Number of Stories	1.03
	(0.15)
Number of Square Feet	1377.62
	(316.23)
Roof Type –Hip	0.33
	(0.47)
Roof Type – Gable	0.54
	(0.50)
Year Built	1972.32
	(9.89)
Built Between 1966 and 1968	0.01
	(0.11)
Built Between 1968 and 1972	0.66
	(0.48)

Note: Standard Errors are in Parentheses.

Table 4 presents the regression results for total dollar loss per parcel and the loss ratio. In one specification we use the variable, *year built*, and in the other specification we use year built dummy variables. Further, this change in specification allows us to check robustness of our general model. We estimated the models using OLS reporting White-corrected standard errors to correct for heteroscedasticity. The first two columns report regression results for total dollar loss with aforementioned two specifications that differed in the way we handled year built. The third and fourth columns report the estimated loss ratio regression model for the two alternative specifications. The results in the first column indicate that, compared to total loss associated with *F-0* damage, loss in market value increases significantly when wind damage is rated *F-1, F-3* or *F-4*. The estimated coefficient for houses with *F-2* damage was also positive but not statistically significant. This finding is not surprising to some extent in that we would expect homes with higher physical damage ratings to be worth less than ones that were subjected to wind capable of causing "Some damage to chimneys; branches broken off trees; shallow-rooted trees pushed over; sign boards damaged." However, a priori, we might expect a more gradual increase in the average loss in market value with increases in the ordinal Fujita scale damage rating. What we appeared to get was a jump in losses.

As we look at building characteristics that may affect losses, the size of a building obviously affects the total value of the property at risk. As expected number of square feet is a statistically significant predictor of total loss. We observe that, if struck by a tornado, a house lost almost $23 per square foot in market value. All other building characteristics, including year built, are statistically insignificant.

Table 4. OLS Regression Results for Losses

Independent Variable	Loss	Loss	Loss Ratio	Loss Ratio
Constant	387716.10	13871.09	-1.423	0.633*
	(365704.30)	(12533.32)	(4.287)	(0.171)
F-1	15683.31*	16153*	0.210*	0.224*
	(4198.36)	(4986.37)	(0.061)	(0.067)
F-2	6916.23	7301.40	0.169*	0.185*
	(4602.01)	(4599.92)	(0.060)	(0.061)
F-3	11860.30*	12119.61*	0.192*	0.190*
	(3615.52)	(3564.96)	(0.055)	(0.055)
F-4	12445.15*	13862.11*	0.201*	0.200*
	(4292.24)	(4231.05)	(0.057)	(0.057)
Number of Stories	-15007.16	-8397.19	-0.105	-0.081
	(9643.82)	(9784.15)	(0.146)	(0.148)
Number of Square Feet	22.74*	23.26*	0.000	0.000
	(6.24)	(6.09)	(0.000)	(0.000)
Roof Type –Hip	3133.96	4251.32	0.007	0.007
	(3125.54)	(2896.47)	(0.039)	(0.038)
Roof Type – Gable	-4942.64	-4002.59	-0.068*	-0.065
	(3125.54)	(2542.61)	(0.034)	(0.035)
Year Built	-183.06		0.001	
	(186.87)		(0.002)	
Built Between 1966 and 1968		1975.51		0.067
		(3820.38)		(0.038)
Built Between 1969 and 1972		6049.65		0.038
		(3383.56)		(0.041)
Number of Observations	89	89	89	89
Adj-R^2	0.3204	0.3314	0.205	0.200

* Denotes 95% significance. Standard Errors are in Parentheses.

The results for the loss ratio regressions are reported in columns three and four. On average a house in the sample suffers a 63% loss if it sustains *F-0* tornado damage. When compared to *F-0* damage, *F-1* or higher damage ratings generate from 18.5% to 22.4% greater loss. Once again, moving between *F-0* damage and all other damage ratings seems to present a statistically significant jump in the loss ratio that is relatively constant whether the damage rating to *F-1, F-2, F-3,* or *F-4*. These results are robust for all model specifications.

CONCLUSION

This paper has examined the relationship between Fujita scale damage ratings and dollar losses resulting from the 1999 OKC tornado. As expected, the tornado had a large negative impact on the property values. More surprising is the near total degradation in market value once damage is rated *F-1* or higher. The damage to structures is apparently severe enough to move the value classification from a "repairable" state to a salvage value-only state with only the lot value remaining for most properties. Further, we find that, with an *F-0* damage rating, damage varies widely with damage ratios ranging from 13% to 91%. This seems inconsistent with the relatively low wind speed estimates 40-70 miles per hour for *F-0* tornado damage. Our results point toward two possible conclusions. One is that there was a wide variation in quality of construction and maintenance that left some homes more vulnerable to even the lower intensity tornado. Phan and Simiu (1998) indicate that wind speeds in the *F-3, F-4* and *F-5* range are not necessary to cause the damage associated with those classes in the Fujita scale. A second possibility is to conclude that the structure of the wind field created by a tornado cannot be adequately described or related to straight-line winds because the change in pressures, uplift, turbulence and change in wind direction have as much to do with the damage as wind speed.

Abbott and Meade (2003) provide a framework to evaluate research activities that are most likely to make the largest contribution to loss reduction efforts. They state that R&D should be focused on "solvable" problems. Our results indicate that the greatest opportunity for improvement in loss reduction is for wind storm damage in the *F-0* and *F-1* range. This is the wind storm intensity at which improvements in construction techniques and engineered mitigation measures can make a big impact. This impact comes in two ways. 1) Relatively simple construction measures such as additional strapping and roof fasteners can substantially reduce the loss and 2) 75% of tornadoes reported between 1950 and 1999 were rated *F-0* and *F-1* [Online Tornado FAQ]. In other words F-0 and F-1 destruction is the solvable problem.

REFERENCES

2000 International Building Code. International Code Council, Inc.

Blong, R. 2003. A Review of Damage Intensity Scales. *Natural Hazards* 29: 57-76.

Fujita, T. T. 1971. *A proposed characterization of tornadoes and hurricanes by area and intensity*. SMRP Paper 91: 42. University of Chicago.

Fujita, T. T. 1992. *Memoirs of an effort to unlock the mystery of severe storms*, Wind Research Laboratory, Department of Geophysical Sciences, University of Chicago.

Huang, D.V. Rosowsky and P.R. Sparks, Hurricane simulation techniques for the evaluation of wind speeds and expected insurance losses. *J. Wind Eng. Ind. Aerodyn.* 89 (2001), pp. 605–617.

Kruse, J. B., Kevin Simmons, and T. Tiglioglu.1999. Nashville tornado-economic damage estimation using tax assessor and insurance data. *Wind Engineering into the 21st Century*, A. Larsen, ed. A. A. Balkema, Rotterdam/Brookfield.

Kruse, J.B., M. Thompson, D. Smith, R. Peterson, E. Shaw, and K. Simmons. *The Oklahoma City Tornado Outbreak: A Wind Damage-Economic Loss Interface.* Proceedings: Americas Conference on Wind Engineering, 9 pages, 2001.

Mani, S., J. McDonald, and K. C. Mehta. 2003. *Elicitation Process of Enhancing F-Scale for Tornado Intensities.* Proceedings of the 11th International Conference on Wind Engineering.

Marshall, T. P. 2002. Damage Survey at Moore, Oklahoma Tornado. *Weather and Forecasting,* 17(3): 582-598.

McCarthy, Daniel. 2003. *NWS Tornado Surveys and the Impact on the National Tornado Database.* Symposium on the F-scale and Severe Weather Damage Assessment. 83rd Annual Meeting of the American Meteorological Society, Long Beach CA.

McDonald, J. R. and K. C. Mehta. 2002. *Summary Report Fujita-Scale Forum*, Texas Tech University.

McDonald, J. R. 2000. *The Need to Refine Wind Speeds Related to Fujita Scale.* White Paper, Texas Tech University.

Meade, C. and M. Abbott. 2003. *Assessing Federal Research and Development for Hazard Loss Reduction.* Prepared for the White House Office of Science Technology and Policy, RAND, Santa Monica, CA.

Minor, J. E., J. R. MCDonald and K.C. Mehta. 1977. *The tornado: An engineering-oriented perspective*, NOAA Tch. Memo., ERL NSSL-82, National Weather Service, Norman, OK. (reprinted as NOAA Tech. Memo. NWS SR-147, 1993).

Online Tornado FAQ, *www.spc.noaa.gov.*

Phan, L.T. and E. Simiu. 1998. *The Fujita tornado intensity scale: A critique based on observations of the Jarrell tornado of May 27, 1997*, NIST Tech. Note 1426, US Dept. of Commerce, Gaithersburg, MD.

Shaw, E., R. Peterson, J. Kruse, M. Thompson, D. Smith, and K. Simmons. Radar-Derived Analysis of the 3 May 1999 *Oklahoma City Tornado and Comparison to Damage Estimates*. Proceedings: Americas Conference on Wind Engineering, 11 pages, 2001.

Sparks, P.R. 2003. Wind speeds in tropical cyclones and associated insurance losses. *J. Wind Eng. Ind. Aerodyn.* 91: 1731–1751.

Sparks, P.R, S.D. Schiff and T.A. Reinhold. 1994. Wind damage to envelopes of houses and consequent insurance losses. *J. Wind Eng. Ind. Aerodyn.* 53: 145–155.

Storm Prediction Center Historical Data Archive. *http://www.spc.noaa.gov/archive/tornadoes/*

ACKNOWLEDGEMENTS

This work was performed under the Department of Commerce NIST/TTU Cooperative Agreement Award 70NANB8H0059. The authors thank Robert Chapman, Emil Simiu, Kishor Mehta, Chris Letchford, Daniel Sutter, Kevin Simmons, and participants at the Southern Economic Association meetings, 2003. Further, the authors thank Mike Means, Mike Morrison, Garry Dotson, Edward Hardison, and Jerry Wood of Oklahoma City Tax Assessor office for their support on this research.

In: Economics and the Wind
Editors: B. T. Ewing, et. al., pp. 25-34
ISBN: 1-59454-280-5
©2005 Nova Science Publishers, Inc.

Chapter 3

ANALYSIS OF LOCAL LABOR MARKET RESPONSES TO TORNADOES

Bradley T. Ewing
Rawls College of Business and Wind Science and Engineering Research Center, Texas Tech University, Lubbock, TX
Jamie B. Kruse
Wind Science and Engineering Research Center, Texas Tech University, Lubbock, TX, and the Center for Natural Hazards Mitigation, East Carolina University, Greenville, NC
Mark A. Thompson
Department of Economics and Finance, Stephen F. Austin State University, Nacogdoches, TX

INTRODUCTION

The objective of this study is to estimate the impact of tornadoes on the time series dynamics of local labor markets. In particular, we examine the local labor market effects of the April 16, 1998, Nashville, TN tornado, the May 3, 1999, Oklahoma City, OK tornado, and the March 28, 2000, Fort Worth, TX tornado. We chose to study the effects of these three tornadoes for several reasons. First, these tornadoes hit major urban areas with a substantial population base and labor force that is diverse and large enough to permit examination of the dynamics of their respective labor markets. Secondly, in addition to a major workforce, these urban areas have many colleges and universities, museums, galleries, and other cultural attractions that contribute to the increasingly important service sector. Third, while there are many similarities among these urban areas, underlying differences in labor market characteristics may lead to a variety of responses to tornadoes.

The Nashville and Fort Worth tornadoes struck downtown business districts causing severe damage to high-rise office complexes, historical buildings, and some residential homes. The estimated damage caused by the Nashville tornado was $100 million, while the Fort Worth tornado was approximately $450 million. Alternatively, the Oklahoma City tornado destroyed many residential homes and some commercial buildings, with estimated damage over $1 billion. Our study focuses on the localized labor market response to tornadoes. We characterize the time series behavior of the total employment growth rate for each urban area and, where appropriate, make allowance for the existence of time-varying (conditional) variability in the employment growth rate. An econometric intervention technique enables us to capture changes in these labor market dynamics and to make comparisons between the pre- and post-tornado periods.

LABOR MARKET INDICATORS

Employment is an input in the production of goods and services in an economy. Given current levels of the capital stock and technology, the amount of output that is produced will rise with increases in employment [Romer (1996)]. Measures of employment are typically used by policymakers and economists to describe the economic condition of a particular labor market. For this reason, employment growth serves as an indicator of how well or how poorly an economy is performing. An increase in employment growth in an area, or a speeding up of the economy, should provide economic benefits to the local economy. This phenomenon is often stated in terms of the income multiplier effect. More jobs means more income for workers. These workers, or their households, spend a portion of this income on goods and services in the local economy. In turn, this spending creates income for local business owners and their workers (in the form of additional jobs and/or overtime pay, etc.). The process generates an increase in total income in the local economy that exceeds the initial infusion of income from the creation of the new jobs and, hence, is referred to as the income multiplier. Of course, a number of constraints exist on a regional economy's growth including existing capital stock, state of technology, and infrastructure, etc. Additionally, other factors may lead to a lower local multiplier. For instance, the use of nonlocal workers by businesses in an area. When nonlocal workers are employed (e.g., construction project where workers may live in the project area only during the duration of the project) some of the income they earn is directed out of the local economy to their families and households living in other areas. This type of phenomenon, and others like it, are called leakages. Variations in income multipliers may be one factor that differentiates local economies.

Another aspect of a local labor market is the characterization of the volatility of the employment growth rate. In the context of unemployment, Ewing and Kruse (2002) used volatility as an indicator of the state of the labor market. The present study incorporates the both the employment growth rate and its variance as indicators. Lower volatility in the employment growth rate, as measured by thevariance, implies a more stable economic environment. A less volatile labor market, all else equal, is preferred to a more volatile labor market. One reason for the preference for stability is that the variance reflects the risk associated with successful labor market matches. For example, determining and planning for future labor force needs is more difficult for firms when they face higher labor market risk. Forecasts and projections can be made with a greater degrees of confidence when there is a low variance in employment growth, all else equal. Moreover, a riskier or less stable labor market may be cause for hesitation to firms deciding whether or not to locate or remain in the area. Increased labor market risk raises the costs associated with assessing and evaluating labor force decisions. A more volatile environment may cause potential workers to be reluctant to migrate to the area while making labor market participants less likely to remain there.

EMPLOYMENT DATA

This study used monthly total employment data for the Nashville, Oklahoma City, and Fort Worth Metropolitan Statistical Areas (MSA) spanning January 1980 to December 2002. The data were obtained from the Bureau of Labor Statistics' Employment and Earnings (various issues). We calculated the seasonally adjusted employment growth rates for each MSA and their respective state-level employment growth rate. Specifically, we used the ratio-to-moving-average method based on the discussion about seasonal adjustment of time series made in Harvey (1994). Growth rates were calculated as $[(e_t - e_{t-12})/e_{t-12}]^{*}100$, where e represents employment. The year-over-year calculation should eliminate any effects of seasonality that may remain in the data.

Table 1. Descriptive Statistics on State and MSA Employment Growth Rates

	Mean	Maximum	Minimum	Standard Deviation
Nashville	3.00	8.04	-3.04	2.34
Tennessee	2.03	6.77	-2.07	3.72
Oklahoma City	1.44	6.39	-6.10	2.25
Oklahoma	1.35	6.38	-6.15	2.40
Fort Worth	2.98	8.72	-1.86	2.28
Texas	2.22	6.50	-3.24	2.16

Note: Growth rates are for January 1980 to December 2002 (264 observations). Data are from the U.S. Bureau of Labor Statistics' *Employment and Earnings* (various issues).

Table 1 reports descriptive statistics for the employment growth variables for each of the local labor markets. On average, all state and MSA employment growth rates were positive. The mean growth rate was highest in Texas at 2.22%, followed by Tennessee (2.03%) and Oklahoma (1.35%). Each state experienced negative growth rates in at least one month with the maximum growth rate in a month being 6.77% (Tennessee). Tennessee's employment growth rate had the largest standard deviation implying that it is the most volatile of the three states. In comparison, the MSA level mean growth rates were higher than the growth rates of their respective states. This is an indication of relatively strong local economies. Only Fort Worth exhibited a standard deviation in employment growth that was larger than the corresponding state measure of volatility. Among the MSAs, Nashville's labor market was the most volatile while also exhibiting the highest mean growth rate. The descriptive statistics illustrate that these regions do behave differently over this time period. Figure 1 illustrates the employment growth rate for each MSA (and their respective state employment growth rate). The shaded areas indicate the post-tornado period. Visual inspection reveals differences in the employment growth variability across the three different urban areas. Based on these cursory findings, we expect to see differences in how these local economies responded to their respective tornadoes. We now proceed with a more formal examination of employment growth using modern statistical time series techniques.

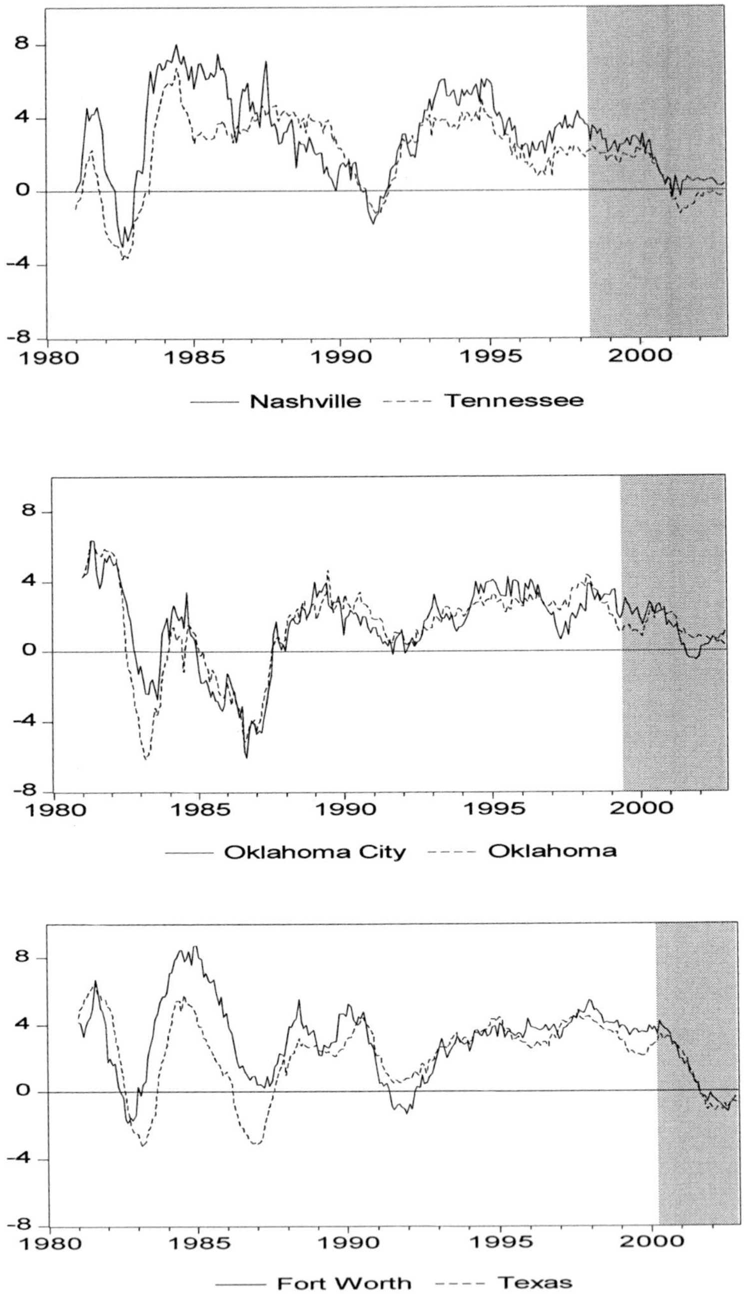

Figure 1. Employment Growth Rates for Nashville and Tennessee.
Note: The shaded area represents the post-tornado period (for Nashville this is May 1998-on; for Oklahoma City this is June 1999-on; for Fort Worth this is April 2000-on).

EMPIRICAL METHODOLOGY

We characterize the dynamics of the Fort Worth, Nashville, and Oklahoma City labor markets by estimating a time series econometric model of employment growth. In order to analyze the impact of the tornadoes on these market, our model includes an intervention variable. The analysis begins with the construction of autoregressive integrated moving average (ARIMA) models of total employment growth for each MSA. However, preliminary analysis indicated that none of the growth rates had a unit root as determined by ADF test of Dickey and Fuller (1981). Thus, in what follows we focus on the standard univariate ARMA model (i.e., no differencing of the growth rate series was required). Many macroeconomic time series exhibit a phenomenon known as momentum and this feature is captured by the autoregressive (AR) term in the model. Momentum implies that an immediate past change (or changes) in the employment growth rate may be a useful predictor of current and future values (Enders, 1995). The ARMA specification also takes into account the prior period's difference between fitted (or expected) employment growth and the actual employment growth rate. This difference is called an innovation and is the residual for a given period. The moving average (MA) term measures the degree to which current employment growth responds to past innovations in employment growth.

It is likely that case that factors other than these innovations or momentum also influence the growth rate of a local economy. However, many of these factors may be highly correlated with the past innovations and/or the momentum and thus it would be redundant to include them in the model. One important factor that is likely to be an important determinant of local employment growth are the state and national business cycles. Earlier work by Payne, Ewing, and George (1999) suggested that individual state and national labor markets were cointegrated. Their finding implies a high and positive long run correlation between the US labor market and state labor market behavior. While the local economy may be influenced by the state business cycle, as can be seen in Figure 1, there are a number of periods in which the local employment growth rates do not parallel the actions of the respective state employment growth rates. It is unlikely that movements in employment in any local area may be predicted solely on movements in their state employment growth rate. In order to avoid the multicollinearity problem, we augment the MSA employment growth models with the rate of total employment growth for their respective state.

Ordinary least squares estimation of the autoregressive moving average model assumes that the variance of the error process is homoscedastic so that the unconditional variance and the conditional variance exist, both are greater than zero, and the current variance is independent of past variance. However, the assumption of constant variance is often violated and estimates obtained using classical linear regression are therefore inefficient. The presence of an autoregressive conditional heteroscedastic (ARCH) error process implies that current and future volatilities of a series can be modeled based on past volatilities. ARCH effects can be determined using the Lagrange multiplier test [Engle (1982)]. When ARCH effects are present, it is appropriate to simultaneously model both the mean and the variance of the series. Engle (1982) showed that efficiency is improved by taking these ARCH effects into account directly when modeling the time series dynamics of a series. For our purposes, if an ARMA model of the mean employment growth rate is determined to have time-varying variance, then we estimate the corresponding ARMA-ARCH model.

The ARMA model includes an intervention variable which enables us to test whether or not the labor market in the pre-tornado period differs from that in the post-tornado period. ***to capture the post-tornado effects. effects of the tornado on employment growth *** The intervention variable is a dummy variable equal to zero before the tornado and one thereafter. Intuitively, the intervention variable captures the effect of the tornado in terms of a shift in the intercept. A statistically significant intervention variable reflects a change a change in the long run time series behavior of the employment growth rate The ARMA model, augmented with the respective state employment growth rate and intervention variable, is given by:

$$\varphi(L)g_t = \theta(L)\varepsilon_t + c_0 + \psi s_t + \lambda\pi_t \qquad (1)$$

The growth rate under investigation is denoted g; the coefficient on the state employment growth rate variable, s, is given by ψ; and λ is the coefficient on the tornado intervention variable, π. $\phi(L)$ and $\theta(L)$ are polynomials in the lag operator and thus represent the coefficients on the autoregressive (AR) and moving average (MA) terms. The intercept is represented by c_0. Equation (1) is used to model the total employment growth rate for Nashville, Oklahoma City, and Fort Worth.

The specification of equation (1) is identified using standard Box-Jenkins techniques that involve examination of autocorrelation and partial autocorrelation functions. Specifically, we follow the Box-Jenkins technique for choosing model specification based on goodness-of-fit measures outlined in Mills (1999). The autoregressive moving average model of order one, zero (ARMA(1,0)) was selected in each case. The ARMA(1,0) is simply the AR(1) model where the absence of a significant MA term suggests that last period's innovation is not an important determinant for constructing a projection of the current employment growth rate. In contrast, a significant predictor of the current rate of employment growth is the last period's growth rate. The degree of momentum in employment growth can be determined by examining the coefficient on the autoregressive term. As stated above, the estimated model also contains the contemporaneous state employment growth rate as well as the tornado intervention variable.

In the conventional OLS model, the error process is assumed to have zero mean and constant variance so that $\varepsilon_t \sim N(0,\sigma)$. However, if the error process has a time-varying variance such that $\varepsilon_t \sim N(0,h_t^2)$, then an alternative estimation method is needed. After first estimating equation (1) via OLS, we examine the residuals to determine if ARCH effects are present [Engle (1982)}. If we fail to reject the null hypothesis of no ARCH effects, then equation (1) is treated as a conventional ARMA(1,0) model and the results interpreted accordingly. If we reject the null of no ARCH effects, then we estimated equation (1) simultaneously with the conditional variance given in equation (2). This simultaneous estimation procedure is conducted using the method of maximum likelihood:

$$h_t^2 = \alpha_0 + \alpha_1\varepsilon_{t-1}^2 + \gamma\pi_t \qquad (2)$$

$V(\varepsilon_t|\Omega_{t-1})=h_t^2$ is the conditional variance of ε_t with respect to the information set Ω_{t-1}. For estimation purposes we computed the quasi-maximum likelihood covariances and standard errors as in Bollerslev and Wooldridge (1992). We further assume that the errors in the model given by equations (1) and (2) are conditionally normally distributed. Note that equation (2) contains a moving average component referred to as the ARCH term. The ARCH term picks up the amount of dependence that exists between current volatility and a past shock. The presence of a significant ARCH term indicates that current volatility may be estimated using a past (squared) innovation. It is possible that equation (2) may contain more than one ARCH term. For those cases in which ARCH effects were present, we found q=1 sufficient to capture all ARCH effects. Economic, political, and naturally occurring events may lead to structural changes in the times series behavior of the conditional variance as well as the mean equation. It is possible that a tornado may alter the risk characteristics of a labor market through changes in infrastructure, behaviors of market participants, etc. For this reason we include the intervention variable is included in the variance equation. γ is the coefficient on the intervention variable, π., in equation (2). Moreover, it is important to allow for this type of regime change in the variance process. In fact, Lastrapes (1989) showed that failing to properly account for regime changes may lead to an overestimation of volatility persistence. In other words, it may appear that the growth rate under investigation exhibits more ARCH effects than is actually the case if the intervention variable is erroneously omitted from the specification.

OLS estimation of equation (1) revealed the presence of time-varying volatility in the total employment growth rates in Nashville and Oklahoma City, but not in the case of Fort Worth. In what follows, we estimated the ARMA-ARCH model for the two MSAs that showed ARCH effects.

Empirical Results and Discussion

The employment growth models were estimated and the empirical results are presented in Table 2. It is important to note that the federal building in downtown Oklahoma City was the site of a domestic terrorist bombing in April 1995. Thus, in what follows, we also estimated the Oklahoma City model including a control variable (equal to one in May 1995 and zero otherwise) to capture any labor market effects associated with this event. Our results and conclusions were not altered by the inclusion of this control variable. We find that that the coefficient on the autoregressive term in each equation (1) is positive and significant for all three urban areas. This finding has several implications. First, the results indicate that there is momentum in MSA-level employment growth rates. If employment growth was rising (falling) last month, then there is a tendency for growth to be rising (falling) in the current month. These momentum effects are estimated to be 0.78 for Oklahoma City, 0.82 for Nashville, and 0.95 for Fort Worth. These estimates suggest a one percentage point change in employment growth last period contributes from around three-quarters to almost a full percentage point change in current employment growth. Second, the results also indicate that labor market activity in Nashville and Oklahoma City is significantly influenced by their respective state business cycle. In contrast, the Fort Worth labor operates more independently of the state labor market. For Fort Worth firms and workers, this finding of economic isolation has several implications. The Fort Worth MSA is not subject to swings in the Texas economy in the same way that the labor market condition of Nashville and Oklahoma City might be linked to the performance of their respective state economy. Along these same lines, any effects of the Fort Worth tornado will be neither be dampened nor magnified by the state economy. Whereas any positive benefits attributable to the tornado would not be "watered down" by a weak state economy, it is also the case that any adverse tornado effects would not be offset by a strong state economy.

Table 2. Results of the Employment Growth Models

	Nashville	Oklahoma City	Fort Worth
Mean			
Constant	0.2021*	0.0427	0.1028
AR(1)	0.8241*	0.7758*	0.9536*
State Growth Rate	0.1605*	0.2023*	0.0199
Tornado	-0.1190	-0.0319	-0.2071*
Variance			
Constant	0.3655*	0.3730*	—
ARCH	0.3003*	0.0803	—
Tornado	-0.2516*	-0.2400*	—
Log Likelihood	-245.51	-231.31	-204.12
ARCH LM	0.0020	0.1266	0.0270
F-statistic	484.87*	544.90*	1537.17*

Note: Growth rates are for January 1980 to December 2002 (264 observations). Data are from the U.S. Bureau of Labor Statistics' *Employment and Earnings* (various issues). * denotes p-value<0.05. The F-statistic tests the null hypothesis that all the explanatory variables in the model (except the intercept) are jointly equal to zero. ARCH LM tests the null hypothesis that there are no remaining ARCH effects.

Table 2 shows how the mean and/or variance of the employment growth rate in each labor market changed following their respective tornado. In terms of an intercept change in equation (1), the estimated coefficient on the tornado intervention variable was negative but insignificant for both the Nashville and Oklahoma City. This indicates the absence of a significant post-tornado change in the mean employment growth rate for either of these MSAs. In contrast, the estimated coefficient on the tornado intervention variable was negative and statistically significant for the Fort Worth model (estimated coefficient = -0.21, p-value < 0.05). The employment growth rate in the Fort Worth MSA has fallen following the tornado. Controlling for the business cycle and other factors, the tornadoes had no significant effect on employment growth in Nashville and Oklahoma City but had an adverse effect on Fort Worth. There are several interesting points that might be made about the Fort Worth labor market. First, this MSA exhibited strong momentum as detected by the AR term. Thus, the immediate adverse impact on the economy would last for a number of period's into the future. Indeed, this is what anecdotal evidence suggests. Downtown Fort Worth has not fully recovered as many of the businesses displaced by the tornado moved. Second, the economic independence of the local labor market meant that Fort Worth did not experience any spillover effects of a strong Texas economy. These two factors help to explain the long run adverse impact that the tornado had on the Fort Worth labor market.

Table 2 also includes the results from estimating equation (2) for the MSAs which exhibited ARCH effect. For both Nashville and Oklahoma City, we found the estimated coefficient on the intervention variable to be negative and statistically significant. This finding indicates that the degree of local labor market volatility or risk is lower after the tornado. In fact, for the case of Oklahoma City, the inclusion of the intervention variable removed the ARCH effects. This underscores the importance of a structural change in the risk measure of the labor market. Overall, while both Nashville's and Oklahoma City's mean employment growth rates remained unchanged, each labor market became more stable. These favorable labor market outcomes may be explained by the rebuilding of businesses, residential areas, and infrastructure in the post-tornado period.

Concluding Remarks

This research explored how three local labor markets responded to tornadoes. Specifically, we examined the labor market effects of the April 1998 Nashville tornado, May 1999 Oklahoma City tornado, and the March 2000 Fort Worth tornado. This study revealed several important insights into how a tornado may alter the mean and variance of employment growth rates in these local economies. The mean employment growth rates in Nashville and Oklahoma City remained unchanged following their respective tornadoes. However, Fort Worth experienced a reduction in mean employment growth following the tornado. Our results also indicated that the post-tornado period was associated with a more stable labor market in both Nashville and Oklahoma City.

References

Bollerslev, T. and J. Wooldridge (1992). Quasi-maximum likelihood estimation and inference in dynamic models with time-varying covariances. *Econometric Reviews*, 11, 143-172.

Dickey, D. and W. Fuller (1981). Likelihood ratio statistics for autoregressive time series with a unit root. *Econometrica*, 49, 1057-1071.

Enders, W. (2004). *Applied Econometric Time Series* (2nd ed.). New York: John Wiley & Sons.

Engle, R. (1982). Autoregressive conditional heteroscedasticity with estimates of the variance of the U.K. inflation. *Econometrica*, 58, 987-1008.

Ewing, B. and J. Kruse (2002). The impact of Project Impact on the Wilmington, North Carolina labor market. *Public Finance Review*, 30, 296-309.

Harvey, A. (1994). *Time Series Models*, Cambridge: MIT Press.

Lastrapes, W. (1989). Exchange rate volatility and US monetary policy: an ARCH application. *Journal of Money, Credit and Banking* 21: 66-77.

Mills, T. (1999). *The Econometric Modelling of Financial Time Series*. Cambridge: Cambridge University Press.

Payne, J., B. Ewing, and E. George (1999). Time series dynamics of U.S. state unemployment rates. *Applied Economics*, 31, 1503-1510.

Romer, D. (1996). *Advanced Macroeconomics*. New York: McGraw-Hill.

U.S. Bureau of Labor Statistics (various dates). *Employment and Earnings*. Washington, D.C: U.S. Bureau of Labor Statistics.

ACKNOWLEDGEMENTS

This work was performed under the Department of Commerce NIST/TTU Cooperative Agreement Award 70NANB8H0059. Ewing and Kruse received financial support from an Advanced Research Program (ARP) grant from the Texas Higher Education Coordinating Board.

In: Economics and the Wind
Editors: B. T. Ewing, et. al., pp. 35-46
ISBN: 1-59454-280-5
©2005 Nova Science Publishers, Inc.

Chapter 4

WIND DISASTERS AND THE INSURANCE INDUSTRY

George R. Walker
Aon Re Australia, Sydney, NSW, Australia

INTRODUCTION

Wind damage is one of the most widely insured forms of losses, but it is also one of the greatest concerns to the insurance industry, as shown in figures 1 and 2. The largest insured property loss from any single event to the end of 2002, in current values, is that due to wind damage from Hurricane Andrew, even taking the World Trade Centre loss into account (Swiss Re, 2003). Between 1970 and 2002, of the 40 mostly costly insurance losses, 22 were primarily due to wind damage accounting for approximately 55 percent of the total loss of US$156 billion from these events in current values (Swiss Re, 2003). 14 of these 22 events were due to tropical cyclones.

Of the 40 largest losses during the period 1970–2002, 68 percent occurred since 1990 incurring 81 percent of the loss, highlighting the increasing scale of the problem, largely as a result of changing demographics.

The insurance industry generally has little difficulty coping with the relatively frequent isolated cases of wind damage from small storms. It is the large-scale events like tropical cyclones that cause the major problems, because, although relatively rare, they produce large aggregations of losses from a single event.

The insurance industry controls its risks through setting premiums and policy conditions, using risk transfer mechanisms like reinsurance, risk-financing mechanisms like contingent capital, and putting aside reserves (Kiln, 1981). One of the cutting edges of modern insurance is the development of sophisticated financial risk management systems that integrate all the risks and enable companies to optimise the management of the control mechanisms in terms of the risk to both the shareholders and the policyholders (Masters, 2001). Important components of these systems are catastrophe loss models that simulate the losses arising from major events like hurricanes and earthquakes.

Where the risk is considered uninsurable by normal means, it may become the subject of government schemes (Kunreuther and Roth, (1998). These operate under different criteria to normal insurance, but, although generally backed by governments, they must also be sustainable in the long term. Consequently the design and operation of these schemes is dependent on reliable modelling of the performance of the schemes a considerable number of years into the future. This can be undertaken using similar integrated financial risk management systems to those required by normal insurance companies.

Color graphics are presented at the end of the chapter.

INSURABILITY OF WIND DAMAGE

To be insurable a risk needs to satisfy several criteria(Berliner, 1982). The risk must be capable of being expressed in clear and unambiguous terms known as the policy conditions, which connect a prescribed financial payment to the occurrence of a defined fortuitous event within a specified period. Generally to be insurable there must be enough knowledge of the risk for intended customers to want to be protected from it, and to enable a premium to be established, which must be low enough to be affordable by the intended customers. To avoid fraudulent use of insurance, processes must be in place for insuring the risk and paying any subsequent claims that minimise the risk of moral hazard.

In relation to general insurance such as householder insurance of homes and their contents, affordability is a key factor. This can best be achieved by having a large number of policyholders at risk from independent events, which, while possibly severe for the individual policyholder, have a low probability of occurrence. Under such conditions the Central Limit Theorem of probability and statistics (known as the Law of Large Numbers in the insurance industry) results in average annual losses for the insurance company that are a very small percentage of the total sum insured, and, just as importantly, have a low standard deviation. This enables the insurance company to set a premium rate with reasonable confidence that the annual premium income will exceed annual claims, but will not be excessive and thus either unaffordable or non-competitive. Fire insurance was developed on this principle.

Wind damage does not fit this pattern because it generally occurs in association with events that cause damage to several properties, sometimes large numbers of properties, from the one event. Under these conditions the risks to different properties are not independent and the benefits from the Central Limit Theorem can be lost. For the more common local storms, the effect is generally small and manageable, but not so for large events.

Wind insurance as an addition to normal fire insurance began about 100 years ago in an environment where local storms were considered the main hazard. During the 20th century insurance became more widespread, and major demographic changes occurred that greatly increased the exposure to severe wind events such as tropical cyclones. One result has been an escalation in the losses from wind damage suffered by the insurance industry, which has continued in many respects to regard wind as a standard risk for insurance cover. However research has led to a much greater understanding of the risk of extreme events (Woo, 1999). This has enabled the industry to cope with the problem. The inherent limitations of the Central Limit Theorem for managing such losses have been recognised, and forms of protection developed, the most common of which is Treaty Excess of Loss Reinsurance (Kiln, 1981). This normally works by ceding the risk above a certain level – the retention level – up to an upper limit generally known in the industry as the Probable Maximum Loss (PML). The risk is ceded to reinsurance companies in portions, with the overall loss to be ceded being first divided into layers, and then sub-divided into smaller portions, so that it can be widely distributed, with no reinsurance company taking an excessive amount of the risk.

As a result, wind damage has continued to remain insurable for many properties exposed to extreme wind events - although not for all. The premiums charged by the reinsurer have to be passed on to the insurer's customers. They can be several times the premium income from customers for insurance against wind damage from local storms. Where risks are high, building construction not very resistant to extreme wind speeds, and customers are not very wealthy, the resulting premiums that need to be charged to the customers can make them unaffordable. When this happens the main solution is a government-controlled scheme.

DISASTER INSURANCE SCHEMES

If normal insurance is unaffordable then there are two options. Allow the householders to remain uninsured and depend on government assistance and charity if they suffer a major loss, or provide insurance, but not necessarily full insurance, through a government controlled scheme. The advantage of the latter is that funds are available, and mechanisms in place for distributing them, to fund repairs and reconstruction when a catastrophic loss occurs. Currently, for this reason, the World Bank, to whom many of the poorer countries turn for reconstruction loans after a major disaster, is increasingly making the development of national disaster insurance schemes a condition of providing such loans (Lester, 1999).

National disaster insurance schemes are different from normal insurance for several reasons. In the first place they are generally restricted to a single line of business – property insurance against specified major hazards. Secondly they are generally operated within an environment in which the insurance industry considers the specified hazards uninsurable. Thirdly their primary function is essentially social welfare, being seen as being a more efficient method of assisting the victims of disaster from the point of view of government and other major institutions than disaster relief aid in the aftermath of disasters.

For normal insurance the policy conditions are usually relatively standard and based on either the replacement cost or the indemnity value, which is the market value of buildings or contents being insured. Premiums are then established in terms of this insured risk. However, in the case of disaster insurance schemes the premiums may be determined by affordability, in which case the policy conditions have to be tailored to meet the premiums – the reverse of the normal insurance approach (Walker, 2003).

Because disaster insurance schemes are designed to handle extreme events that by their nature are also very rare events, they must be sustainable. This means that in the long-term premium income must be sufficient to cover the risk, and the schemes must be financially well managed.

FINANCIAL RISK MANAGEMENT TOOLS

Historically insurers and reinsurers managed their risks from catastrophic events by a combination of intuition, subjective opinion based on personal experience, and empirical heuristic procedures that had stood the test of time. The rapid changes in the characteristics of the risks, such as those due to changing demographics, and the changing nature of the insurance and reinsurance industry due to globalisation, have made these historical methods much less reliable than they used to be. They are being replaced by complex analytical tools that enable the financial behaviour of insurance and reinsurance organizations (figure 3) to be simulated on a computer to produce statistical forecasts of performance for differing financial risk management decisions. These tools are in many ways the financial equivalent of the structural engineering computer systems for analysing the performance of structures for different design parameters.

These systems essentially comprise three main components – an insurance loss risk modelling component, a financial asset risk modelling component, and a dynamic financial analysis (DFA) component which integrates the various risks, combines them with the proposed risk financing and risk transfer programs, and outputs information of the performance of the insurance entity in probabilistic terms (figure 4). Using such systems, reinsurers can optimise their selection of risks and the price to be charged subject to meeting company and regulatory criteria is respect of sustainability, and insurers can optimise their reinsurance programmes, premium structures and policy conditions to maintain solvency and meet shareholder expectations in terms of annual balance sheet parameters.

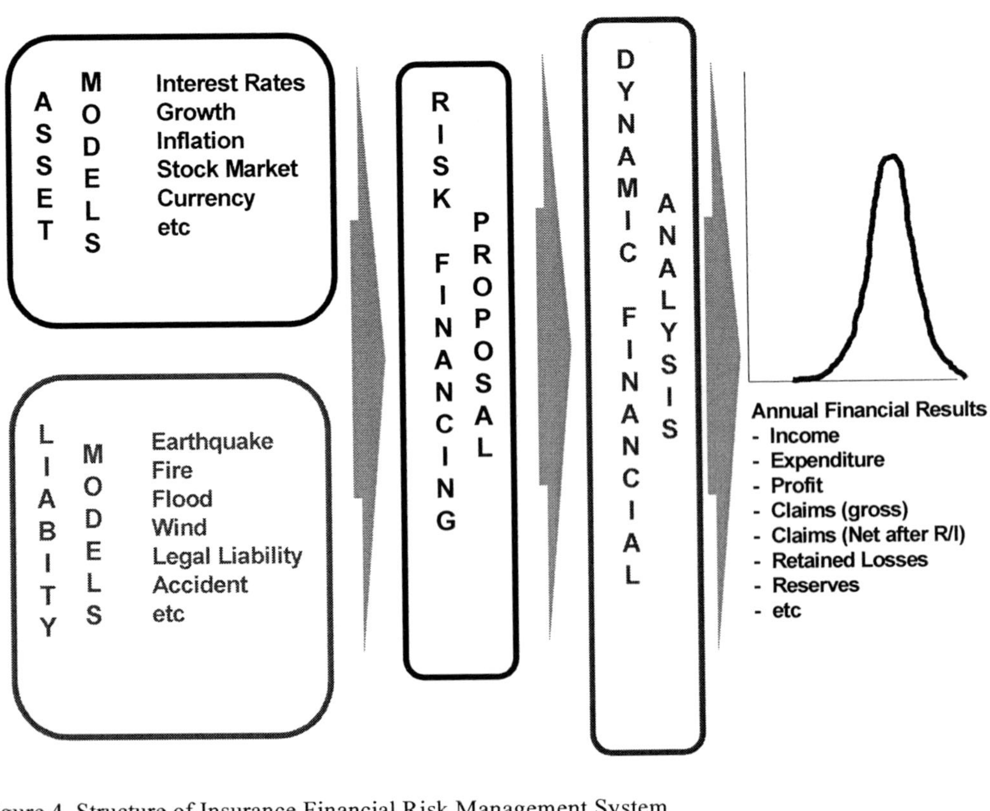

Figure 4. Structure of Insurance Financial Risk Management System.

An example of such a system is the Minerva financial risk management system (Middleton 2001) that has been developed for the New Zealand Earthquake Commission, the Government entity that manages the New Zealand earthquake insurance scheme. This system forecasts in statistical terms the performance of the New Zealand Disaster Fund, which underpins the scheme, ten years into the future, providing information on a wide range of parameters of which the most important are probably the fund size and the probability that the fund will be exhausted. The system allows differing assumptions regarding premiums, policy conditions, reinsurance arrangements, and economic variables related to growth, to be input, and incorporates tools for estimating reinsurance costs, and estimating the number, size and geographical distribution of claims if an earthquake occurs. It includes a full probabilistic earthquake loss model covering all New Zealand households, both present and forecast into the future, and asset models that model the effect of financial variables such as interest rates, share market fluctuations, inflation and currency exchange rates on the performance of the Disaster Fund.

In such systems, the asset models and DFA models are the province of actuaries and other financial risk management specialists in the financial industry. The insurance loss models are the province of engineers and scientists. These financial risk management systems are therefore expert systems incorporating the expertise of a range of disciplines from structural engineering to financial securitisation. The use of these tools is still in its infancy and their full potential has yet to be realised, but they will almost certainly form the core of decision making in the insurance industry of the future. Consequently any future orientated research directed at the insurance industry needs to be formulated and undertaken in the context of these systems.

CATASTROPHE LOSS MODELS

Catastrophe loss models are the foundation blocks of modern financial risk management of insurance risk from major catastrophic hazards both natural and man-made. Their principal output are tables of estimated event losses as a function of frequency of exceedance for the different identified hazards (figure 5). In this form they can be readily combined statistically with other hazard risks, to produce multi-hazard loss risk tables or curves, or input into DFA models to analyse system performance. From the derived loss curves reinsurance programmes can be designed and the price of reinsurance estimated. By selective modelling in terms of location, building type and building use, risk based premium structures can be designed.

The term "catastrophe loss model" normally refers to the modelling of major hazards such as earthquakes and tropical cyclones using Geographic Information System (GIS) based simulation of the hazards and the resulting insurance losses from damage arising from them. (Walker, 1999) Friedman pioneered the approach in the 1970's (Friedman, 1975). Smaller more frequent losses are usually modelled using statistical analysis of past losses. Modelling losses using GIS based hazard simulation models requires expert input on the characteristics of the hazard and its effects on buildings and other structures. Modern models generally comprise four main components – hazard simulation; the occurrence in terms of track, frequency, central pressure and size; the vulnerability of the buildings; and the insured portfolio.

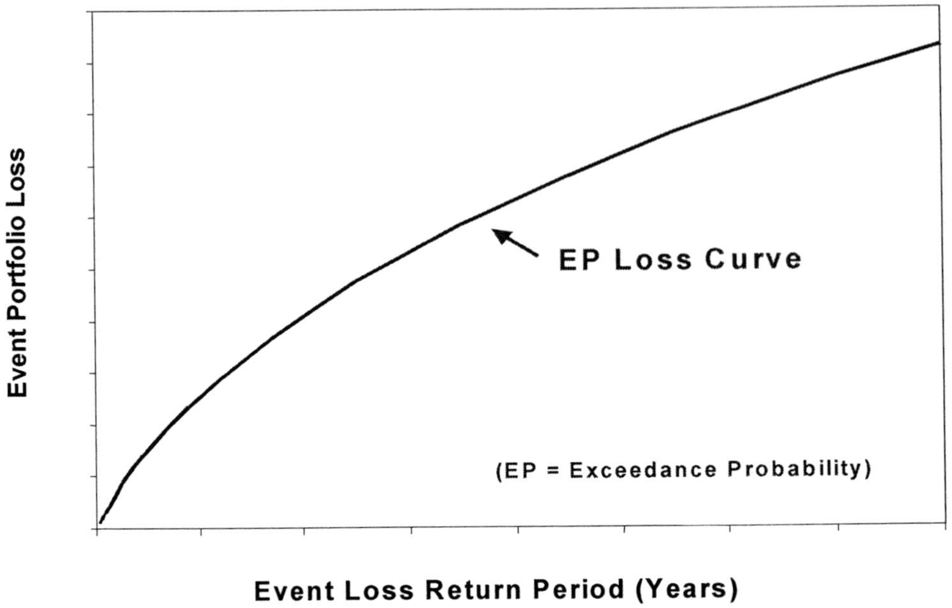

Figure 5. Graph of Typical Output from Catastrophe Loss Model.

For tropical cyclone wind loss models the hazard simulation is concerned with modelling wind characteristics such as maximum gust speed, or mean 10 minute wind speed, and direction, at a particular height, at the locations of the insured property, as a tropical cyclone of prescribed central pressure and radius to maximum wind speed moves along a prescribed path. Such modelling needs to take into account the effect on tropical cyclone intensity of moving over land, and terrain and topographic effects.

Modelling the occurrence in terms of track, frequency, central pressure and size is generally based on a statistical analysis of historical data, and using the resultant statistical parameters to model by Monte Carlo techniques a representative sample of all the tropical cyclones that could impact on the insured properties at risk.

To date most of the modelling of vulnerability of insured property to wind has been based on the analysis of actual insured losses as a function of building characteristics and the estimated wind speeds causing the loss. This is a relatively crude approach dependent on limited information from past wind damage. A developing approach is the development of engineering based vulnerability relationships that are a function of design criteria as well as other characteristics, and incorporate the estimation of damage using engineering principles, and the estimation of insured loss based on damage.

The portfolio model is the GIS representation of the insured risks in terms of location, insurance class (e.g. building or contents), insured value, policy conditions, building characteristics, and building use. The location may be in terms of actual geographical location (e.g. latitude and longitude), but more often is in terms of a small area such as the postcode, and sometimes is only in terms of a large area such as the Cresta Zone – a standardised region used by insurers for measuring accumulation of insured values at risk from a single event. The building characteristics should be characteristics relevant to the hazard (eg in the case of wind losses the building age, roof type and shape, structural type, envelope characteristics, etc) as also must the building use.

The determination of almost all of the parameters required to model the loss risk is based on limited information and involves a measure of knowledge uncertainty, which is also modelled. Many of the algorithms and parameter values used in the models are the result of expert opinion, not accurate scientific analysis. Consequently for all their complexity and scientific input, they are in essence systems that integrate expert opinion, and just as expert opinion varies from one expert to another, so do the results from different models for the same insurance portfolios. It is not uncommon for these to vary by a factor of two or more, with the result that further expert opinion is required to interpret the results! This will only change as the science underlying the models is improved. In the case of wind loss models, much of this science is wind engineering science.

IMPLICATIONS FOR WIND ENGINEERING RESEARCH

The greatest source of uncertainty in present wind loss models is probably the modelling of vulnerability. There are two main sources of this uncertainty. One of these is the categorisation of building characteristics by insurance companies, which often bears little relationship to the characteristics that significantly affect wind damage. This occurs because the traditional insurance industry approach to classification of buildings has been in relation to fire, so the emphasis tends to be on materials of construction, rather than roof geometry, age of construction, or relative area of windows, that can be more important in regard to wind damage. This is not so much an engineering science problem as an insurance company data management problem, although it requires input from wind engineers on suitable building characteristics to use as the basis for modelling vulnerability. The latter is not a trivial problem as the characteristics need be ones that ordinary policyholders can readily identify when filling in an insurance policy form, and for general use there needs to be a degree of standardisation of these characteristics across the industry.

However it is the development of a better understanding of the relationships between wind characteristics and damage loss where wind engineering researchers can probably make their greatest contribution to the improvement of current wind loss models. The relationships used in current models have been largely developed by analysing insured losses from major events using estimated values of maximum wind speeds causing the loss, and building classifications largely dependent on current insurance practice, although more appropriate classifications are used if the information is available. This approach results in average losses and, if enough loss data is available, statistical information on the spread of losses about the average loss, as a function of wind speed and building type. The weakness of this approach it that it requires a major loss to produce data, and because building practices vary greatly from one region to another, even within large countries, the vulnerability models developed from an event in one location may have limited significance for other areas. Furthermore most major wind disasters result in changes in building codes directed at mitigation of wind losses, rendering the vulnerability curves derived from the damage of limited use for estimating loss to new construction.

The modelling of vulnerability in the current commercial models used widely throughout the world is probably very dependent on analyses of insurance losses sustained in Hurricane Andrew, with adjustments made based on expert opinion for application to other parts of the world. In Australia major changes in building regulations followed the destruction of Darwin by Cyclone Tracy in 1974. But there have been only a few significant wind loss events since then, and they mainly occurred in the 1980's when the number of buildings built to the new regulations was small. On the evidence available the effect of the new regulations has been dramatic in reducing wind damage, but the sample is too small for statistical analysis as a function of wind speed and building type, so the models used tend to be heavy on expert opinion and light on scientific data.

The solution to this dilemma is the adoption of an engineering approach where damage is related to the engineering strength relative to wind loads, and losses are estimated from the damage based on building costs. These are two separate issues that require separate treatment. Such models are likely to have much more universal validity, being much more amenable to customisation to differing local situations. Some modellers have begun using this approach, but much more needs to be done for its use to become universal.

To be useful these vulnerability models must be relatively simple since they need to be applied to a large number of buildings in a single analysis. For researchers this often poses a dilemma because of the inherent complexity of the actual phenomenon being modelled. However the systems are risk based, and consequently allow for the uncertainties associated with simplification to be incorporated. The likely course of development will be the development of initially very simple models with a large band of uncertainty, followed by increasing complexity of models with decreasing uncertainty.

It needs to be remembered that the objective is insurance loss risk, not damage risk. Although they are related, the relationship between damage and loss can be highly non-linear, and needs to be a subject of research in its own right. Insured loss is also a function of the cover conditions, which usually include a deductible and may also include a limit on the size of the claim and limitations on the nature of the cover. These also need to be incorporated in the modelling. This approach will have special importance for disaster insurance schemes where policy conditions need to be tailored to meet premiums limited by affordability. The current empirical models are implicitly based on normal policy conditions, and hence not very amenable to modelling policy conditions that may involve claims only being paid if the damage exceeds certain limits – e.g. unsafe for occupation, which is the type of criteria used in some cases.

Although the modelling of vulnerability is probably the weakest part of current models, there is considerable scope for refinement of the other components. The behaviour of tropical cyclones as they cross from ocean to land is still the subject of considerable study, with the effect on ground level winds as a result of changing eye dynamics, the interaction with major topographical features, and the decrease in intensity with passage over land, being areas of research which have the potential to lead to considerable improvements in catastrophe loss modelling. The effects of climate variability, both natural and man-made, on the occurrence characteristics of tropical cyclones, is another area of research that has considerable potential use for loss modelling, which is still largely based on the assumption of a stationary random process. The modelling of terrain and topographical effects is another source of uncertainty in current models.

Another problem with current models, but one which may be outside the scope of most wind engineers, is the losses in tropical cyclones due to damage from other hazards than wind, particularly damage from heavy wind driven rain, flooding and storm surge. The concern of insurance companies in disasters is the total loss they may sustain, not the loss they will sustain due to one specific hazard. A major weakness of most current tropical cyclone loss models is that they only model wind losses. In some areas of world the primary insured losses are due to water damage, not to wind damage, although they often occur in conjunction with each other. Modelling of the combined effects is an urgent need in some areas, particularly Southeast Asia.

Currently the modelling of losses from severe storms, including tornadoes, is still in its infancy. Severe storms do not have the same potential to produce large losses as tropical cyclones but they can produce losses that can severely dent the balance sheets of insurance companies. In Australia the largest historical insured loss is from a hailstorm, despite the country's vulnerability to tropical cyclones and the destruction of Darwin by Cyclone Tracy. For financial risk management purposes, insurers and reinsurers would like to have a better understanding of the risks associated with these, but modelling them requires much more research if reliable models are to become common use in the insurance industry.

Another weakness of current modelling is business interruption. Business interruption losses are increasing as a percentage of total losses, but most are due to infrastructure failures, not damage to the insured property on current modelling of business interruption is based. Proper modelling of business interruption losses will involve modelling infrastructure damage and its impact on business. This is a major modelling challenges, which needs to be resolved in the next few years.

The continuing development of catastrophe loss models poses a challenge to the wind engineering research community. The development of models underpins the practice of engineering, and a characteristic of engineering research is the improvement of models to reduce uncertainty. However the traditional engineering approach to uncertainty has been to provide deterministic models incorporating levels of conservatism consistent with the levels of uncertainty, recognising that in general over-design is safe. Insurance loss models require a different approach since uncertainty is explicitly incorporated into the models, and the basic model is required to give the expected result without significant conservatism, since uncertainty is being already addressed. Furthermore engineering models are generally produced for engineers to use directly, whereas these models are for incorporation in a multi-disciplinary system for use by non-engineers.

Funding this development poses another challenge. The developments to date have been largely funded by the commercial companies that produce and market the models, and by governments through publicly funded research generally undertaken for other reasons, but which has had application to the modelling. With government funds for wind engineering becoming scarcer, and the limited resources of commercial companies to fund research without a clear cost benefit to them, new approaches will be needed if reliable models for use around the world are to be developed. The large market in the United States and Europe for modelling services will probably ensure continuing development of models relevant to these regions, but the situation looks much bleaker for the rest of the world, since much of the cost is concerned with customisation to local conditions. National approaches by Governments and the insurance industry working together to produce nationally acceptable publicly available models of occurrence and vulnerability that all commercial modelling companies can use may be the most effective approach.

CONCLUSION

To date wind damage has generally been regarded as insurable, at least in the wealthier countries where there is a high level of insurance. Increasing insured wind losses being sustained due to changing demographics, and increasing pressure for property to be insured against wind in countries where insurance is low and the risk of major wind disasters relatively high, are posing a challenge to the insurance industry. Technology is providing powerful tools to meet this challenge. One of these tools is GIS based wind loss modelling. These models are very dependent on wind engineering research. Although now being used very widely, in most countries there are many uncertainties attached to them. Resolving these uncertainties poses a significant challenge to wind researchers.

REFERENCES

Berliner, B. (1982), *Limits of Insurability of Risks*, Prentice-Hall.

Friedman, D. G. (1975), *Computer Simulation of Natural Hazard Assessment*, Institute of Behavioural Science, University of Colorado, Boulder.

Kiln, R. (1981), *Reinsurance in Practice*, Witherby & Co., London.

Kunreuther, H., R. Roth (ed.), (1998), *Paying the Price*, Joseph Henry Press, Washington.

Lester, R. The World Bank and Natural Catastrophe Funding, In N.R. Britton (ed.) (1999), *The Changing Risk Landscape: Implications for Insurance Risk Management,* Aon Re Australia Ltd.

Masters, T. Asset/Liability Modelling as a Tool for Financial Risk Management, In N.R. Britton (ed.), (2001), *Enhancing Shareholder Value Through Capital Risk Management*, Aon Re Australia Ltd, Sydney.

Middleton, D. 2003. The EQC – A Case Study in the Use of Modelling for Financial Risk Management, In N.R. Britton (ed.) (2001), *Enhancing Shareholder Value Through Capital Risk Management*, Aon Re Australia Ltd, Sydney.

Walker, G.R, Engineering Disaster Insurance Schemes for the 21st Century, Proceedings, 2003 Pacific Earthquake Engineering Conference, CD-Rom, University of Canterbury, Christchurch.

Walker, G. R, Current Developments in Catastrophe Modelling, In N.R. Britton & J. Oliver (eds.) (1999), *Financial Risk Management for Natural Catstrophes,* Aon Group Australia Ltd.

Woo, G (1999), *The Mathematics of Natural Catastrophes*, Imperial College Press, London.

"Alternative Risk Financing", Jim Banister Developments Ltd, London, 1998.

"Natural Catastrophes and Man-Made Disasters in 2002", Sigma No.2: 37, Swiss Re, Zurich, 2003.

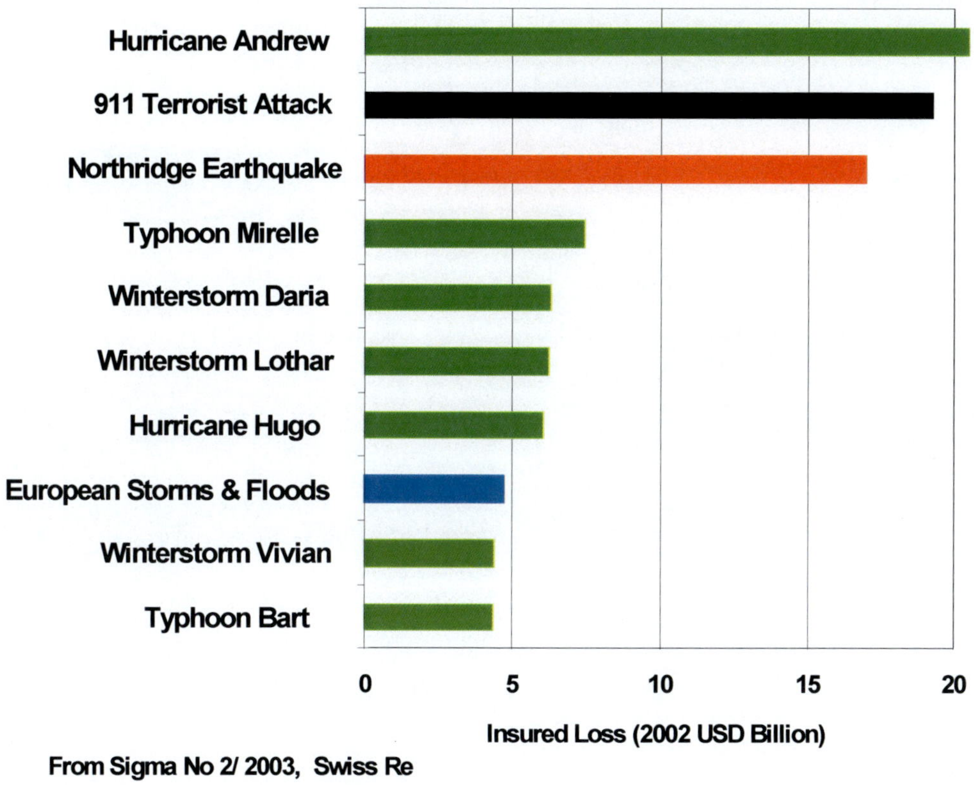

Figure 1. Largest 10 Insured Property Losses 1970-2002.

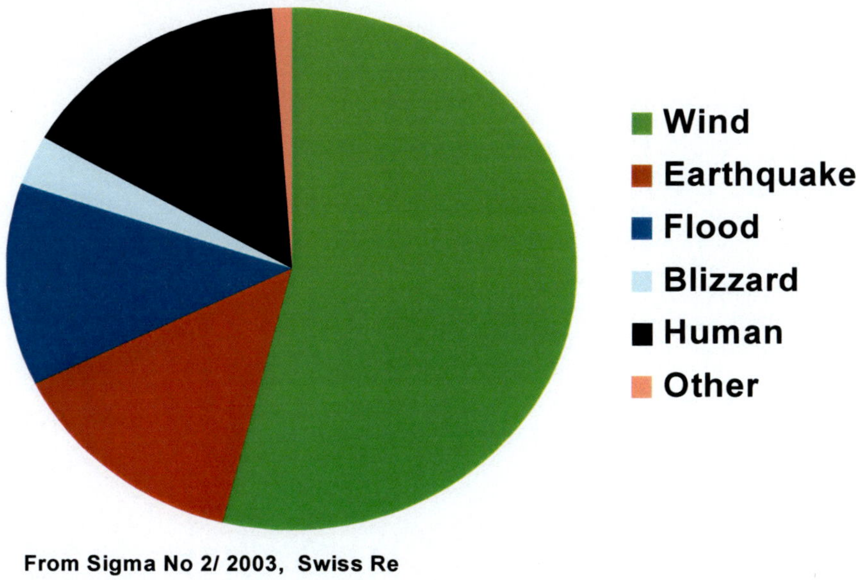

Figure 2. Relative Contribution to 40 Largest Insured Property Losses 1970-2002.

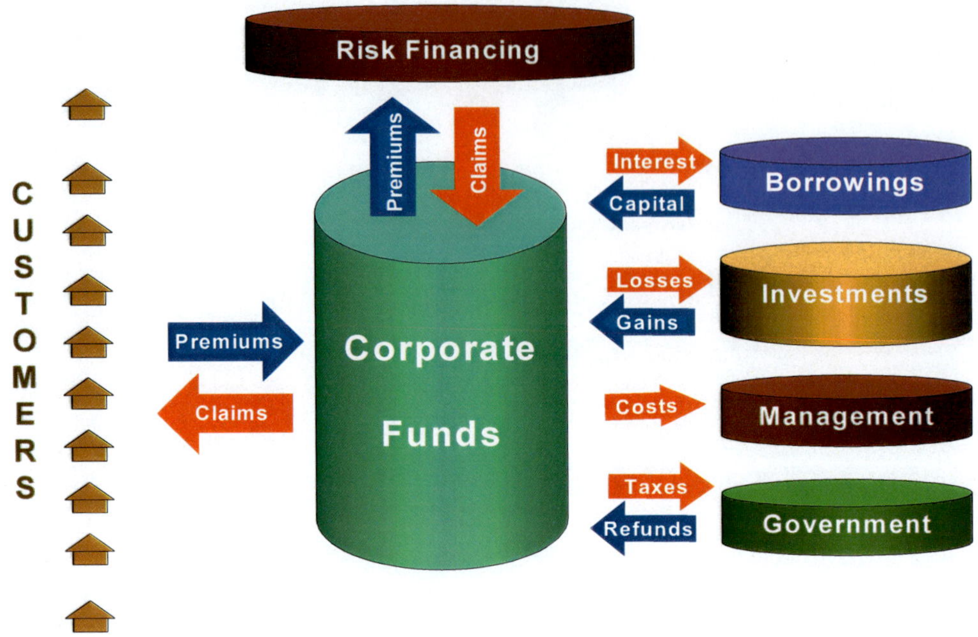

Figure 3. Financial Structure of Property Insurance Company.

In: Economics and the Wind
Editors: B. T. Ewing, et. al., pp. 47-61
ISBN: 1-59454-280-5
©2005 Nova Science Publishers, Inc.

Chapter 5

EFFECT OF UNCERTAINTIES IN MODELING TROPICAL CYCLONES ON PRICING EXCESS OF LOSS REINSURANCE

Siamak Daneshvaran and Robert E. Morden
Aon Impact Forecasting, Chicago, IL.

INTRODUCTION

Recently, improved understanding of catastrophe exposure is providing the private sector with better tools to quantify their risk. Many insurance companies realize the level of their exposure concentration and reinsurance companies immediately respond to this increase in exposure by radically raising rates. This increase in rate along with the increase of the attachment points/retentions pressures the insurance companies and as result the policyholders. The probable scenario losses estimated by catastrophe models for Florida are on the order of $70 billion. Given their capacity, insurance industry in general is reluctant/unable to absorb losses due to such large events and the majority of the loss will be self insured by the owners. In an effort to reduce/mitigate this risk, reinsurance is widely used. In this study the focus is a typical excess of loss reinsurance. Among the benefits of the excess of loss reinsurance is helping to stabilize the losses to the primary insurers and enable them to write larger risks. Catastrophe modeling software is generally used as an input to estimate the price of insurance layers. These models, in a probabilistic framework, use science and engineering methods in combination with the observed/recorded data. These models are capable of producing scenario results as well as probabilistic results (PML curves). Both the average annual loss and PML curves (results of probabilistic analysis) are important in pricing reinsurance layers

The methods used by the catastrophe models follow a cause and effect analysis logic to determine where the events occur, what magnitude and intensity they have, at what frequency they occur, how their damaging forces propagate in time and space, what and how local conditions amplify or de-amplify the effects at the site of the built environment, and how the built environment responds and the degree of damage caused. Due to randomness as well as uncertainty in data and models, these methods use probabilistic methods to estimate the potential losses due to future events. Randomness includes natural variability and inherent randomness that cannot be easily reduced via collection and analysis of more experience or experimental data. The location, time, and intensity of the next major hurricane that may landfall on the US coast can all be considered to be random quantities. Uncertainty, also referred to as epistemic uncertainty, thus comprises knowledge variability, data variability, and model uncertainty that can be reduced by better data or use of better and more refined models. With variability sources defined in this fashion, using a probabilistic framework, randomness on the underlying parameters is used to develop probability distribution functions on loss and uncertainty is used to define confidence intervals on these probability distributions.

The limited amount of reliable historical data on storms (from around 1945 till present) along with subjective assumptions on the assets at risk makes the statistical results generated by hazard and damage models unreliable. On the hazard side, the limited data on the storms generates two sources of uncertainty one being the reliability of the moments of the distributions used in the modeling process and the other one the uncertainty on the annual rate of occurrence (depending on the status of the climate). The resulting uncertainty associated with short record of data in combination with generic assumption on assets at risk (such as uncertainty on the damage models), when propagated through the insurance structure brings about the issue of credibility on the PML results. This is more pronounced as we try to model high severity-low frequency events at the tail of the distribution; this is usually the area where catastrophe options are more appealing to the investors. The focus of the paper is to quantify the effect (in order of magnitude) this combined uncertainty has on the loss distributions (both frequency and severity-wise) and the effect on pricing a typical excess of loss reinsurance.

EXAMPLE PORTFOLIO

The portfolio data used in this paper is based on the one provided by the Florida Commission on Loss Projection Methodology (Florida Hurricane Catastrophe Fund aggregate exposure data, 2002). A deductible of $250 is assumed per coverage and the rest of the input data follows the FHCF exposure. Figure 1 shows the spatial distribution of exposure.

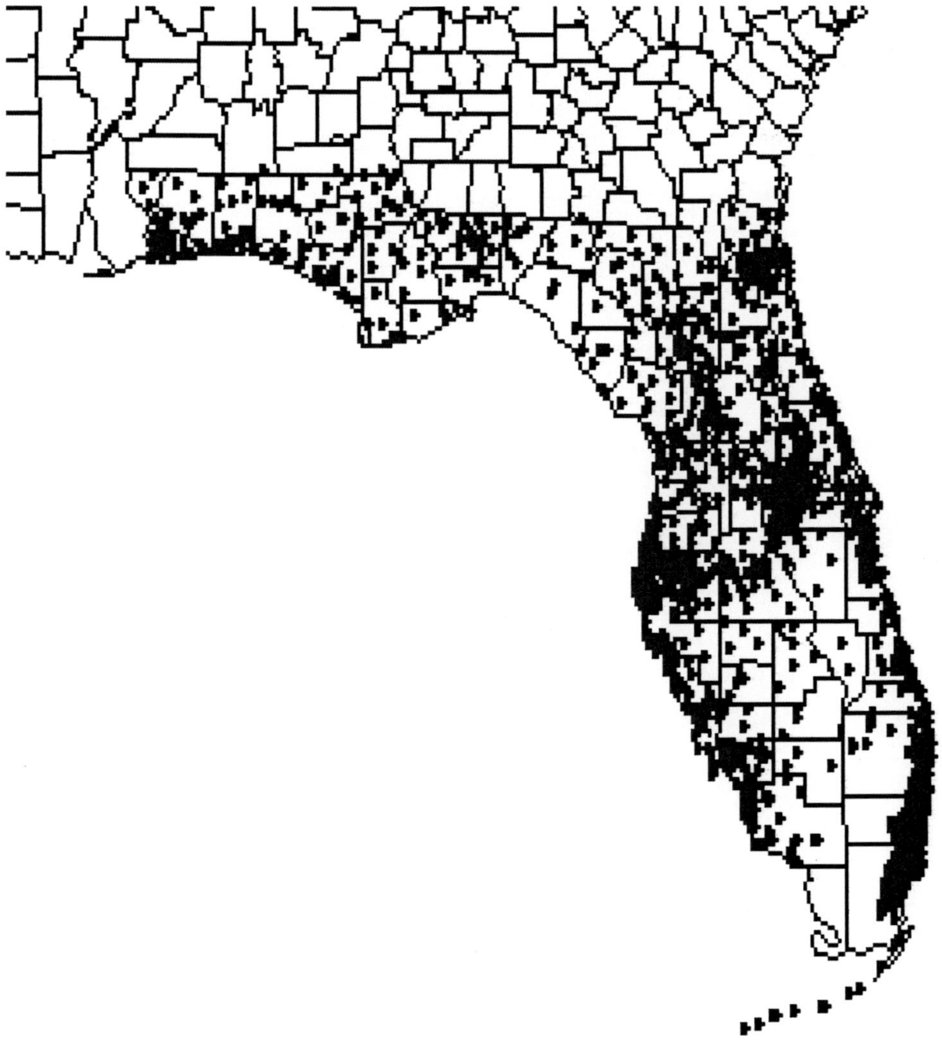

Figure 1. Example portfolio used to carry out the knowledge uncertainty analysis.

Hurricane Wind Risk Analysis

A numerically based hurricane wind-field model was used to estimate the wind speeds at the zip code level in the portfolio. The model has been extensively validated using actual storm data in recent years. Using GIS, the US Gulf, Florida peninsula, and Atlantic coasts are linearized and coastal segments are treated as sources of land falling convective storm events. Distributions are developed for Δp and R_{MAX} for each segment. The distributions of Δp and R_{MAX} are assumed to be Weibull and lognormal respectively (Georgiou, 1985; Vickery and Twisdale, 1995). The distributions for V_t (track speed), Θ (heading), and X (point of landfall measured from the beginning of a segment) are assumed to be log-normal, normal, and uniform, respectively (Georgiou, 1985; Daneshvaran et al., 1997).

The correlation between hurricane parameters is considered using the information from the National Hurricane Center and results reported by Ho et al (1987). Among the hurricane parameters, the prediction of wind speed is the most sensitive to the correlation between Δp and R_{MAX}. This correlation was considered by fitting an empirical equation to the mean of $\ln(R_{MAX})$ versus Δp for all of the land falling hurricanes. A constant standard deviation is used to model the segment-based random scatter around the mean. This is similar to the methods used by Georgiou (1985) and Vickery and Twisdale (1995).

Using the orthogonal decomposition method it is shown (Daneshvaran and Morden, 1997) that among the physical hurricane parameters, Δp contributes the most to the mean square wind speed (90%) and ultimately loss, with the mean response being captured by the first mode. The lack of measured data on Δp (about 60 years) indicates that its statistics is not highly reliable. The same argument holds for the annual rate of occurrence of the storms. Although in this case we have about 100 years worth of data, however this presents another source of knowledge uncertainty. The occurrence model used to temporally simulate the events is Poisson distribution. The rate of occurrence λ is small (about 3.7), however the parameter λT ($T \cong 100$ years) is large and it is assumed to have a normal distribution with mean and variance equal to λT. The confidence on the mean and variance of these parameters and their effect on the predicted wind speed were also addressed by Twisdale and Vickery (1993). In this study a similar model is used to propagate the effect of this variability on the loss and pricing of the catastrophe option. Based on the small number of samples in each coastal segment, error on the mean values of Δp is considered to follow Student's t distribution and it is possible to build distributions with different confidence levels on these parameters and eventually weight them according to their significance. Figure 2 shows the three branches of distribution for central pressure drop(expressed in milibar) corresponding to 10% mean and 90% confidence intervals (lower bound, central and upper bound distributions). The uncertainty in the wind-field model was considered as a source of random variability and was not considered as knowledge uncertainty.

By combining different states of central pressure distribution (with the their corresponding weights) and different states of occurrence (with their corresponding weights), several event sets were generated. These event sets were used to estimate the wind speeds at the locations of interest. Finally, using the weighted probabilities at each return period, distribution of wind speed at different return periods were obtained. Figure 3 presents the effect of knowledge uncertainty described above on the return period wind speeds at a site close to Miami Florida. The 10% and 90% confidence intervals along with mean wind speed are shown for different return periods. The coefficient of variation (CoV) on the wind speed is about 9% and reduces at higher return periods. Wind speed uncertainty is more sensitive to uncertainty in Δp compared with uncertainty in rate of occurrence. The method used to quantify the knowledge uncertainty is approximate since it is using the probability mass functions along with conditional distributions. The site used for wind speed calculations has a terrain factor of 0.89.

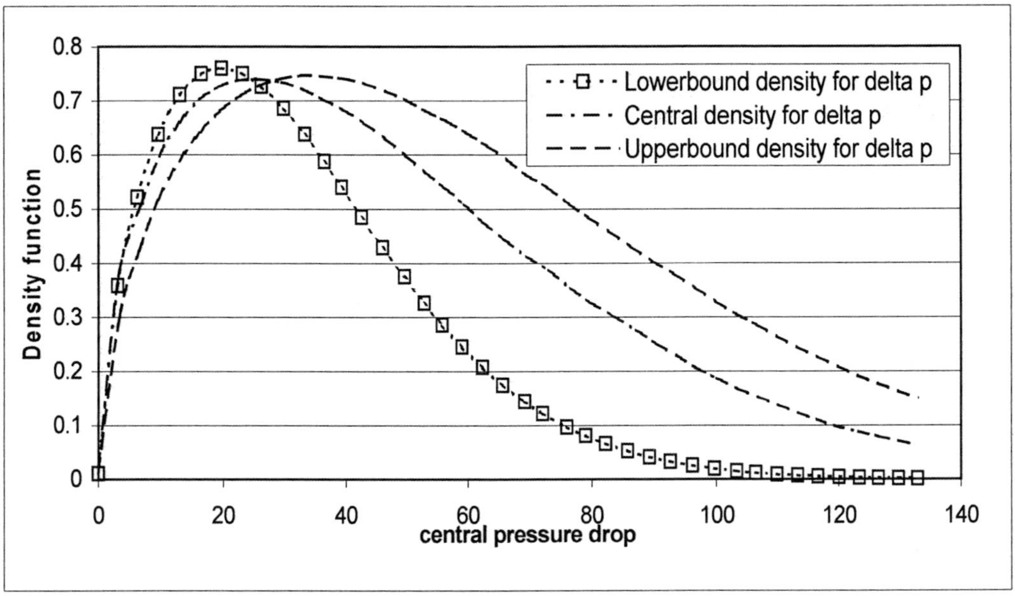

Figure 2. Probability density functions for central pressure drop (in millibar) used for expected and 10% and 90% confidence intervals.

PHYSICAL DAMAGE MODELING OF ASSETS AT RISK

The wind damage model used in this study computes physical damage to building and contents. The time element damage function estimates the time necessary to bring the building to its pre-loss level. No demand surge or loss adjustment expenses are modeled. The estimated physical damage covers damage to roof covering, roof sheathing, roof framing, wall envelope, openings, and garage doors. The methodology is based on ultimate strength of the components, where the component capacities at failure are converted into equivalent component failure velocities. The wind loading data is incorporated using the extensive amount of wind tunnel tests performed both in US and in Canada. Pressure distributions are developed for different areas of the roof and wall systems. Strength characteristics are developed based on manufacturing data and standards. The random variability as shown in Figure IV is coming from various building geometries, building exposure (terrain), load and strength characteristics. Monte Carlo simulation is used to predict the wind speed required to cause failure of individual building components and its likelihood of occurrence. The damage simulation process is repeated until a stable mean and standard deviation for damage at a range of wind speeds has been achieved (Sciaudone, et al, 1997).

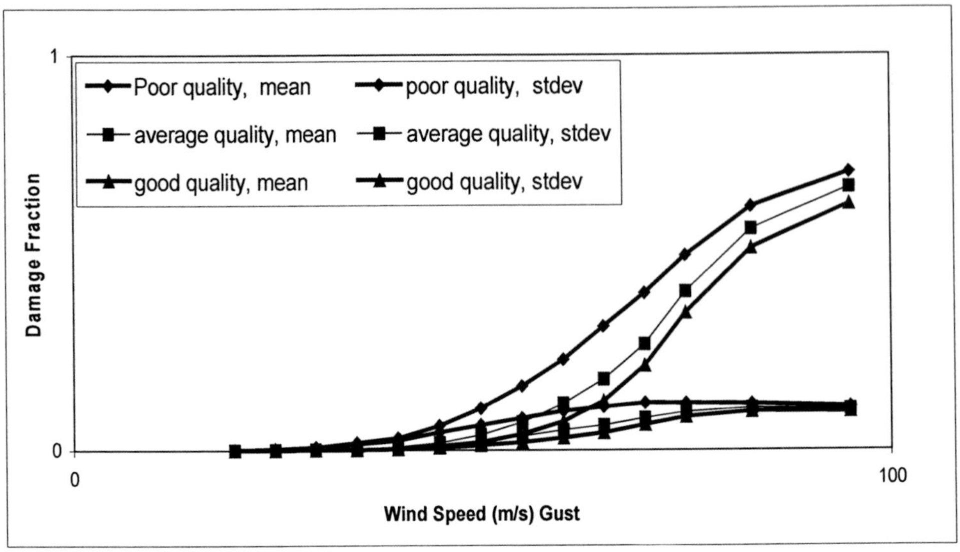

Figure 4. Typical damage functions representing three population of buildings in the portfolio

In this study, in order to reflect the uncertainty associated with different types of quality of buildings in a portfolio (for example it is known to be wood frame but no other information about its' wind resistive characteristics are available), the effect of knowledge uncertainty of the vulnerability functions within each class of buildings is considered. Please note that this uncertainty is different from the random variability within a given quality of construction/performance level. The component-based damage function is used to generate 3 sets of damage functions representing 3 different levels of vulnerability called poor, average and good construction. The criteria to estimate these performance levels are a combination of parameters that reflect different wind-resistivity levels of the buildings. These include the effectiveness of roof covering, roof sheathing, wall envelope, openings and garage doors. Figure 4 shows a comparison of these damage functions. They are used in a full probabilistic analysis in order to factor in the contribution of this part of portfolio uncertainty to the overall knowledge uncertainty. To propagate this uncertainty it is assumed that the average quality building has a weight of 60% and each of the good and poor quality buildings carry a weight of 20%. The damage functions are generated to more or less reflect these weighting factors given the population of buildings in a typical portfolio. The mean component resistance characteristics for the upper bound and lower bound damage functions (poor quality and good quality) correspond to 90% and 10% values of the parent distributions. The coefficient of variation (CoV) was assumed to stay constant. The mitigated/demitigated components used in the analysis were roof covering, roof to wall connections, amount of missing connectors, opening and garage door. Generally when wind speed increases there is a transition range for wind speed where damage to a building can be both small and large and the distribution of simulated damage fractions shows two separate clusters of damage population (a bimodal behavior). This is out of the scope of this paper and is not considered in this analysis, as its effect is not significant.

MODELING UNCERTAINTY

In summary, Table 1 presents the treatment of uncertainty in this study. The c, and k are the parameters of the Weibull distribution (all of the distributions are truncated at 133 mb). Beta distribution is used to model the conditional damage at a given wind speed. Both Lognormal and Beta distributions generated satisfactory results when fitted to the conditional simulated damage values, however since the upper bound of physical damage to the building is 100%, Beta was used. A tree structure is used to propagate the uncertainty throughout the analysis for all of the results. The weights represent the weight of each branch in the tree. So together 27, (3x3x3), event loss sets are generated with their corresponding weights. Generally the loss PML curves presented in portfolio analysis results are those associated with the central branch (shaded branch in Table 1). We refer to this as central branch results. The uncertainty due to the other random variables (such as Rmax and Track speed) is assumed to be less significant, as shown in a different study Daneshvaran and Morden [1997]. The method used to quantify the knowledge

Table 1. The Tree Structure Used to Propagate the Uncertainty via the 27 Branches.

ΔP Weibul(c,k)	Occurrence Poisson(μ)	Damage Beta ($\mu_{D\vert V}$, $\sigma_{D\vert V}$)	Weight			
			ΔP	Occurrence	Damage	Total
Lower Bound C_L, k_L	Lower μ_L	Lower $\mu^L_{D\vert V}$, $\sigma^L_{D\vert V}$	.2	.2	.2	0.008
		Central $\mu^C_{D\vert V}$, $\sigma^C_{D\vert V}$	.2	.2	.6	0.024
		Upper $\mu^U_{D\vert V}$, $\sigma^U_{D\vert V}$	.2	.2	.2	0.008
	Central μ_C	Lower	.2	.6	.2	0.024
		Central	.2	.6	.6	0.072
		Upper	.2	.6	.2	0.024
	Upper μ_U	Lower	.2	.2	.2	0.008
		Central	.2	.2	.6	0.024
		Upper	.2	.2	.2	0.008
Central Bound *C_C, k_C*	Lower	Lower	.6	.2	.2	0.024
		Central	.6	.2	.6	0.072
		Upper	.6	.2	.2	0.024
	Central	Lower	.6	.6	.2	0.072
		Central	.6	.6	.6	0.216
		Upper	.6	.6	.2	0.072
	Upper	Lower	.6	.2	.2	0.024
		Central	.6	.2	.6	0.072
		Upper	.6	.2	.2	0.024
Upper Bound C_U, k_U	Lower	Lower	.2	.2	.2	0.008
		Central	.2	.2	.6	0.024
		Upper	.2	.2	.2	0.008
	Central	Lower	.2	.6	.2	0.024
		Central	.2	.6	.6	0.072
		Upper	.2	.6	.2	0.024
	Upper	Lower	.2	.2	.2	0.008
		Central	.2	.2	.6	0.024
		Upper	.2	.2	.2	0.008

Note: The shaded branch is the central branch which is traditionally used to report portfolio losses.

LOSS ANALYSIS AND PRICING RISK

Figure 5 presents the total portfolio insured loss as a function of return period. The mean loss along with standard deviation (left axis) and CoV (on the right axis) as a result of combining 9 event sets together with 3 sets of damage functions representing the portfolio population of building is shown. The CoV of loss for larger return period is about 40% and is dominated by the contribution of the knowledge uncertainty induced by portfolio building vulnerability.

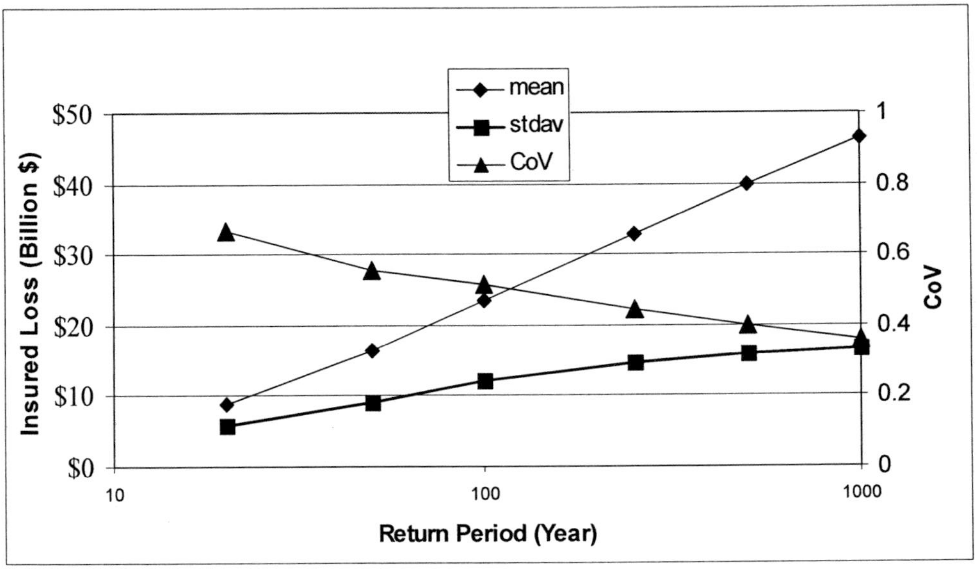

Figure 5. Expected Insured loss, its standard deviation and its CoV vs. return period.

Analysis of insurance/reinsurance risks indicates that the distribution of the losses in a cover is skewed and simple first order analysis is not able to capture the tail of the distribution. We use two models for reinsurance pricing:

1. The two-parameter standard deviation load model

$$ROL = EL + k\sigma \tag{1}$$

   Where ROL is total premium normalized by the layer limit and, k is the loading coefficient, EL is the expected loss, and σ is the standard deviation of the layer under consideration.

2. Single parameter, nonlinearly proportional to EL: $ROL = (0.47)(EL^{0.53})$ (Major and Kreps, 2002)

Lane (2000) also used an empirical two-parameter model to estimate price of catastrophe bonds (Daneshvaran and Morden, 2003). This model will be used in this paper to compare the price of a typical catastrophe bond option with reinsurance pricing models presented in equation 1. The two parameters in Lane's model are the conditional expected loss of the layer

(CEL) estimated based on the events attaching from the lower bound of the layer, and probability of attachment, PA, which is the probability that the cover will attach and the principal and interest will be impaired. In this case the price consists of the summation of the following two terms, which is called spread.

$$EL = PA \times CEL. \tag{2}$$
$$EER = 0.55(PA)^{0.495} \times (CEL)^{0.574}$$

The first term, EL, is the same in both reinsurance and bond pricing: The second term accounts for the profit for assuming the risk. The financing markets refer to this profit factor as expected excess return (EER). Reinsurance pricing is generally similar however the second term (k σ) is called loading term. The higher the safety factor the higher is the price. In this paper these formulas are used to propagate the event uncertainties to quantify the level of uncertainty in modeling the total price. The authors believe the results presented in this study are applicable irrespective of the pricing model used.

ESTIMATION OF PRICE BY LAYER

Loss due to an event, in a given excess layer with attachment Ai and limit Li, is given by:

$$Y(x) = \begin{cases} 0 & x < A_i \\ x - A_i & A_i < x < A_i + L_i \\ L_i & x > A_i + L_i \end{cases} \tag{3}$$

The expected loss over all events and variance for each layer is calculated by numerically integrating the simulated event losses on a non-exceedence probability curve. The CEL (conditional expected loss) and variance is later estimated by rescaling the probability for each layer to make them conditional: The formulation to calculate the first and second moments of each layer for each of the 27 branches is given by:

$$Y = (x - A_i)_+ - (x - (A_i + L_i))_+ \tag{4}$$
$$E(Y) = E((x - A_i)_+ - (x - (A_i + L_i))_+) = \mu(A_i) - \mu(A_i + L_i)$$

where $(x - A_i)_+$ is a ramp function. It is greater than zero only when x is larger than A_i and is zero otherwise. The second moment is:

$$E(Y^2) = E((x-A_i)_+ - (x-(A_i+L_i))_+)^2 = E((x-A_i)^2_+ - E(x-(A_i+L_i))^2_+ - 2(L_i)\mu(A_i+L_i)$$

The loss axis is divided in to 10 equal excess layers starting from a threshold of \$3.50 billion. The layer limits (\$6.65 billion) are selected to be equal to enable easier presentation and comparison of the results. Table 2 shows for each of the excess layers the following quantities: expected loss, EL, for the central branch (no uncertainty), weighted average of expected loss over all of the branches (includes uncertainty), standard deviation of loss for central branch and total standard deviation including uncertainty which is given by:

$$\sigma(Layer_i) = \sqrt{\sum_{j=1}^{27} w_j \sigma^2{}_{i,j} + \sum_{j=1}^{27} w_i (\mu_i - E_{i,j}(Y))^2} \quad (5)$$

(mean of the variances plus variance of the means). w_i is the weight for each branch, $E_{i,j}$ is the expected loss for layer i and for branch j, and $\sigma^2_{i,j}$ is the variance for layer i for branch j.

Table 2. Statistics of Expected Loss with and without Knowledge Uncertainty

Layer	Excess Layer BN	EL w/o uncertainty	Mean EL w uncertainty	St. Dev. w/o uncertainty	St. Dev.w uncertainty
1	6.65 XS 3.5	5.358%	7.687%	20.0%	25.3%
2	6.65 XS 10.2	2.038%	3.290%	13.2%	17.0%
3	6.65 XS 16.8	0.980%	1.739%	9.2%	12.5%
4	6.65 XS 23.5	0.481%	0.999%	6.6%	9.6%
5	6.65 XS 30.1	0.239%	0.592%	4.6%	7.4%
6	6.65 XS 36.8	0.131%	0.369%	3.4%	5.8%
7	6.65 XS 43.5	0.055%	0.218%	2.2%	4.5%
8	6.65 XS 50.1	0.030%	0.132%	1.6%	3.5%
9	6.65 XS 56.7	0.014%	0.082%	1.1%	2.7%
10	6.65 XS 63.4	0.005%	0.048%	0.7%	2.1%

As can be observed, knowledge uncertainty increases both quantities (EL, σ) as we go to higher layers. Table 2 shows the expected loss for the central distributions (without uncertainty) and expected loss when uncertainty is included along with corresponding standard deviations. Let's look at layer 6 for some comparison. The EL for layer 6 is almost 3 times larger when the uncertainty is accounted for. The same table also shows that the standard deviation for layer 6 is about 70% larger when the uncertainty is included in the analysis. These differences definitely have an impact when we price the layer for the reinsurance. Figures 6 and 7 present this information in graphs. The vertical axis in Figure 6 is shown in log to stress the difference in higher layers.

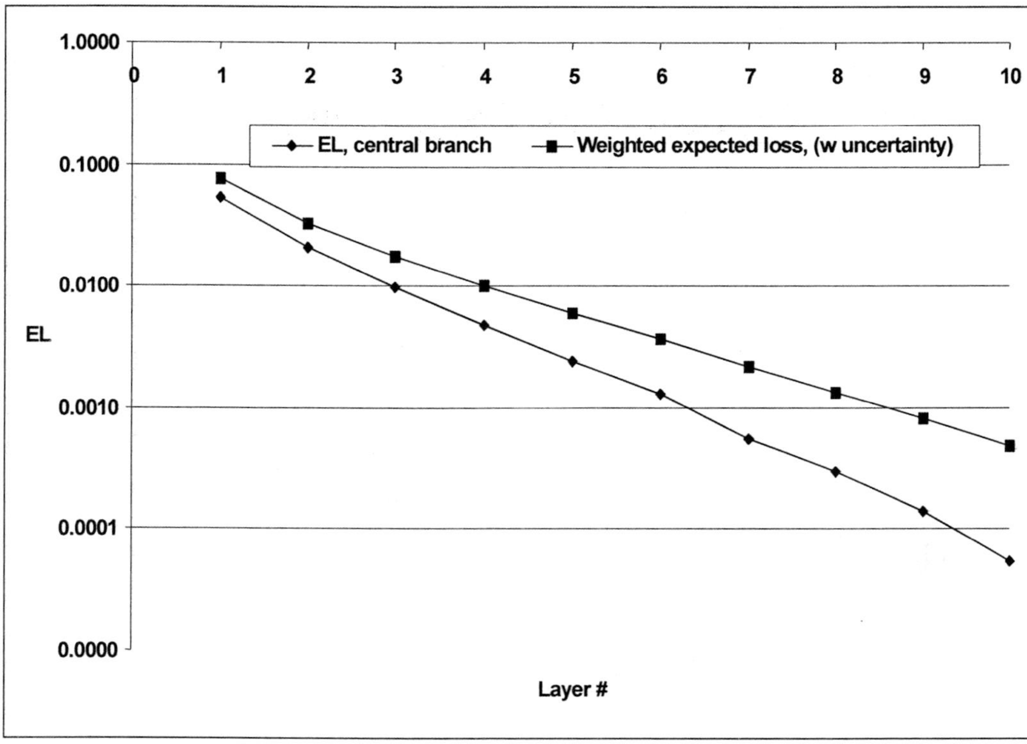

Figure 6. Expected loss for central branch (no uncertainty) and with uncertainty

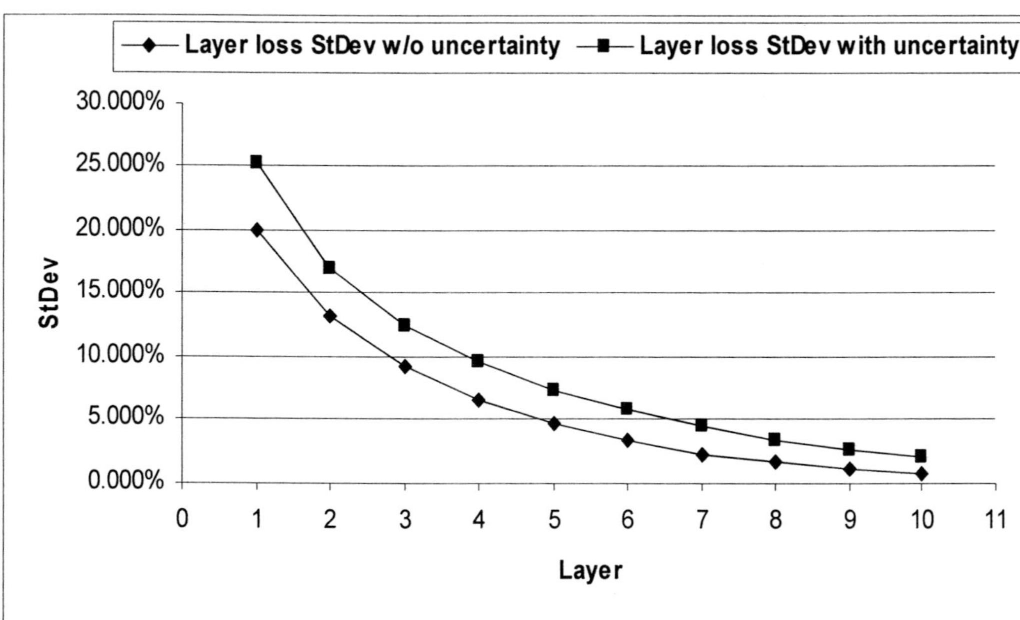

Figure 7. Standard deviation of loss for central branch (no uncertainty) and with uncertainty

REINSURANCE PRICING

In previous section we briefly discussed the layer EL and standard deviation (Figures 6, 7) Using those results we can analyze some reinsurance pricing models in the light of existing uncertainty. The traditional reinsurance model expressed in equation 1: $ROL = EL + k\sigma$ is used as the first example. The uncertainty, in this case, affects the price both through EL and σ. Figure 8 presents comparison of ROL calculated both ways with and without uncertainty. The coefficient k (load factor or Sharp ratio) is assumed to be 0.25.

The ratio of rate-on-lines varies from 1.35 for layer one to about 3 for layer 10 (Table 3). For layer 6 this ratio is 1.86. In other words the premium increases by 86% when uncertainty is considered. Now, one may argue that individual companies will calibrate the coefficient k to account for this uncertainty. In other words account for under-prediction in standard deviation (by not modeling the uncertainty) by increasing k factor. However, this is not correct when one tries to define a risk consistent pricing model.

Table 3. Layer price with and without Uncertainty

Layer	Excess layer BN	Price w/o uncertainty (%)	Price w uncertainty (%)
1	6.65 XS 3.5	10.37	14.02
2	6.65 XS 10.2	5.33	7.55
3	6.65 XS 16.8	3.28	4.87
4	6.65 XS 23.5	2.12	3.39
5	6.65 XS 30.1	1.40	2.44
6	6.65 XS 36.8	0.98	1.83
7	6.65 XS 43.5	0.60	1.34
8	6.65 XS 50.1	0.44	1.00
9	6.65 XS 56.7	0.28	0.73
10	6.65 XS 63.4	0.18	0.57

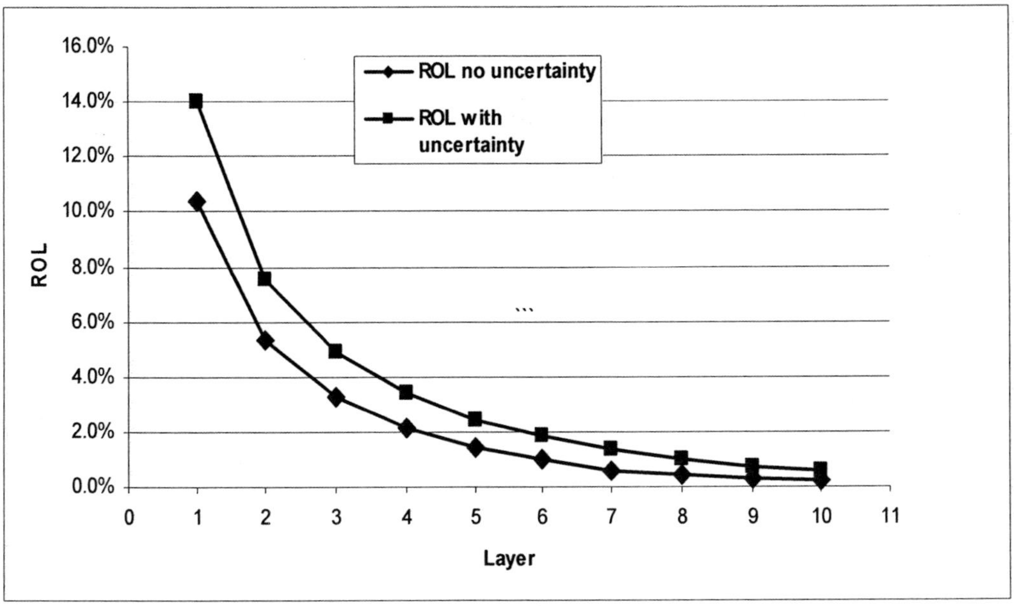

Figure 8. Rate on Line with and without uncertainty.

Figure 9 compares the ROL derived using four different formulas. All models results presented include uncertainty. The graph includes **1**-Lane's regression model for total spread EL+EER for catastrophe bonds (Daneshvaran and Morden, 2003), **2**-Equation 1 for pricing reinsurance **3**-Only EER (equation 2, Lane), **4**-The regression model reported by Major and Kreps (2002). The Figure suggests that catastrophe bonds are generally more expensive than the similar reinsurance programs. Models 4 and 3 both asymptotically approach model one as we move to higher layers. Model 1 and 2 results are almost parallel in log space. This means that model 1 results (catastrophe bond) consistently is about 60% larger than model 2 results (reinsurance). It should be mentioned that catastrophe bond trenches generally span the higher return period region of PML curves. Layer 6 corresponds to 500-year loss return period (PA=0.002) and from this layer up the prices suggested by models 1,3, and 4 are almost asymptotically converging (all proportional to EER in equation 3).

Table 4 shows the difference in mean PA calculated based on the original distributions (central branch) and the one estimated when including uncertainty in the underlying parameters (this study's approach). Table also shows the coefficient of variation of PA for each layer which increases rather drastically as we proceed to higher layers. Also, looking at the ratio of column 4 to column 3, it is obvious that the probability of attachment at layer one is 38% larger when uncertainty is included and this ratio for layer ten is bout 10 times (1000%). This stresses the fact that inclusion of uncertainty in estimating PA is essential.

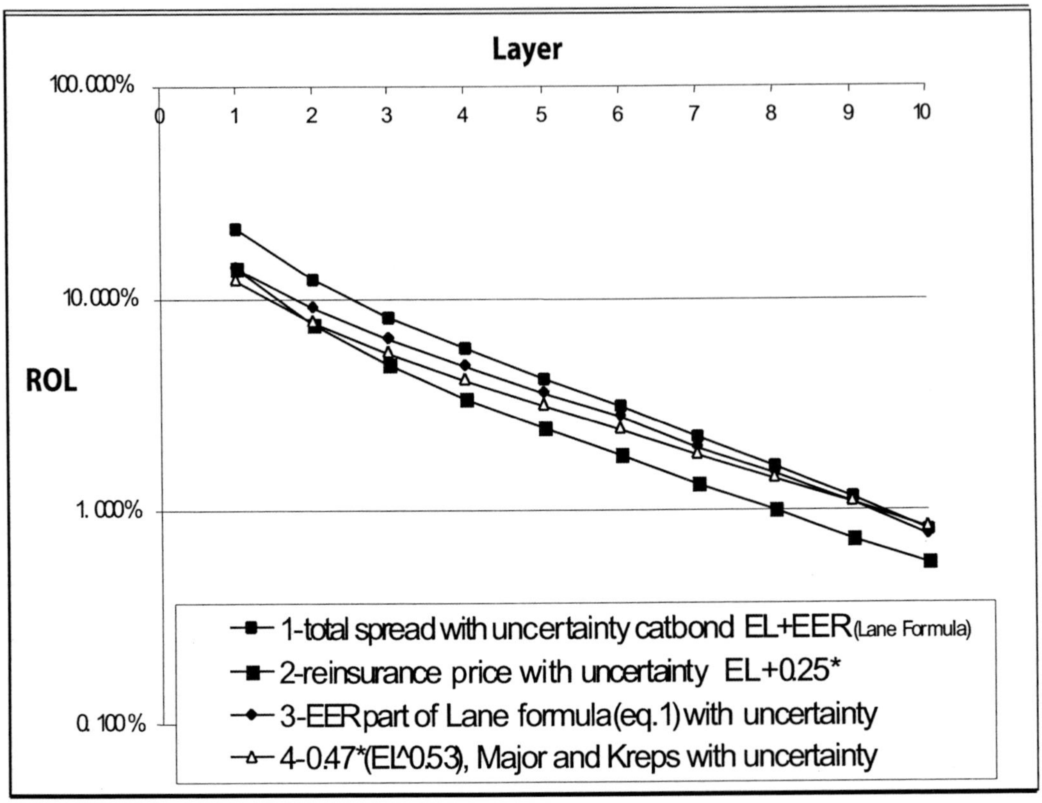

Figure 9. A comparison of the effect of uncertainty on the different pricing models

Table 4. Mean Probability of Attachment (PA) with and without Inclusion of Uncertainty

Layer	Excess layer $BN	Mean w/o uncertainty (%)	Mean w uncertainty (%)	CoV PA w uncertainty (%)
1	6.65 XS 3.5	9.845	12.833	68.19
2	6.65 XS 10.2	2.948	4.679	92.06
3	6.65 XS 16.8	1.391	2.298	102.13
4	6.65 XS 23.5	0.645	1.285	116.79
5	6.65 XS 30.1	0.330	0.756	127.97
6	6.65 XS 36.8	0.176	0.459	144.09
7	6.65 XS 43.5	0.082	0.282	161.87
8	6.65 XS 50.1	0.038	0.169	187.00
9	6.65 XS 56.7	0.019	0.101	208.34
10	6.65 XS 63.4	0.006	0.061	223.72

Note: Also, coefficient of variation of PA is shown

CONCLUSIONS

Knowledge uncertainty introduces rather large uncertainty in to the pricing of risk in a typical reinsurance layer. This increases both layer expected loss and layer variance. It is recommended to account for this increase in a risk consistent framework. Using the methodology presented in this paper, it is possible (as an example) to calibrate the k factor in the traditional standard deviation load model (equation 1) when pricing insurance and reinsurance products.

Introducing knowledge uncertainty (parametric uncertainty) on hazard and damage parameters increases the layer mean probability of attachment. This is true even if the mean of the underlying parameters stays the same.

REFERENCES

Daneshvaran, S, R. Morden (2003), "Effect of Uncertainties in Modeling Tropical Cyclones on Pricing catastrophe bonds" *International Wind Engineering Conference*, Texas Tech University.

Daneshvaran, S., T. Yao, R. Morden, M. M. Zadeh and Y. K. Wen (1997), "A parametric model for efficient hurricane risk analysis of large portfolios", *International Conference of Structural Safety and Reliability (ICOSSAR) '97*, Kyoto, Japan, November 24-28.

Daneshvaran, S., and Morden R. (1998), "Fast Hurricane Wind Analysis Using the Orthogonal Decomposition Method", *Journal of Wind Engineering and Industrial Aerodynamics*, Vol.77&78.

Sciaudone, J. C., D. Feuerborn, G. N. Rao, and S. Daneshvaran (1997), "Development of Objective Wind Damage Functions to Predict Wind Damage to Low Rise Structures" *8th US National Conference in Wind Engineering.*

Lane, M.N. (2000), "Pricing Risk Transfer Transactions", *ASTIN Bulletin*, Vol.30: 2.

Georgiou, P.N. (1985), "Design wind speeds in tropical cyclone-prone regions," *Ph.D. Thesis, Boundary Layer Wind Tunnel Laboratory*, The University of Western Ontario, Canada.

Ho, F.P., J.C. Su, K.L. Hanevich, R.J. Smith, and F.P. Richards (1987), "Hurricane Climatology for the Atlantic and Gulf Coasts of the United States" *NOAA Technical Report NWS 38.*

Major J., R. E. Kreps (2002), *Alternative Risk Strategies: Catastrophe Risk Pricing in the Traditional Market,* Risk Books.

Twisdale, L.A., P.J. Vickery, M.B. Hardy (1993), "Uncertainties in the prediction of hurricane wind speeds" *ASCE Conference.*

Vickery, P.J., L.A. Twisdale (1995), "Wind-field and filling models for hurricane wind speed predictions" *ASCE, J. of Structural Engineering.*

In: Economics and the Wind
Editors: B. T. Ewing, et. al., pp. 63-71

ISBN: 1-59454-280-5
©2005 Nova Science Publishers, Inc.

Chapter 6

WEATHER AND SHOCKS TO INSURANCE STOCK PRICES: VOLATILITY AND PERSISTENCE

Bradley T. Ewing
Rawls College of Business and Wind Science and Engineering Research Center, Texas Tech University, Lubbock, TX
Guillermo Covarrubias
Department of Economics, Texas Tech University, Lubbock, TX

INTRODUCTION

There are several reasons that one may want a model that accounts for regime shifts to forecast volatility. First, it may help one asses more accurately the risk of holding an asset or have a better estimate of the value of an option by using the improved forecast of volatility on the Black-Scholes framework. Second, for risk managers it is important that they incorporate in their hedging strategies forecast confidence intervals that are time-varying, so that more accurate intervals can be obtained by modeling the variance of the errors. Third, more efficient estimators can be obtained if heteroskedasticity in the errors is handled properly.

A model of volatility that provides a better fit for the data can also be helpful for analysts in shedding some light on the behavior of management in response to shocks. This paper is concerned with the effectiveness of insurance companies' management of industry specific risk. As weather related events that have economic consequences occur, the profitability of insurance companies is adversely affected and this reflects on the firm's asset price.

LITERATURE REVIEW

ARCH models were introduced by Engle (1982) and generalized as GARCH (Generalized ARCH) by Bollerslev (1986). These models are widely used in financial time series analysis. Malik (2003) examines exchange rates using a GARCH model accounting for regime shifts in volatility and finds that the persistence in volatility is reduced. Aggarwal, Inclan and Leal (1999) also using a GARCH model accounting for regime shifts in volatility on emerging stock market returns find a reduction in volatility persistence as well. It is important to incorporate the regime shifts in the model for improved forecast. Accurate forecasts are important to financial market participants wishing to hedge risk. A financial instrument that is creating interest is weather derivatives. The Demand for these instruments is created by the need to hedge against weather surprises.

METHODOLOGY

Identifying Regime Changes in Volatility

This paper uses the ICSS algorithm introduced by Inclan and Tiao (1994) to detect sudden discrete changes in volatility. Their analysis focused on detecting breaks in volatility due to a sudden shock in a given time series. It is standard practice in finance to use variance as a proxy for volatility. Malik (2003) describes their methodology as follows; let ε_t be a series with zero mean and with unconditional variance σ_t^2. Let the variance within each interval be given by σ_j^2, j=0,1... N_T, where N_T is the total number of variance changes in T observations, and $1 < \kappa_1 < \kappa_2 < \ldots < \kappa_{NT} < T$ are the change points,

$$
\begin{aligned}
& 1 < t < \kappa_1 \\
&= \tau_1^2 \quad \kappa_1 < t < \kappa_2 \\
&= \tau_{NT}^2 \quad \kappa_{NT} < t < T
\end{aligned} \tag{1}
$$

Inclan and Tiao use a cumulative sum of squares to detect the number of changes in variance and the time point of each variance shift. Let $C_k = \sum_{t=1}^{k} \varepsilon_t^2$ k=1...T be the (mean–centered) cumulative sum of squared observations from the first observation to the kth point in time. Define the D_k statistic as follows

$$D_k = (C_k / C_t) - k/T \quad k=1,\ldots,T \text{ with } D_0 = D_T = 0 \tag{2}$$

Significant changes in variance are detected based on the critical values obtained from the distribution of D_k under the null hypothesis of constant variance. Specifically, the null hypothesis of homogeneous variance is rejected if the maximum absolute value of D_k is greater than the critical value. Let k^* be the value at which $\max_k |D_k|$ is reached. If $\max_k$

$\sqrt{(T/2)}\,|D_k|$ falls outside the predetermined boundary, then k^* is taken as the time point of a variance change in the series. The term $\sqrt{(T/2)}$ is required to standardize the distribution.

A critical value of 1.36 is used, which is the 95th percentile of asymptotic distribution of $\max_k \sqrt{(T/2)}\,|D_k|$. Therefore, in the D_k plot, the upper and lower boundaries are set at ± 1.36. A change point in variance is identified if it falls outside these boundaries. However, if the series has multiple change points then these are difficult to detect due to the "masking effects". To overcome this problem Inclan and Tiao (1994) designed an algorithm that looks at different pieces of the series for identification of change points in variance. The ICSS algorithm works by evaluating D_k over different periods of time, and those different periods are determined by the break points that are identified by the D_k plot.

GARCH Model

Once the regime changes have been detected, we want to incorporate them in a volatility model. We begin with the estimation of a simple GARCH model. In developing a GARCH model, you will have to consider two distinct specifications—one for the conditional mean and one for the conditional variance. In the standard GARCH(1,1) specification:

$$Y_t = \mu + \varepsilon_t,\ \varepsilon_t \,|\, I_{t-1} \sim N(0, \sigma_t^2) \tag{3}$$

$$\sigma_t^2 = \omega + \alpha\varepsilon_{t-1}^2 + \beta\sigma_{t-1}^2 \tag{4}$$

where N is the conditional normal distribution with a zero mean and variance σ_t^2. I_{t-1} is the information set available up to time t-1. In the GARCH specification, the sum of α and β measures the persistence of volatility for a given shock and would have a value of 1 for an *integrated* GARCH (IGARCH) process. Shocks to an IGARCH process have a permanent effect on the variance of a series.

Table 1. Descriptive Statistics for Excess Returns

	Mean	Std. Dev	Skewness	Kurtosis	J-B
Insurance Composite	.034456	2.120685	.248327	5.606785	181.0379
Life and Health	-.079542	2.326719	.010202	5.217422	126.4176
Property Casualty	-025073	2.584322	.400591	6.373753	309.1197
Multiline	.105926	2.476853	.102841	5.384782	147.2957
Insurance Brokers	-.015236	2.511791	.276471	5.111236	122.4504

Note: There are 617 observations.

Combined Model of Sudden Changes with GARCH

Lamoureux and Lastrapes (1990) argue that persistence in volatility is overestimated when standard (G)ARCH models are applied to a series with underlying sudden changes in variance. These shifts in volatility could be due to regime/structural changes that are caused by weather, political, social or economic events. To get reliable parameter estimates of the conditional variance equation, regime shifts should be incorporated in the standard GARCH model. The present study uses a GARCH model with sudden changes in variance, which were identified by using ICSS algorithm. The Marquardt algorithm was used to maximize the log likelihood function. All calculations were performed using RATS version 4.31 (Regression Analysis of Time Series).

$$Y_t = \mu + \varepsilon_t,\ \varepsilon_t \mid I_{t-1} \sim N(0,\ \sigma_t^2) \tag{5}$$

$$\sigma_t^2 = \omega + d_1 D_1 + \ldots + d_n D_n + \alpha\, \varepsilon_{t-1}^2 + \beta\, \sigma_{t-1}^2 \tag{6}$$

where $D_1, \ldots, D_n$ are the dummy variables taking a value of one from each point of sudden change of variance onwards, zero elsewhere.

Data

This paper uses weekly data for the Wednesday close of the S&P insurance composite index, S&P insurance sub sector indices, and the S&P 500. The sample period spans from January 3,1990 to October 24, 2001. In case of a holiday on Wednesday, the closing level of the index on the previous day of trading was used. The data are transformed to returns by taking the natural log of the index at time t and subtracting the log of the level of the index at time (t-1). Data are from Global Financial Data.

Regime Changes in Volatility

Time periods in which a regime shift in volatility occurs were identified using the ICSS algorithm. Three different regimes were identified in the insurance composite excess returns data and in the insurance sub indices. The first breaking point in volatility for the insurance composite excess returns data occurs in May 4, 1994 where a significant decrease in volatility is identified by the ICSS algorithm. The second breaking point occurs in October 7, 1998 where a significant increase in volatility is observed. Table 2 shows the breaking points for the insurance composite excess returns volatility and for the insurance sub sectors tracked by S&P. Similar results are seen in the sub sectors excess return volatility series. The sub sectors also have three different regimes. In all cases the ICSS identifies an initial significant decrease in volatility followed by a significant increase in volatility for the third regime. Figure 1 presents a graph of the volatility regimes.

Table 2. Sudden Changes in Volatility

	Number of Change Points	Time Period	Standard Deviation
Insurance Composite	2	Jan 3, 90-May 4, 94^{+}	1.88134
		May 4, 94-Oct 7,98^{++}	1.35827
		Oct 7, 1998-Oct 31,01^{+++}	3.1246
Life and Health	2	Jan 3, 90-Oct 27,93+	2.02051
		Oct 27, 93-Sep 9, 99^{++}	1.54082
		Sep 9, 99-Oct 31, 01^{+++}	3.44056
Property Casualty	2	Jan 3, 90-Apr 20, 94+	2.10530
		Apr 20, 94-Oct 14, 98^{++}	1.54171
		Oct 14, 98-Oct 31, 01^{+++}	4.04364
Multiline	2	Jan 3, 90-May 4, 94+	2.26358
		May 4, 94-Jul 8, 98^{++}	1.59769
		Jul 8, 98-Oct 31, 01^{+++}	3.485338
Insurance Brokers	2	Jan 3, 90-Sep 22, 92^{+}	2.32796
		Sep 22,92-Sep 2,98^{++}	1.66736
		Sep 2,98-Oct 31, 01^{+++}	3.71528

$^{+}$ denotes period of normal weather.

$^{++}$ denotes period of mild weather.

$^{+++}$ denotes 1997-1998 when El Nino was very strong.

Insurance Brokers

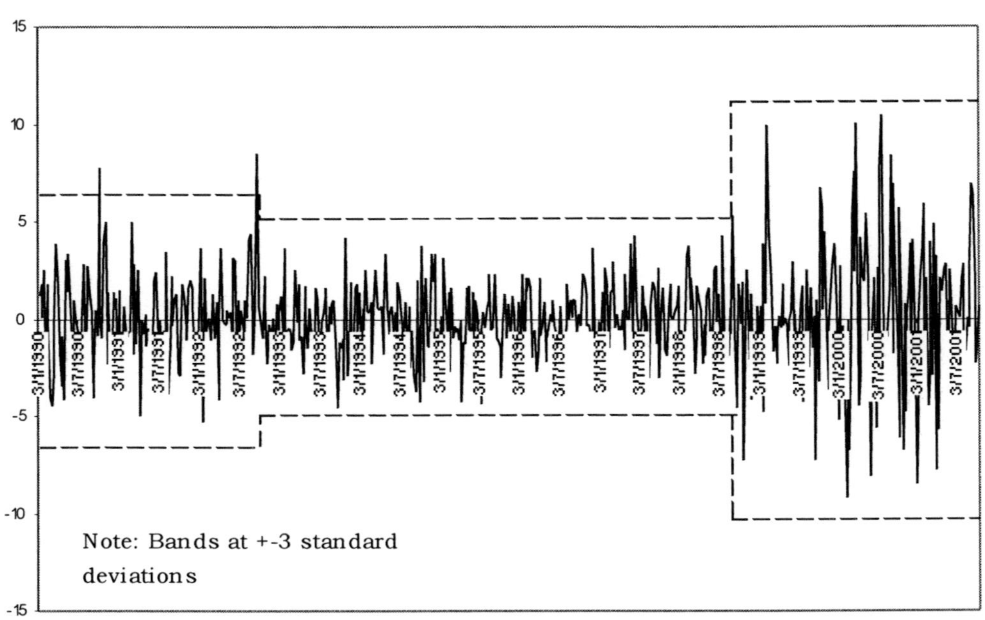

Figure 1. Insurance Composite Indices Excess Returns Volatility.

Insurance Composite

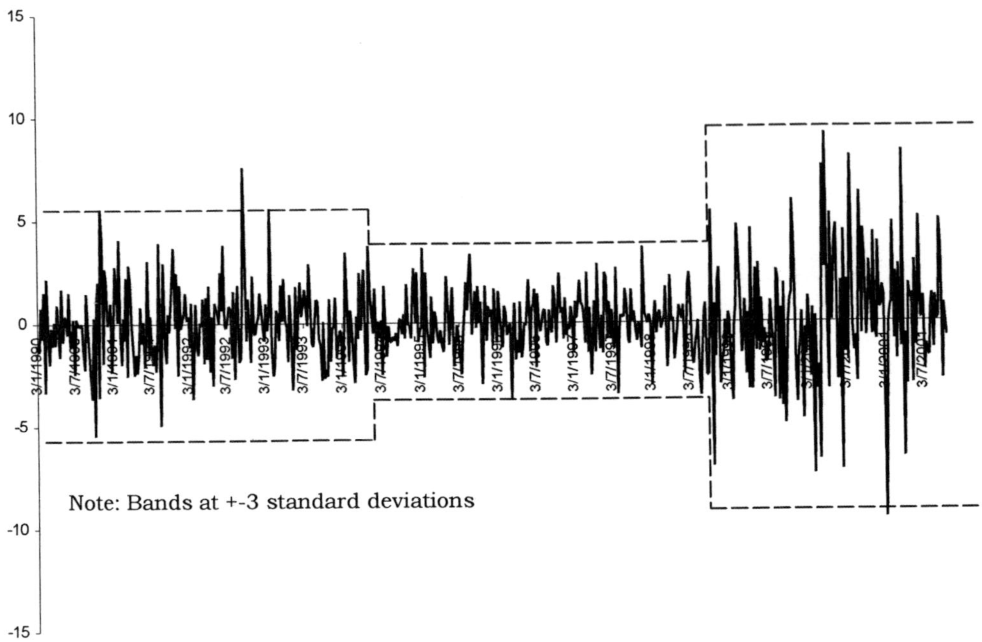

Life and health

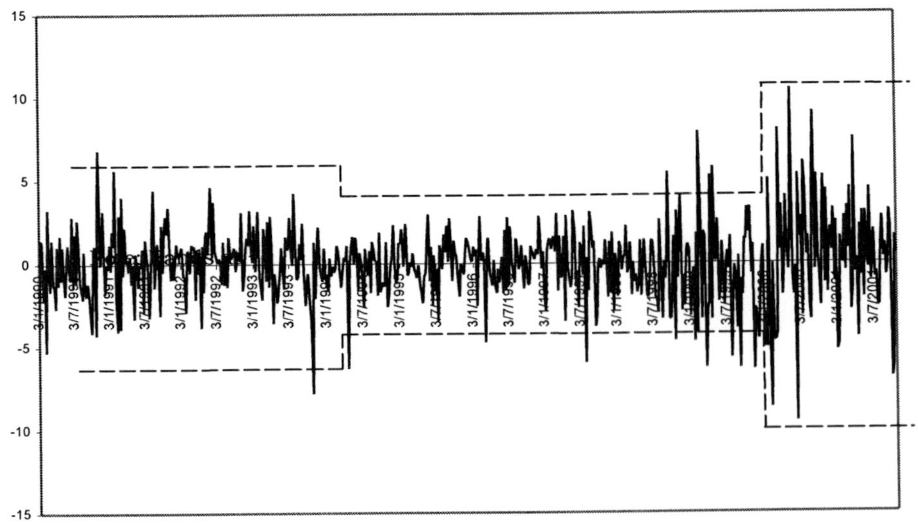

Figure 1. Insurance Composite Indices Excess Returns Volatility (Continued).

Multiline

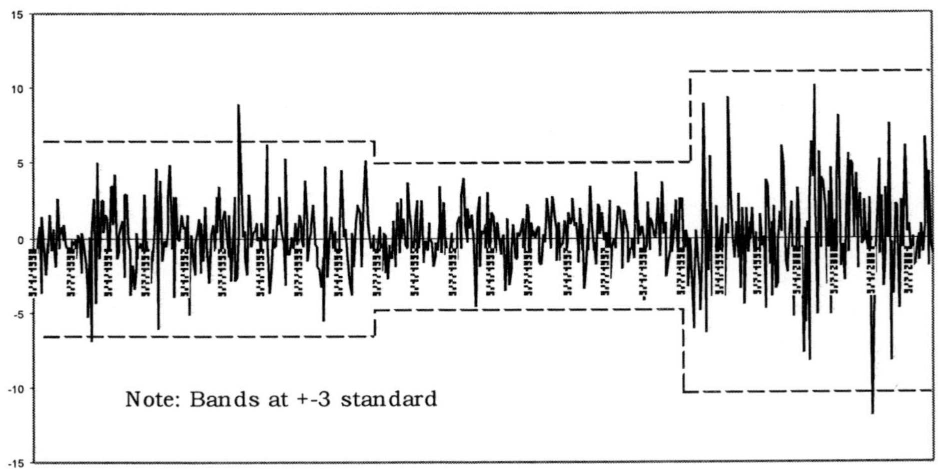

Property Casualty

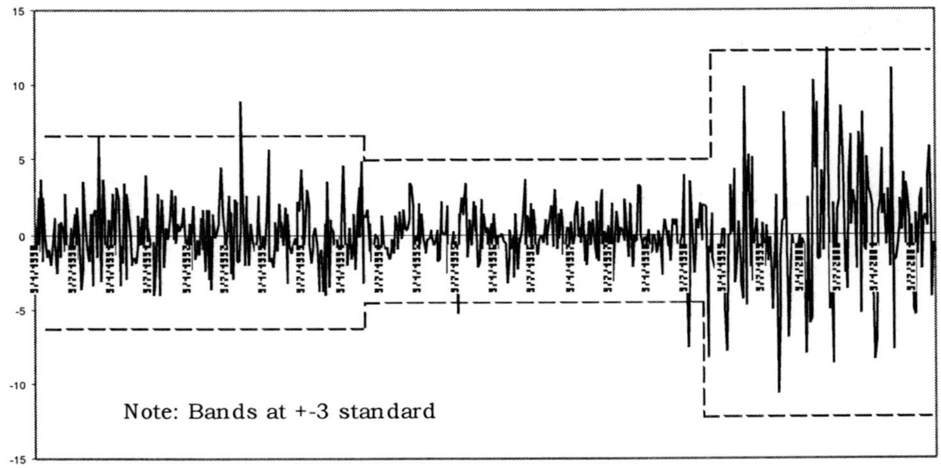

Figure 1. Insurance Composite Indices Excess Returns Volatility (Continued).

The three periods identified by the ICSS algorithm correspond to periods of time characterized by different amounts of weather related damage. Anecdotal evidence suggests that the first period in our sample has a normal amount of severe weather events. In fact, 11.37 billion dollars in damage is the average from 1955 to 1999 according to data compiled from the National Climatic Data Center. The second regime is characterized by weather that was relatively mild, at least as compared to the norm. The third regime may be associated with a very strong El Nino effect that occurred in 1998. El Nino is associated with changes in global weather patterns including windstorms, droughts or winter weather variations. In 1998 the amount of damage created by windstorms jumped to over 16 billion dollars. The increase in weather related damages may be responsible for the increase in volatility in insurance stock prices in this time period.

GARCH Model Taking into Account Regime Changes in Volatility

Dummy variables were included in the variance equation to account for breaks in volatility as detected by the ICSS algorithm. Table 3 shows that the persistence of shocks as measured by the sum of α and β was significantly reduced in all cases. The persistence of volatility declined from 0.99293 to .37337 for the insurance composite index. Note that in the GARCH specification that excludes dummy variables, the ARCH and GARCH parameters were significant at the 1% level. When regime shifts are accounted for in the model, these two parameters are insignificant at the 5% level. The loss of significance in the parameters is consistent with the notion that time varying volatility may be a manifestation of regime shifts. ARCH LM test and Ljung-Box statistics were performed on standardized residuals ($\varepsilon_t/\sqrt{h_t}$) from both models. Neither model reveals any ARCH effects or autocorrelation after fitting the model.

Table 3. GARCH (1,1) Results

	GARCH (1,1) Model				GARCH (1,1) Model with dummy variables				
	α	*β*	*α+β*	*TR²*	*α*	*β*	*α+β*	*Persistence decline*	*TR²*
Insurance	.05387	.93905	.9929	1.1821	.06250	.31081	.3734	.6196	.04705
Composite	(.0000)	(.0000)		(.5537)	(.1314)	(.4019)			(.8283)
Life and Health	.05735	.93276	.9901	.0966	.07537	.85086	.9262	.0639	.3280
	(.0000)	(.0000)		(.7560)	(.0002)	(.0000)			(.8488)
Property Casualty	.05592	.93994	.9959	.3967	.09166	.34638	.4380	.5578	.0409
	(.0001)	(.0000)		(.8201)	(.1001)	(.2463)			(.8397)
Multiline	.04512	.94923	.9944	1.3971	.00757	.77412	.7817	.2127	.7167
	(.0000)	(.0000)		(.4973)	(.7161)	(.0021)			(.6988)
Insurance Brokers	.05345	.94001	.9935	.6330	.03093	.74837	.7793	.2142	1.6890
	(.0001)			(.7287)	(.2913)	(.0000)			(.4298)

P-values in parentheses.

TR^2 is an ARCH LM test.

Note: Persistence decline column shows the decrease in value of α+β after fitting the GARCH model with dummy variables.

The insurance sectors exhibited declines in volatility persistence consistent with that found for the insurance composite. The least amount of decline is found in the Life and Health sector while the Property-Casualty sector showed the largest decline. Thus, in general, the evidence suggests that weather related patterns impact excess insurance stock return volatility in terms of when regime changes occur. However, additional research may be directed at determining how and why differences among sectors exist. Moreover, having found that regime changes have occurred in the past, future research should now focus on detecting probable regime changes before they occur. Variations of the Markov-type and other regime-shifting models may help in this endeavor.

CONCLUSION

This paper finds regime shifts in volatility and accounts for them in a GARCH specification. The results show that omitting a variable that controls for regime shifts will give an inaccurate forecast which overestimates the persistence of volatility. This is an important finding for risk managers and analysts whose actions depend on the best forecast available. The persistence in volatility is generally driven by a drop in the magnitude of the GARCH parameter as opposed to the ARCH parameter. This term represents the degree of momentum as reflected in the autoregressive nature of volatility since the AR term is simply a compact way of writing a higher order MA model. Thus, it suggests that much of the predictability comes from period's further back in the past as opposed to the immediate past squared error term. The Life and Health sector exhibits the least decline in persistence once regime are taken into account. This is consistent with the general finding that, in dollar terms, weather related events are more likely to cause extensive property damage and the like as opposed to loss of life and injury.

REFERENCES

Aggarwal, R., C. Inclan and R. Leal (1999), "Volatility in Emerging Stock Markets", *Journal of Financial and Quantitative Analysis*, Vol.34: 33-55.

Andersen, T. G. and T. Bollerslev (1998), "Answering the Skeptics: Yes, Standard Volatility Models Do Provide Accurate Forecasts", *International Economic Review*, Vol.39: 885-905.

Bollerslev, T. (1986), "Generalized Autoregressive Conditional Heteroskedasticity", *Journal of Econometrics*, Vol.31: 307-327.

Bollerslev T., R. Y. Chou, and K. F. Kroner (1992), "ARCH Modeling in Finance: A Review of the Theory and Empirical Evidence", *Journal of Econometrics*, Vol.52: 5–59.

Cai, J. (1994), "A Markov Model of Switching-Regime ARCH", *Journal of Business and Economic Statistics*, Vol.12: 309-316.

Engle, R. F. (1982), "Autoregressive Conditional Heteroskedasticity with Estimates of the Variance of U.K. Inflation", *Econometrica*, Vol.50: 987-1007.

Engle, R. F. and T. Bollerslev (1986), "Modeling the Persistence of Conditional Variances", *Econometric Reviews*, Vol.5: 1-50.

Hamilton, J. D. and R. Susmel (1994), "Autoregressive Conditional Heteroskedasticity and Changes in Regime", *Journal of Econometrics*, Vol.64: 307-333.

Inclan, C., and G. C. Tiao (1994), "Use of Cumulative Sums of Squares for Retrospective Detection of Changes of Variance", *Journal of the American Statistical Association*, Vol.89: 913-923.

Lamoureux, C. G. and W. D. Lastrapes (1990), "Persistence in Variance, Structural Change and the GARCH Model", *Journal of Business and Economic Statistics*, Vol.68: 225-234.

Malik, Farooq, "Sudden Changes in Variance and Volatility Persistence in Foreign Exchange Markets 2003", *Journal of Multinational Financial Management*, No.3: 217-230.

Porterba, J. M. and L. Summers (1986), "The Persistence of Volatility and Stock Market Fluctuations", *American Economic Review*, Vol.76: 1143-1151.

In: Economics and the Wind
Editors: B. T. Ewing, et. al., pp. 73-87

ISBN: 1-59454-280-5
©2005 Nova Science Publishers, Inc.

Chapter 7

RISK MITIGATION: INDIVIDUAL AND MARKET BEHAVIOR

Jamie Brown Kruse
Wind Science and Engineering Research Center, Texas Tech University, Lubbock, TX, and Director of the Center for Natural Hazards Mitigation, East Carolina University, Greenville, NC

Kevin M. Simmons
Department of Business and Economics, Austin College, Sherman, TX

INTRODUCTION

Wind research has focused mainly on the meterological aspects of storms and the engineering challenges to construct resistant structures. Over the last several years, however, an effort has been launched to understand the behavior of people living in areas threatened by violent windstorms. The aftermath of a significant windstorm event brings instant media attention to the affected area and government aid is usually forthcoming to lessen the financial blow to residents and businesses. It is rare, but some storms produce damage so severe that it alters the economic conditions, not only of those living and working in the path of the storm but third party insurers as well. Hurricane Andrew is a relatively recent example. As losses from these events mount, several questions continue to arise. What can be done to lessen the effect of a tornado or hurricane? And second, will people adopt mitigation measures that may be available to them?

The second question has been of interest to economists and there is some debate on the potential response of people living in vulnerable areas. These events are rare and it is possible that people simply ignore the risk. If this tendency prevails, then storm resistant construction will not be adopted due to the increased cost. Essentially, the safety offered by the storm resistant engineered structures is a form of insurance and the value placed on that insurance may or may not correspond to the perceived risk of an event. This paper uses experimental economics techniques to examine the human response to changes in risk and how this response aggregates to become market demand for risk mitigation measures.

We will examine the relationship between individual bidding behavior and the aggregative properties of a market for full insurance. We utilize a Vickrey auction to sell from one to six policies. A Vickrey auction is a sealed-bid auction in which participants each simultaneously submit bids. The auctioneer discloses the identity of the highest bidder(s) who is declared the winner. The price paid by the winning bidders is equal to the highest bid that does not win the object(s). This format is named after William Vickrey who first described it and pointed out that bidders have a dominant strategy to bid their true values. Participants in the laboratory experiment reported here either acquire one of the available insurance policies in the auction or face exposure to the risk of a two-dollar loss. There is a rich literature in Psychology and Economics that has contributed to our current understanding about decision under risk. We describe a few of the important papers in the next section. This is followed by our experimental design, results and conclusions.

Review of Related Literature

An early lab experiment performed by Slovic, Fischhoff, Lichtenstein, and Corrigan (1977) tested the attractiveness of insurance to consumers at various probability levels. The subjects were given an amount of money, which was put at risk through the drawing of a ball from an urn filled with red and blue balls. If a blue ball was drawn the subject lost his/her money. A red ball would signal that there would be no penalty. Full insurance was available for purchase at a fixed premium equal to the expected value of the loss. The results of this experiment indicated that as the probability of loss increased, the percentage of subjects purchasing the insurance increased. At low probabilities, only about 20% of the subjects purchased the insurance. When the probability of loss increased to over 0.2, the percentage of subjects purchasing insurance increased to over 80%. A second treatment studied was the level of the premium. It was found that as the premium was lowered, through a subsidy, the percentages purchasing insurance at all probability levels increased. Finally, the authors tested the effect of compound lotteries. A compound lottery has nested probabilities. The subjects were told that the probability of loss on each draw was the same, for instance 5%, but the number of draws increased thus increasing their overall probability of loss. An interesting finding resulted from this manipulation of the experiment. At a probability level of 0.01, little change was observed in the percentage purchasing insurance. However, beginning at the .05 level, almost all subjects purchased the insurance. The general conclusion of the study was that as probabilities increased either directly or through a compounding effect, consumer's willingness to purchase insurance also increased.

Shoemaker (1979) reports the results of an experiment that explored several issues regarding insurance. First, the experiment was designed to measure the level of aversion to a high-probability-low-loss event versus a low-probability-high-loss event. Second, the willingness to pay for varying premium/deductible combinations was elicited and finally, the willingness to pay for comprehensive insurance was measured. Subjects for the experiment came from two sources. One group was undergraduate students at the University of Pennsylvania. The other group was solicited by mail from the client list of a Philadelphia insurance agency.

To test differences concerning risk aversion, the subjects were asked to choose between a 60% chance of losing $100 or a 1% chance of losing $6,000. Losses to the subjects were hypothetical in contrast to the first experiment, which used real money losses. The expected value of both choices is the same. The majority of students chose the low probability, high loss option. The majority of insurance clients, mostly adults, chose the high probability, low loss option. A possible explanation for this difference, offered by the authors, was that the adults had a larger accumulated wealth. This increased wealth influenced their decision in that they had more to lose than young college students.

The second group of questions tested various premium/cost combinations of insurance policies. It is interesting to note that for both groups, there was a clear preference for very low deductible and very high deductible policies. The least preferred policies were those in between the two extremes. One possible explanation for this result is the inability to process choices rationally with two variables, premiums and deductibles.

Regarding the willingness to pay for comprehensive insurance, the subjects were asked the amount they were willing to pay for insurance to cover each of three losses. They were then asked how much they would be willing to pay for a policy to cover all losses. Of the student group, 49% indicated that they would pay less for the comprehensive policy. Similarly, 53% of the client group also said they would pay less.

A final set of questions tests preferences for policies where the only difference is in scale. Two choices are offered to the subjects: a premium of $100 to mitigate a 25% chance of a $500 loss or a premium of $1 to mitigate a 25% chance of losing $5. The expected value of the two choices is the same but 49% of the clients and 47% of the student subjects preferred the $1 premium. Only 13% of the students and 7% of the clients indicated consistent choices.

More recently, an experiment performed by McClelland, Schulze, and Coursey (1993) used a Vickrey auction to allocate four insurance policies that protect the subject from a negative result in a lottery. Similar to the urn experiments of Slovic et al., the subjects could earn monetary awards based on the results of the lottery. This differed from the Slovic et al. (1977) study in that the price of the insurance policy could vary whereas in the earlier study the price was fixed. Once the four policies were allocated to the highest bidders, the lottery was held. If a red chip was drawn, all subjects without a policy lost $4. The draw of a white chip resulted in a gain of $1 for all subjects. Six levels of probabilities were used ranging from .01 to .9. Ten rounds for each probability level were conducted.

A bid to EV ratio was calculated for each individual in each round. These ratios were then compared at the different levels of loss probability. One result of the study was that mean Bid/EV declined as the probability of loss increased. Further, in low probabilities (less than 0.10) a bi-modal distribution was observed with a zero bid forming one node and Bid to EV ratios greater than 1 forming the other extreme. At low probabilities, subjects either ignored the risk and bid zero, or focused predominately on the loss and submitted a bid in excess of the expected value of the loss. As probabilities increased the distribution of Bid/EV began to take the shape of a normal distribution.

A second experiment was used to test differences in bids as the subjects gained experience with the lottery. Fifty rounds, all at a probability of 0.01, were conducted. On round 33, a red chip was deliberately drawn from the jar. The authors observed that as the subjects gained experience with the process, the bids began to drop. Subsequent to the drawing of a red chip in round 33, bids began to increase. Decreased bids prior to round 33 were attributed to the subjects lowering their perception of the risk until a loss occurred. The increase in the bids after the loss was attributed to a fear that once a loss has occurred, it seems more likely to happen again.

Ganderton, Thurston, Brookshire, Stewart, and McKee (1997) used lab experiments to test consumers' willingness to purchase insurance protection from a disaster such as a flood. The authors created three possibilities in the lottery. One possibility was no event, the second was a periodic flood and the third was an episodic flood that results in severe damage. Further, in many disasters, some homes are destroyed while neighboring structures suffered little damage. To model this possibility, once the nature of the event was determined by the lottery, a second drawing was held to determine if the damage was slight or severe.

Prior to each treatment, the subjects were told the possibilities for each event, potential losses and the cost of the insurance to protect them from the losses. A total of eighteen treatments were tested with different combinations of probabilities, losses, and cost of insurance. The authors found that as the level of expected loss increased, subjects purchased more insurance. Also, at a given level of loss, insurance was more likely to be purchased as the cost of the policy decreased.

One of the benefits of experimental research is the ability to identify individual behavior that determines the characteristics of a market. Market data aggregates the many decisions made by market participants. It is quite possible, that individual decisions may violate rational decision rules while the market does not. A study by Evans (1997) constructs a set of experiments where participants bid on a set of choices with the same expected value. If their choices exhibit inconsistency the author calculates the deviation of the individual bid from the expected value. These deviations are violations of a form of rationality known as the "betweenness property" of the *independence axiom* of Expected Utility Theory. The study concluded that betweenness violations were high for individuals.

Evans (1997) examined market behavior using a fifth price Vickrey auction. A fifth price auction is a device, which assigns the fifth highest bid as the market price in an auction. In the market setting, while betweenness violations continued to exist, the magnitude of the violations dropped dramatically. One of the reasons, suggested by the author, for the improved market behavior was the mechanism to set the market price. A fifth price auction selects a price from the middle of the bid distribution. This ignores the tails of the distribution that yield most violations. Evans states that it may be that research on individual bidding behavior is less relevant to market behavior than previously thought. Market mechanisms, which target the middle of the bid distribution, perform well. By this logic, other mechanisms which choose extreme bids, for instance a first price auction, may not perform as well.

Camerer (1987) examines the role of probability bias in setting market prices. In this experiment, participants were allowed to bid on lottery tickets that paid a state dependent dividend. The expected value of the dividend could be determined by multiplying the payoff by the state probability. Bids for the tickets were compared to the expected values to determine individual bias. Several competing theories were tested to determine which theory did the best job of predicting market price. The first theory uses Bayes Rule to determine the probability. The probability was determined by a compound lottery. Participants using Bayes Rule to determine the probability needed to correctly assess the state probability in the initial drawing. Competing theories assume participants either overestimate or underestimate the probability in the initial drawing.

Results indicated that while individual bias was prevalent, generally market prices converged to Bayesian expected values. This convergence occurred more quickly with experienced subjects than with inexperienced subjects. As each type of subject participated in additional rounds, bids more closely tracked expected values. This result suggests that participants learn from the market.

METHODOLOGY

The experiment we report was divided into five sessions with 8 to 12 participants in each session. Subjects were recruited from undergraduate and graduate courses at Texas Tech University as well as the local community. A total of 50 volunteers participated in the three sessions. There were 17 women and 34 men who participated in the experiments. All subjects were offered the same incentives. The length of each session ranged from 1½ to 2 hours. Payment per subject ranged from $18 to $25.

Each session began with volunteers signing an alphabetical participant list for the session. Volunteers were then given a copy of the Consent Form to read and sign. When all subjects had arrived and signed the consent form they were assigned a seat and given an envelope containing the experiment instructions, bid forms and their individual record sheet. The instructions were explained and a time for questions regarding those instructions was allowed prior to the session.

Each session contained 11 rounds, 1 practice and 10 actual rounds. After the practice round, each participant received $2.00 at the beginning of each round. Before they could claim the money, a lottery was held in which 1 ball was drawn from a bingo cage containing 100 balls numbered sequentially 1-100. Every participant was assigned a range of numbers on his/her record. If the ball drawn was within the assigned range, the subject must forfeit the $2.00. The probability for loss was the same for all participants in each round, however, the range of numbers was different for each individual. Five different loss probabilities were used in the experiment, 1%, 5%, 10%, 15%, and 20%. These probabilities were not explicitly given on the record sheets, but could be calculated by examining the range of numbers assigned. Each probability level was used in one of the first five rounds and the last five rounds. The sequence of probabilities in each half of the experiment was randomly determined prior to the experiment.

Prior to the lottery, all participants were given an opportunity to purchase a license (an insurance policy), which would protect their $2.00, regardless of the outcome of the lottery. A Vickrey auction mechanism was used to allocate 1, 2, 3, 4, 5, or 6 licenses. Bids were posted from highest to lowest. All bids were public knowledge but the identity of the bidder was not. After the bids were posted, a six-sided die was rolled to determine the number of licenses available in that round. With the protocol we used, subjects did not know the number of available licenses at the time they submitted their bids. The license price was the bid whose rank was one more than the number of available licenses in that round. For example, if the roll of the die was 3, three licenses were sold to the highest bidders. The price of the license was equal to the fourth bid. In the event of a tie, tied bids were randomly queued for license allocation purposes.

Once the number, price and allocation of licenses were determined, the bid forms were returned with an indication of whether the participant had purchased a license. A ball was then drawn from the bingo cage, its number announced, displayed, and then returned to the bingo cage. For those with a license, the earnings for that round were $2.00 minus the price of the license. All other participants were exposed to the results of the lottery and thus had earnings of $2.00 or zero depending on the draw from the bingo cage. At the conclusion of the round, the participants were asked to total their earnings, update their accumulated balance and prepare their bid form for the next round. After all ten rounds were complete, the participant earnings were verified and paid in cash.

RESULTS

In a previous study, McClelland et al. (1996) demonstrated that Bid/EV at low probabilities exhibited a bi-modal distribution. One node was at zero Bid/EV and the second node was a Bid/EV ratio well in excess of 1. Our study corroborates this finding. As is shown in Figure 1, there is a large cluster of bids at zero, few bids at middle ranges and a second cluster at Bid/EV in excess of 5. In fact at a probability of 1%, three quarters of the bids were zero. This confirms the observation made by McClelland et al. (1996) that at very low levels of probability, subjects either ignore or exaggerate the risk. The effect of subjects who exaggerate the risk is particularly noteworthy at these very low levels of probability. Since the expected value of the loss is minimal, it takes a small increase in the bid to increase dramatically the Bid/EV ratio at low probabilities. This fact is illustrated in Figure 2. The average Bid/EV at a probability of 1% is almost 3 while the percentage of zero bids was 75%. Some of the participants submitted bids in which the Bid/EV ratio was over 40. There are actually two forces at work here. First, as noted in McClelland et al. (1996), subjects who value mitigation at low probabilities exaggerate the risk. A second reason for the high Bid/EV ratio is the fact that the Bid/EV measure at low probability levels is extremely sensitive to very small changes in the bids. As the probability increases, the bid distribution begins to take a more normal shape. Again, two reasons account for this. First, the number of subjects bidding zero declines and second, the sensitivity of the Bid/EV ratio to small changes in the bids is lower. As Figure 2 indicates, beginning at a 5% probability, average Bid/EV tracks closer to one. In fact, at 20% probability, average Bid/EV is not significantly different from 1 [t-statistic = 1.35589 assuming unequal variance. P(T<=t) = .08911 (one tail test)].

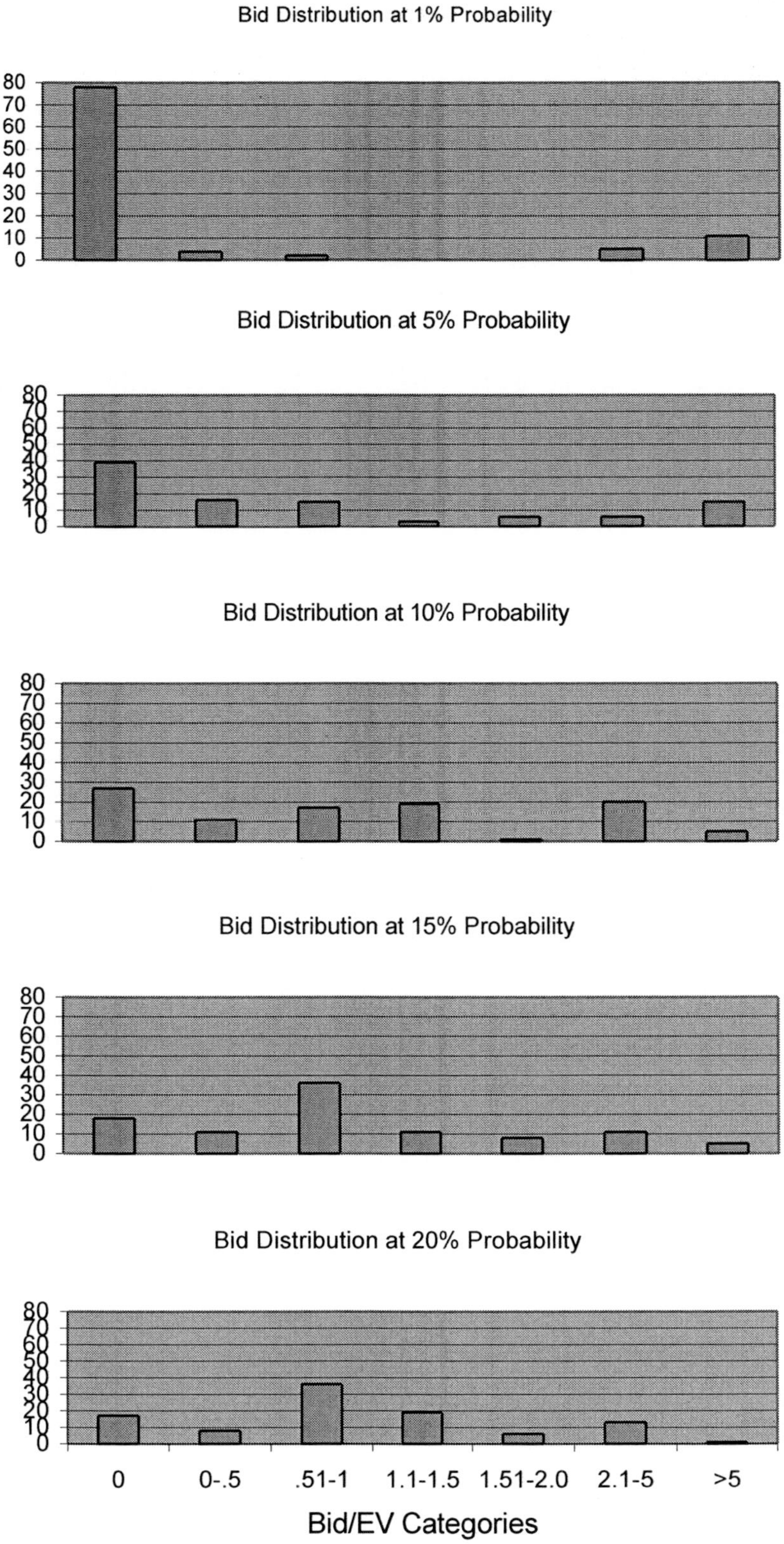
Bid Distribution at 1% Probability
Bid Distribution at 5% Probability
Bid Distribution at 10% Probability
Bid Distribution at 15% Probability
Bid Distribution at 20% Probability
0 10 20 30 40 50 60 70 80
0
0-.5
.51-1
1.1-1.5
1.51-2.0
2.1-5
>5
Bid/EV Categories

Figure 1.

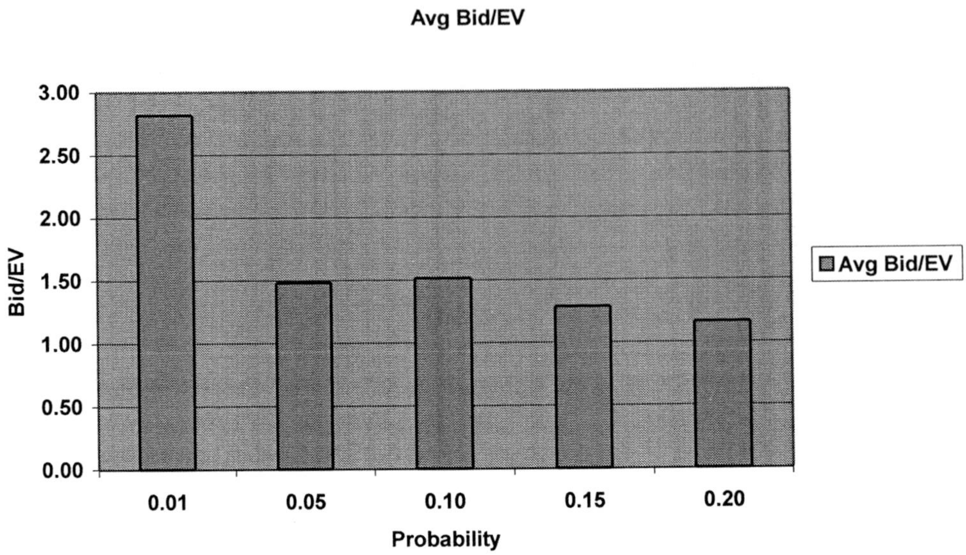

Figure 2.

To address the question of whether the subject bidding behavior responds to increases in probability we performed a regression with bid as the dependent variable and probability as the independent variable.

$$\text{Bid} = \beta_0 + \beta_1\text{Prob} + \beta_{2\text{-}51}\text{Subject} + \text{Error}$$

Even though our database contains 500 bid decisions by the experiment participants, the sample contains only 50 individuals. To control for the small number of participants we used a fixed effects regression model. This model controls for possible error correlation within the observations for a given individual by adding a dummy variable for each individual in the experiment. As can be seen in Table 1 the regression is significant. The intercept is very close to zero, although it is not significant. Probability is highly significant. The 2.196 coefficient of Probability indicates a Bid/EV ratio of 1.098 over the entire distribution, since EV = \$2.00 x Probability. This corresponds to the observation seen in the graph in Figure 2. Clearly, an increase in probability motivates subjects to increase their bid for the license.

Since the zero bids are prominent in this analysis, we plotted the changes in the percentage of subjects bidding zero at increasing probabilities. McClelland et al. (1996) noted that the number of zero bids declined as probability increased but never disappeared entirely. This observation is consistent with the results of our study. As shown in Figure 3, zero bids at 1% probability are 78% of the total bids. The percentage of zero bids decreases as probability increases but never completely disappears. Small increases in subjects bids translate to large increases in Bid/EV. A similar effect is created by the zero bids. Since negative bids were not an option the bid distribution has a floor, which at low probabilities creates a distribution that is asymmetrical. As probability increases, the effect of the floor diminishes.

Table 1. Regression Results

	Parameter Estimate	Std Error	T Value	Prob>T	R-Sq	Adj.R-Sq
Bid/Probability Model (All Participants)						
Intercept	0.0470	.0999	0.475	.6353	.5003	.4446
Probability	2.1961	.2016	10.892	.0001		
Bid/Hit Model (All Participants)						
Intercept	0.0752	.1018	0.739	.4606	.4818	.4220
Probability	2.3550	.2438	9.661	.0001		
Bid/Hit Model (Participants which Experienced a Hit)						
Intercept	0.0860	.1056	0.815	.4157	.5016	.4448
Probability	2.2206	.2029	10.944	.0001		

EV = 2.00 X
.01 = .02

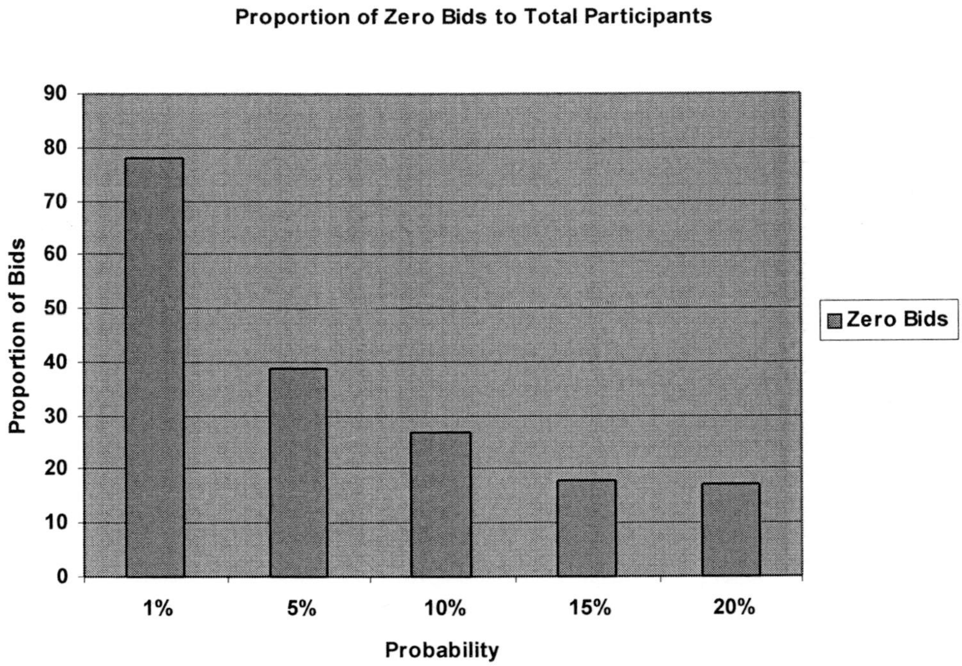

Figure 3.

This experiment used a Vickrey auction to allocate licenses. A unique feature of the study was to withhold information about the allocation of the licenses. Subjects did not know the number of available licenses until their bids were submitted. As a result, we can examine the behavior of prices at each probability for six possible allocations. Figure 4 shows the behavior of the prevailing price, averaged across sessions, for each of six allocation possibilities. As expected, prevailing price declines as allocation increases. This models the effect of the scarcity of the license. When only 1 license is allocated, price begins and remains high. As the probability increases, price rises, although for 1 license the relationship is more erratic than when 2, 3, 4, or 5 licenses are available. When six licenses are available, the price increase across probabilities begins to lose some stability. This is an interesting result and it reflects the effect of bids on price at the upper and lower end of the bid distribution. As noted by Evans (1997), individual bids do not always track expected value. However, the market price is remarkably consistent. Her study used a fifth price auction to determine market price. The design of our study allows for analysis of six different prices and confirms her result at the middle of the bid distribution. As allocation of licenses increases, the price function approaches a linear function. But when allocation exceeds 4 licenses, the instability seen in the 1 license allocation reappears. At these high levels of available licenses, price is largely determined by the low and sometimes zero bids. To examine this effect further, we performed regressions on each allocation using price as the dependent variable and probability as the independent variable. (Table 2) These regressions contain few observations, so only the general behavior of the relationship between price and probability can be examined. Each of the six regressions indicated that probability was highly significant and the value of the intercept was very close to zero. The difference seen in the graph, however, is reaffirmed by differences in the value of the adjusted R-Square, for each regression. R-Square for the 1 license and 6 license allocation was .31 and .32. The middle allocations, 2 through 5 licenses, had adjusted R-Square values ranging from .41 to .48. These middle allocations minimize the effect of the high and low bidders on price and indicate that market price responds well to increases in the probability of a loss.

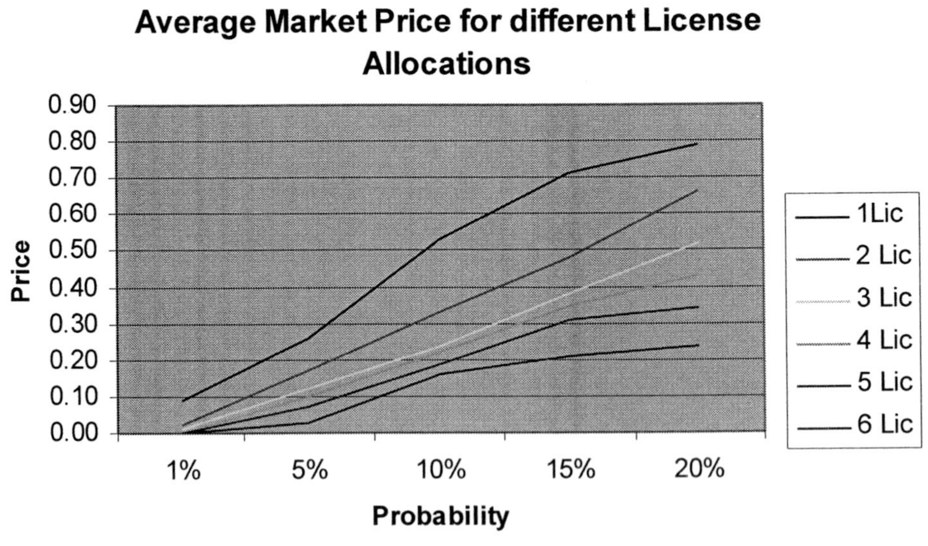

Figure 4.

Table 2. Regression Results: Market Price/Probability Model for Different License Allocations

	Parameter Estimate	Std. Error	T Value	Prob>T	R-Sq	Adj. R-Sq
One License Allocation						
Intercept	0.0866	.0974	0.889	.3786	.3244	.3103
Probability	3.8176	.7951	4.801	.0001		
Two License Allocation						
Intercept	-0.0079	.0682	-0.117	.9075	.4261	.4140
Probability	3.3232	.5567	5.96	.0001		
Three License Allocation						
Intercept	-0.0186	.0541	-0.310	.7577	.4313	.4194
Probability	2.6626	.4413	6.033	.0001		
Four License Allocation						
Intercept	-0.0186	.0446	-0.416	.6790	.4596	.4483
Probability	2.3231	.3636	6.389	.0001		
Five License Allocation						
Intercept	-0.0167	.0346	-0.482	.6321	.4933	.4827
Probability	1.9302	.2824	6.836	.0001		
Six License Allocation						
Intercept	-0.0109	.0342	-0.320	.7502	.3370	.3232
Probability	1.3801	.2794	4.939	.0001		
Total Regression						
Intercept	0.0026	.0274	0.095	.9241	.3083	.3060
Probability	2.5728	.2232	11.525	.0001		

While the main focus of this study was the response of subjects to increases in the probability of loss, two side issues were examined. First, does experiencing a "hit" from the lottery have an effect on subsequent bidding behavior? McClelland et al. (1996) devised a scheme to test this effect by contriving a hit to all subjects on the 33rd round of a 50-round experiment. Their observation was that bids increased after the loss. Our study tests the effect of a loss, but the hit is allowed to occur naturally from the lottery itself. For all subjects, we create a variable whose value is zero if no loss occurs in the previous round and has a value of 1 if a loss does occur in the previous round. We also created a variable that had a value of 1 in every round subsequent to a loss. This variable is analogous to the method used by McClelland et al. (1996). A graph comparing the Bid/EV ratio for subjects experiencing a hit and those who did not is shown in Figure 5. We used a fixed effects regression model similar to the one described earlier to test the effect of a hit on bidding behavior.

$$\text{Bid} = \beta_0 + \beta_1\text{Prob} + \beta_2\text{Hit} + \beta_{3\text{-}53}\text{Subject} + \text{Error}$$

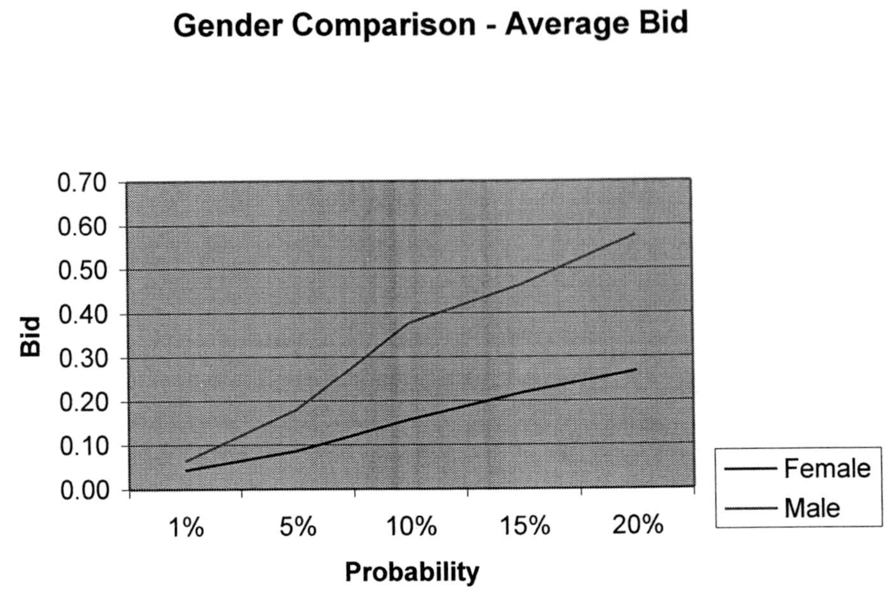

Figure 5.

The first model regressed bid against hit for all participants in the study, regardless of whether they experienced a hit. Secondly, we regressed bid against hit for only the participants who experienced a hit. As can be seen in Table 1, HIT is not a significant explanatory variable for bidding behavior in either model. We therefore conclude, that experience with a hit in the lottery has no effect on subsequent bidding behavior.

A second issue was the effect of gender on bidding behavior. We assigned a value to each subject indicating whether the subject was male or female. It was then possible to compare the bids by gender. Figure 6 shows average bids by women and by men at increasing probability levels. At every probability, bids by women were lower than the bids submitted by men. To test the strength of this observation, we ran a regression where bid was the dependent variable and the independent variables were probability and whether or not the subject was female.

$$\text{Bid} = \beta_0 + \beta_1\text{Prob} + \beta_2\text{Gender} + \text{Error}$$

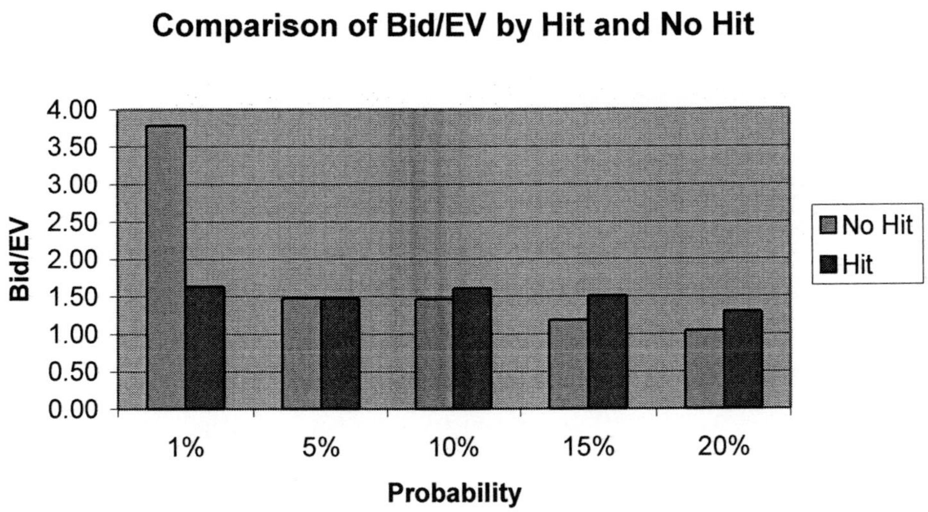

Figure 6.

The variable for female was highly significant and the sign of the coefficient was negative. We also conducted a t-test on the bids of men and women. As Figure 6 shows, the bids submitted by men generally increased as probability increased. However, the increase was large between 5% and 10%, declined at 15% and then increased again at a probability of 20%. Compared to the pattern for women, these increases were more erratic. Some of this difference can be seen in the variances for bids from women and bids for men. The variance for women's bids was under \$0.03 whereas the variance for men's bids exceeded \$0.23. Further, men submitted bids that were consistent with higher risk aversion (Figure 7). This result is consistent with other experimental results and gives an instance where men appear to be more conservative toward risk than women. Our conclusion is that there is a significant difference in the bidding behavior between men and women.

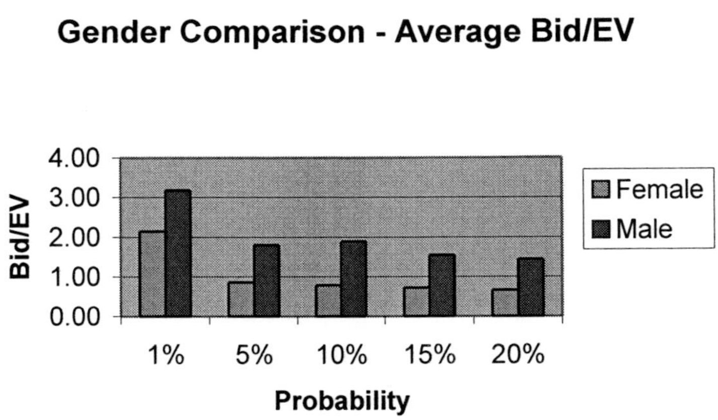

Figure 7.

CONCLUSION

This study generated three important results. First, individual bids and consequently market price are affected by probability of loss. As shown in the McClelland

et al., subjects do respond to increasing loss probabilities in their willingness to buy protection. This behavior, at low probabilities, indicates a bimodal response to risk with most subjects ignoring the risk and a minority over-valuing the risk. At higher probabilities, the distribution appears to take a shape similar to a normal distribution. Further, bid/EV ratios correspond closely to the expected value of the loss.

Second, in contrast to the McClelland et al. study, we find that experience with a hit in the lottery has no discernible effect on subsequent bidding behavior. This may be due to the contrast in the way that a loss was implemented in the two studies. Although the probabilities for an individual were the same for the two studies, in McClelland et al., when a loss occurred, it hit everyone whereas a hit was isolated to only one or two individuals in our study. This could be likened to when a single property is damaged by a tornado versus an entire community that could be damaged by a hurricane. Finally, we find a difference in the bidding behavior of men and women. Men tend to bid higher than women indicating that men value the protection of the license more highly than women do.

Extreme wind events such as hurricanes and tornadoes are low-probability-high-consequence events. The annual probability that a tornado will touch down at a given location is less than 1% even in the states in "tornado alley." The annual probability that a hurricane force storm will strike a location is 10% or less even in hurricane-prone regions. The results of this study give us insight on mitigation investment behavior when the probability of loss is low. Admittedly, a two dollar loss in the laboratory is not a high consequence event. However, the preponderance of zero bids at low probabilities match up with the syndrome the Kunreuther calls "it can't happen to me." Likewise, those individuals that overweight the probability are likely to be the first to adopt mitigation measures that otherwise fail cost effectiveness tests. Individuals that overweight the probability are likely to unnecessarily evacuate when a hurricane threatens and contribute to congestion on evacuation routes. Public policy that takes into account individual biases will be more effective in managing mitigation efforts and protecting the population when a disaster occurs.

REFERENCES

Camerer, Colin F. (1987). "Do Bias in Probability Judgment Matter in Markets? Experimental Evidence," *American Economic Review*, Vol. 77, No. 5, pp. 981-977.

Evans, Darla A.(1997). "The Role of Markets in Reducing Expected utility Violations," *Journal of Political Economy*, Vol. 105, No. 3, pp. 622-636.

Ganderton, P., Thurston, H., Brookshire, D., Stewart, S., and McKee, M. (1997). "*Buying Insurance for Disaster-Type Risks: Experimental Evidence,*" Manuscript. Albuquerque: University of New Mexico.

McClelland, Gary H., Schulze, William D., and Coursey, Don L. (1993)."InsuranceFor Low-Probability Hazards: A Bi-Modal Response to Unlikely Events," *Journal of Risk and Uncertainty*, Vol. 7, pp. 95-116.

Schoemaker, Paul J. H., and Kunreuther, Howard (1979). "An Experimental Study of Insurance Decisions," *The Journal of Risk and Insurance*, Vol. 46, No. 4, pp. 603-618.

Slovic, P., Fischhoff, B., and Lichtenstein, S. (1977). "Behavioral Decision Theory," *Annual Review of Psychology*, Vol. 28, pp. 1-39.

ACKNOWLEDGEMENTS

This work was performed under the Department of Commerce NIST/TTU Cooperative Agreement Award 70NANB8H0059.

In: Economics and the Wind
Editors: B. T. Ewing, et. al., pp. 89-104
ISBN: 1-59454-280-5
©2005 Nova Science Publishers, Inc.

Chapter 8

RISK PERCEPTION AND THE VALUE OF SAFE ROOMS AS A PROTECTIVE MEASURE FROM TORNADOES: A SURVEY METHOD

Ozlem Ozdemir
Department of Economics, Yeditepe University, Istanbul, Turkey

INTRODUCTION

Over the past thirty years, researchers have developed a theoretical framework concerning risk and the protective mechanisms chosen by individuals (e.g. insurance, seat belts, storm shelters) against disasters (Kunruether, 1978, 1996; Quiggin, 1992; Shogren and Crocker, 1999; Ehrlich and Becker, 1972; Lewis and Nickerson, 1989; Shogren 1990; Viscusi, 1992; Cook and Graham, 1979; Hirshleifer, 1966, Dong and Wong, 1996; Dixit, 1990; Arrow, 1972, 1996; Slovic, 1977). In most of these models, buying insurance is studied as the protective mechanism and monetary loss is taken as the damage from the hazard.

Since the theoretical models are not fully adequate to describe people's reactions under some uncertain and risky situations, particularly low-probability events (Camerer and Kunreuther, 1989), empirical investigations become crucial. As McClelland, Shulze, and Coursey (1993) stated, "both field and lab studies provide complementary information that will lead to a fuller understanding of insurance purchase and other protective behaviors for low-probability risks."

Numerous survey studies have examined risk perception for low-probability, high-consequence (LPHC) hazards (Smith and Devousges, 1987; Fischoff, Watson, and Hope, 1984; Slovic, 1987; McDaniels, Kamlet and Fischer, 1992; Slovic, Fischoff, and Lichtenstein, 1980; Kunreuther, 1976, 1978; Camerer and Kunreuther, 1989; Kunreuther, 1996; McClelland, Schulze, and Hurd, 1990; Kunreuther, Onculer, and Slovic, 1998). Most found divergence in risk perceptions and mitigation actions taken by individuals. While some individuals focus on the probability of the risky event, others act by looking at the extreme loss. These studies call for further investigation of the relationship between the valuation of risk and perception of risk.

The purpose of the current study is to investigate the relationship between risk perception and willingness-to-pay for increased safety in LPHC risk situations. A tornado is chosen as the LPHC risk and willingness-to-pay for an in-residence storm shelter (safe room) is specified as the mitigation measure. The probability that a damaging tornado will strike a given location is miniscule, even in "high" tornado risk areas. However, the prospect of injury or loss of life due to a tornado is frightening. Brown, Kruger and Bos (2000) place tornadoes "among the most violent and lethal of all natural disasters."

An in-residence storm shelter or "safe room" has been proposed to reduce injuries and loss of life in the event of a tornado. One such safe room design by the Wind Engineering Research Center at Texas Tech University has been promoted by The Federal Emergency Management Agency (FEMA)(2000). A safe room is an integral part of the interior of a house and located in the basement or in an interior room on the first floor of a house without a basement. The room is constructed to endure strong winds, windborne missiles, and falling objects.

Brown, Kruger and Bos (2000) report the results of on-site interviews of persons in communities that were severely damaged during the May 3, 1999, Oklahoma City tornado outbreak. 78% of the 614 persons interviewed were inside their homes when the tornado struck. The safe room provides a haven that is consistent with human behavior because it is accessible from within the home.

The question remains whether perception of risk is sufficient to prompt a several thousand-dollar investment in this protective device if it were commercially available. In that respect, first, a theoretical model is developed that uses the severity of risk (magnitude), the probability of occurrence and the protective ability of safe rooms to explain the maximum amount people are willing-to-pay. Different from previous models, the effect on health status as well as monetary loss outcomes are considered in the utility function. In addition, the independent effect of probability and magnitude of risk on WTP are investigated.

Then, a mail survey was conducted to test the conceptual model that explores the relationship between individual tornado risk perception and willingness to pay (WTP) for safe rooms. Different from other empirical research, I examine the willingness-to-pay as two independent components (whether people are willing to buy or not with an undisclosed price and the maximum amount they are willing to pay) that makes a distinction between the choice and payment decision. For perceived risk measurement, perceived exposure, perceived severity, perceived control over risk, and perceived responsibility are chosen as the components of perceived risk (Kunreuther et.al, 1990; Slovic et.al., 1980; Smith, 1986).

The rest of the paper is organized as follows. In the next section I describe prior studies related to this paper. I follow with a description of the theoretical model, the survey instrument and the data collection procedures and relate them to the conceptual model. Results and regression analysis follow with conclusions and suggestions for future research in the last section.

RELATED RESEARCH

The theoretical models used to explain behavioral responses to risk are subject to much debate. Some scholars support the use of expected utility theory to describe the judgments and choices made in LPHC risk situations (Brookshire, Thayer, Tschirhart, Schulze, 1985; Gould, 1989), while others do not (Tversky, Sattath, and Slovic, 1988; Schoemaker, 1982; Robertson, 1974; Kunreuther, 1978; Slovic, 1987; Harless and Camerer, 1994). Thus, researchers have offered alternative theories to expected utility (extended expected utility theories, generalized expected utility and prospect theory) that incorporate a behavioral tendency to overweight low-probabilities (Machina, 1982; Kahneman and Tversky, 1979).

Answering the need for empirical investigation of choice under LPHC situations, many survey studies have investigated the value of mitigation i.e. WTP for reducing the loss from hazards. Each study either has taken different risks (natural disasters, hazardous waste, accidents etc.) or different methodologies to investigate valuation of risk i.e. WTP (e.g., Randall, 1993; Bishop and Heberlein, 1990; Mansfield, 1998; Hammitt, 1990; Smith, Desvousges, and Freeman III, 1985; Brookshire and Coursey, 1987; Crocker and Shogren, 1991; Viscusi and Evans, 1990).

Willingness-to-pay for mitigation measures is highly dependent on perceptions about the uncertain hazard. For many reasons (e.g., the probabilistic information may be a challenge for humans), there has been a gap between public perceptions of risks and the real risks. For instance, members of the League of Women Voters and students were asked to estimate the number of deaths per year in U.S. from automobile accidents. Women estimate 28,000 deaths while students' estimation is 10,500 deaths. In fact, the real number was 50,000 deaths (Slovic, Fischhoff, and Lichtenstein, 1979).

The reasons for biased judgments of risk have always been an interesting research question in many fields (Fischer, Morgan, Fischhoff, Nair, and Lave, 1991; Slovic, Kraus, Covello, 1990, and many others). Slovic (1987) states that risk perception is affected by the length of delay between cause and effect, the degree of control over the risk, the potential magnitude of its effect, and whether the risk is faced voluntarily. Additionally, biased evaluations of risks may be because of unfamiliarity with an event, overconfidence about judgments, and the divergence of opinions about risk (Slovic, et. al, 1980). Whatever the reasons behind the gap between the statistical risk and perceived risk, we are compelled to accept it and must search for an appropriate measurement of perceived risk.

Previous studies determine the perceived risk by stating different components. In Kunreuther, Easterling, Desvousges, and Slovic (1990), four components of perceived risk are: perceived seriousness, control, dread, and trust of the federal government. Slovic, Fischoff, and Lichtenstein (1980) not only claim" perceived risk is quantifiable", but also they list five determinants of perceived risk: frequency of death, subjective fatality estimates, disaster potential, qualitative characteristics, judged seriousness of death. According to Smith (1986), perceived attributes of hazards can be identified as: the extent of knowledge about a hazard, whether it is a source of dread, and the perceived exposure to the hazard.

Alternatively, a "risk ladder," a numerical base comparing risks in terms of their annual mortality probabilities is used in some studies to detect perceived risk (Hammitt, 1990; Mitchell and Carson, 1989; Smith, Desvousges, and Freeman III, 1985; McClelland, Schulze, and Hurd, 1990). A "risk ladder" is a numerical base comparing risks in terms of their annual mortality probabilities (Hammitt, 1990; Mitchell and Carson, 1989; Smith, Desvousges, and Freeman III, 1985; McClelland, Schulze, and Hurd, 1990). Respondents estimate the annual number of deaths per million from tornadoes [the basic premise is the same as the "determinants of perceived risk" from Slovic, Fischoff, and Lichtenstein (1980, page 190)]. Providing the information to respondents in the form of a "risk ladder" has not been examined precisely by previous studies. However, Camerer and Kunreuther (1989) argue that the degree of uncertainty associated with these risk estimates should be explained; otherwise, people may distrust the entire analysis. Slovic, Kraus, and Covello (1990, p.389) offer the following comment on the usage of a "risk ladder":

> .... simplicity and intuitive appeal of comparisons of unrelated risks may be highly deceptive. Many factors appear to play a role in determining whether such comparisons will be useful. Whether these kinds of comparisons ultimately generate more light than heat will depend on the degree to which both the context of risk communication and the content of the messages are sensitive to those factors.

In order to see whether using a "risk ladder" fits the current study, I included a risk ladder question in the survey and concluded that it is statistically inappropriate for this case. One possible reason behind this may be the high variation in the values stated for perceived number of deaths per million per year for tornadoes compared to other risks. Further, the stated number on the risk ladder may capture the combination of exposure and severity; however, the inability to separate exposure from severity seriously limits the explanatory power of this measure.

Previous studies of low-probability, high-consequence risks find divergence in risk perceptions and mitigation actions taken by individuals. While some individuals focus on the probability of the risky event, others act by looking at the extreme loss. For example, Indians near Santa Barbara, California, still live without any fear next to a liquefied natural gas terminal that is shown to be dangerous to health by experts (Kasper, 1980). Individuals tend to buy insurance only when the probability is above some threshold (Camerer and Kunreuther, 1989; Kunreuther, 1996). On the other hand, people "perceive other technological risks, such as a nuclear plant accident, to be more likely than do experts" according to Camerer and Kunreuther (1989). Slovic, Fischoff, and Lichtenstein (1980) explain the overreaction to low-probability risks by emphasizing the importance of the amount of loss rather than the frequency. Consistent with their result, Slovic, et. al (1980, p. 184) states tornadoes to be among the most overestimated risks in terms of the gap between judged frequency and actual number of deaths.

The inconsistent perception of low-probability risks becomes more remarkable in McClelland, Shulze, Hurd (1990). They find some people to perceive the risk of a hazardous waste site as if no hazard exists, while others rate a low-probability risk equal to more frequent risk exposure. These studies call for further investigation of the relationship between WTP and perceived risk.

THEORETICAL AND CONCEPTUAL MODELS

For this study, a theoretical model is developed in the spirit of Ehrlich and Becker (1972) to generate testable hypotheses regarding the value of mitigation measures (willingness to pay for increased safety) in risky situations. The theoretical model can be found in Appendix I. Adoption of a safe room is taken as self-insurance type of mitigation, since having a safe room does not affect the probability, but can influence the consequences of the risk. Monetary compensation would not necessarily restore health status in the same way other physical assets can be replaced, thus, market insurance is not a perfect substitute for self-insurance. The theoretical model yields three testable implications: (1) maximum willingness to pay for the protective measure is increasing in the probability (exposure) of the harmful event, (2) maximum willingness to pay for the protective measure is increasing in the magnitude (severity) of the loss and, (3) maximum willingness to pay is increasing in the protective ability of the measure (safe room).

For the empirical investigation, first a conceptual model is built to test in our hypotheses.

$$WTP = \alpha + \sum_{n=1}^{n}[B_{1n} Exposure + B_{2n} Severity + B_{3n} Experience + B_{4n} Control + B_{5n} \mathrm{Re}sponsibility + B_{6n} Age +$$
$$B_{7n} Sex + B_{8n} Education + B_{9n} Children + B_{10n} Riskaversion + B_{11n} Timeinresidence + B_{12n} \mathrm{Pr}otectivebility$$
$$+ B_{13n} \mathrm{Pr}ecaution + B_{14n} Possess + \varepsilon$$

In this model the maximum amount that people are willing to pay for a safe room is described as a function of perceived risk of a tornado and some socioeconomic variables. Then a survey described in the following section is constructed.

SURVEY DESIGN AND MEASUREMENT

In this section, important variables used in the survey are classified by topic and discussed with their associated survey questions.

DEGREE OF RISK AVERSION

Do you have a smoke alarm?	YES_____	NO_____
a burglar alarm?	YES_____	NO_____
a car alarm?	YES_____	NO_____
natural disaster insurance?	YES_____	NO_____
life insurance?	YES_____	NO_____
emergency items/ food	YES_____	NO_____

This question is a modified version of the one used for a "risk index variable" in Singh and Thayer (1992). The index is calculated by summing "yes" responses to yes/no questions for six different "revealed preferences about risk behavior." These are listed precautions *already taken* against potential risks that a person/family may be exposed to in daily lives. According to their "relative risk aversion" measurement, the individuals that possess 5 or 6 items are considered "relatively risk averse" and those who have 0,1, or 2 index values are risk lovers.

In the present risk index version, I first modify the items that an individual possesses for protection. For that reason, I chose natural disaster insurance vs. earthquake home insurance, then add life insurance for health concern, and finally include the possession of emergency items/food as the last category. This measurement of risk aversion differs from the previous study in the sense that it uses an ordinal scale. In addition, each individual is placed on a risk attitude scale in terms of the relative degree of risk aversion. For example, a person who has 5 items is considered to be more risk averse than people who scored 0, 1, 2, 3 or 4.

Perceived Exposure to Tornado Risk

In your view, how likely is it that *your house* will be hit by a tornado?

	Not Very Likely				**Very Likely**
This Year	1	2	3	4	5
Within the next 5 years	1	2	3	4	5
Within the next 10 years	1	2	3	4	5

Personal exposure is considered rather than public exposure for two reasons; first, it is a common sense that "the individual is primarily concerned with its own exposure to danger" (Bohnenblust and Pretre, 1990). This is different from McDaniels, Kamlet, and Fischer's study (1992). The authors use seven-point psychometric scale reflecting exposure to measure subjective probability. It is also important to note that a similar exposure question was used in "South Florida Mitigation baseline Survey" (1998) by DCA. International Hurricane Center, Institute for Public Opinion Research. Second, it is more appropriate to detect the effect of perceived probability of occurrence on the willingness-to-pay for in-residence shelter, because purchasing a shelter is considered to be an individual decision. Factor analysis (factor scores for each period) is used to determine the linear combination of three periods. Factor scores are not found to be significantly different from each other (and are not shown here). Accordingly, the direct average of three periods is deemed appropriate for the regression analysis.

PERCEIVED SEVERITY OF RISK

Please rank the following activities in terms of the threat (risk) they pose on human life in general.

(1=highest risk, 5=lowest risk)

Motor vehicle accident _______
Airline crash _______
Floods _______
Tornadoes _______
Home accident _______

In Slovic, Fischoff, and Lichtenstein (1980), 110 people were asked to rank 30 different risks ("activities, substances, and technologies") from each activity/technology from least to most risky. The ranking is by the death rate in the U.S. population. Risks included in their list were unrelated in terms of the exposed setting/ cause of the risk.The ordinal scale question in the present study focuses on the individual's perceived severity of tornado generally compared to the other selected risks from the "safety" category. The risk category "safety" is one of the risk classifications in Fischer, Morgan, Fischoff, Nair, and Lave (1991). In their study, subjects were asked to rank five risks "of greatest concern" ranging from "1=greatest concern to 5=least concern" and their categories were: health, safety, environment, society, and other. I use two natural hazards, including tornadoes, and three other selected risks from "safety category." The reason for selecting the risks from the same category is to eliminate the fact that "the simplicity and intuitive appeal of comparisons of unrelated risks may be highly deceptive" (Slovic, Kraus, and Covello, 1990). Note that rank is coded as (6 – the number stated for tornado) for the analysis.

CONTROLLABILITY OF TORNADO RISK

To what extent do you feel that you can *do something (anything)* to protect yourself and your family from a possible tornado?

I can't do much I can do a lot
1 2 3 4 5

This question is a reworded version of the question used to measure perceived "personal efficacy" in Fischer, Morgan, Fischoff, Nair, and Lave (1991).

PERCEIVED RESPONSIBILITY

In your opinion, what degree of responsibility each individual/institution below has to undertake to protect you and your family from the damage of a possible tornado?

Not Responsible At All				Very Responsible Myself	
Local/state government	1	2	3	4	5
Federal government	1	2	3	4	5
Media (newspaper, TV)	1	2	3	4	5
Homebuilders/owners	1	2	3	4	5
Others (Please specify)	1	2	3	4	5

I not only modified the alternatives of responsible entities, but also measured the degree of responsibility each individual/institution has to undertake from Fischer, Morgan, Fischoff, Nair, and Lave (1991) study.

PERCEIVED PROTECTIVE ABILITY OF SAFE ROOM

Do you think this shelter can protect you and your family from a possible tornado? (Please circle one).

Not at all Very much
1 2 3 4 5

Individuals that have a response below 3 are assumed to be *weak believers* of a shelter's protective ability, above 3 to be *strong believers*, and the ones who circled 3 are considered to be *neutral believers*.

WILLINGNESS-TO-PAY (WTP) MEASURES

Would you be willing to purchase the safe room (in-residence shelter) described above?

Certainly Not Certainly
1 2 3 4 5

How much, *at most,* would you be willing to pay for *a safe room inside your house?*

- ❑ Less than $1000
- ❑ $1000-$2000
- ❑ $2000-$3000
- ❑ $3000-$4000
- ❑ $4000-$5000
- ❑ $5000-$6000

- ❑ $6000-$7000
- ❑ $7000-$8000
- ❑ $8000-$9000
- ❑ $9000-$10,000
- ❑ More than $10,000

Consistent with the previous survey studies, contingent valuation method is used for the value of WTP. Different from the studies that used an open-ended question (e.g., McDaniels, Kamlet, and Fischer, 1992; Brookshire and Coursey, 1987) or a percent stated as a portion of current income or a dichotomous type of question (e.g., Bishop and Heberlein, 1990) to measure WTP, for this study, the payment-scale is found to be more appropriate. One reason is that respondents do not have any idea about ranges of safe room price (safe rooms were not available in the market when this study was done). In addition, an open-ended question can be appropriate for a well-known good, but the range of the values that individuals state may become so diverse for a new good that the researcher may not be able to interpret the result (Donaldson, Thomas, and Torgerson, 1997).

In addition to the maximum willingness to pay question, before giving monetary information about the safe room, subjects are asked to indicate whether they were likely to purchase this kind of good regardless of its price (with an undisclosed price). While the former is considered to be a choice decision, the latter is a payment decision.

Sampling Procedure

A sample of one thousand homeowners from Lubbock was selected to be the potential respondents to the mail survey. The addresses were randomly selected from the population of homeowners by a research company called "InfoUSA". A tornado hit Lubbock on May 11, 1970, killing 27 people. The city is considered by FEMA to be in a high-risk wind zone where shelter is suggested as an effective protective mechanism for tornadoes.

The response rate is 20% with no compensation provided to respondents and with no follow-up method used. According to Dillman (1978), this rate is acceptable as an initial response In order to assess sample representative ability, I conducted two different tests. First, I compared the demographics of the homeowners in the general sampling frame (homeowners in the city of Lubbock) with those of my respondents. This test resulted in no significant differences. Second, in order to evaluate the degree of non-response bias in my data, I compared the early (n1=125) and late (n2=75) respondents in the sample in terms of the mean values of the variables in the research. This test is also suggested that non-response bias may not be a critical problem in the data since I found no statistically significant differences.

Descriptive Statistics

There are 138 male and 62 female respondents in the data pool. The median age of a respondent is 38. Almost half of the respondents have a college education (42.33%). The median family income is $45,000. Thus, the demographic description of the respondents is very similar to the general makeup of Lubbock's population. It is interesting to note that less than 15% of the respondents have any kind of shelter. However, 85% report that they would choose to go to safe place *inside* their houses after notice of an approaching tornado. This is consistent with the evidence reported by Brown, Kruger and Bos (2000). Individuals responding to the survey perceive themselves as the most responsible entity to protect themselves and their family from the damage of a possible tornado (68.5% of respondents). The average maximum willingness to pay in the sample is $2449. This amount is lower than the estimated average cost of building a safe room ($4000).

The correlation matrix (not shown) gives the strength of the association between variables. We find a highly positive correlation between willingness to purchase and maximum willingness to pay (p-value of 0.000). Relative severity and perceived exposure are uncorrelated and thus useable for the two-component measure of risk perception. Numerous survey and experimental studies suggest that women are more risk-averse than men in financial decisions (for a review see Schubert, Brown, Gysler, and Brachinger, 1999). The correlation of the degree of risk aversion and gender variables is -0.066 with p-value of 0.360 indicating no strong gender component of risk attitude here. However, the presence of children has a significant positive relationship to willingness to purchase and maximum willingness to pay (Max WTP).

REGRESSION ANALYSIS

The focal variable of the present study is risk perception; however, in order to conduct a stronger test of the effects of risk perception on willingness to pay, several control variables are included. The analysis is based on estimated linear regressions after checking the OLS assumptions. Two regression equations are estimated with dependent variables, willingness to purchase and maximum willingness to pay. The effect of perceived severity and perceived exposure that are the two main components of perceived risk out of four, are examined both as a multiplicative effect and independent effect of each separately.

The multiplicative effect of perceived exposure and severity is found to have a positive effect on willingness to purchase a safe room however no statistical significance is detected for maximum willingness to pay. McDaniels, Kamlet, and Fischer (1992) note that empirical studies have shown that it is applicable to use additive and multiplicative functions for eliciting multi-attribute utility and value. Slovic (1987) describes the similarity between the multiplicative model and analytical representation of risk perceptions.

The results of the regression analysis are summarized in Table 1. Perceived exposure has a significant positive effect on willingness to purchase the safe room, but not on the maximum willingness to pay (p-values are 0.012 and 0.354 respectively). Perceived severity has a significant positive influence on the maximum amount respondents are willing to pay, but not their willingness to purchase the shelter (p-values are 0.136 and 0.038 respectively).

For the analysis on the control variables, the degree of risk aversion has no significant effect on either of the WTP measurements. The belief that individuals can exert some control over the losses from a tornado has a significant positive effect on their maximum willingness to pay. If people believe that safe room protects them from a tornado, then they respond with higher values for both WTP measurements. Income does not have a significant effect on the

WTP measurements. The presence of dependent children is a significant factor with a positive influence on the maximum WTP (p-value 0.018). Contrary to many previous studies but consistent with Fischer, Morgan, Fischoff, Nair, and Lave (1991), male respondents stated higher values for WTP measurements. The maximum amount male respondents are willing to pay for the shelter is $500 higher on average than the amount stated by females. Finally, Max WTP is positively related to the level of education (p-value 0.010).

Table 1. Regression Results

	WTP (Choice Decision)	**MaxWTP (Payment Decision)**
Intercept	1.560	-3535.0
Expected time to live in residence	-0.019	-7.6
	(0.058)	(0.668)
Risk Aversion	-0.093	51.0
	(0.231)	(0.711)
Severity	0.1510	373.0
	(0.136)	(0.038)
Experience	-0.026	-328.0
	(0.879)	(0.277)
Controllability	-0.206	98.0
	(0.013)	(0.503)
Precautions	0.188	42.0
	(0.011)	(0.744)
Protectivity	0.411	315.0
	(0.000)	(0.093)
Have any shelter	-1.006	-68.0
	(0.000)	(0.878)
Income	-0.000	0.009
	(0.232)	(0.110)
Have Children	0.272	995.6
	(0.249)	(0.018)
Age	0.003	22.9
	(0.688)	(0.088)
Sex	-0.178	-506.6
	(0.311)	(0.104)
Education	0.020	475.0
	(0.844)	(0.010)
Exposure	0.217	140.0
	(0.012)	(0.354)
R-square	27.5%	18.0%
F-statistic	4.62	2.67
p-value	0.000	0.001

CONCLUSIONS

The present study examines the relationship between individual risk perceptions and willingness to pay for a safe room for tornado protection. The theoretical model based on expected utility predicts that the probability of loss, the severity of loss, the protective ability of the safe room have a positive effect on the willingness to pay for a safe room. The empirical results are consistent with the theoretical predictions in some dimensions but not in others. The results of the survey study are based on a small segment of the population and so may not generalize. However, they are remarkable in many aspects.

First, theory predicts a positive relationship between perceived protective ability of the safe room and willingness to pay. Empirically, individuals who have a stronger belief about the protective ability of the shelter i.e. strong believers stated significantly higher values for both WTP measures. Second, the theory predicts a positive relationship between the probability of the harmful event and willingness to pay. Accordingly, willingness to purchase the shelter (choice decision) is positively related to perception of the hazard's probability (perceived exposure). Third, theory predicts that willingness to pay is increasing in the size of the loss (severity of the hazard). Empirically, there exists a significant positive relationship between perceived severity and maximum willingness to pay (payment decision). Lastly, the presence of dependent children has important explanatory power on both WTP measures. On average people with dependent children in the home state a maximum willingness to pay nearly $1,000 higher than other respondents.

One of the most interesting facets of this study is the distinction evidently made between the action (or choice) decision and the valuation (or payment) decision embodied in the different descriptions of WTP. Economic theory does not distinguish the WTP measures along these lines. However, respondents do distinguish and react to the two components of risk differently depending on whether they are making a choice or a payment decision. Further research is necessary in many aspects. First, the determinants of perceived risk needs deeper investigation for a precise and more exploratory identification of risk. Second, the questionnaire can be conducted on different samples with a better follow-up procedure. In addition an analysis of different types of disasters (e.g. hurricanes) would be useful.

APPENDIX 1
THEORETICAL MODEL

Let $U(H_i,W_i)$ represent preferences in state i, where U(. , .) is an increasing concave function of health status, H_i, and wealth level, W_i.. For the following analysis, there are two states of the world, 0 and 1. In state 0, a damaging tornado occurs. The probability of state 0 is *p*. The maximum loss of health status due to tornado as loss of life is denoted as $H_0=0$. Further, assume $H_1\geq H_0$, $W_1\geq W_0$ and $U(0,W)=0$.

Expected utility of the tornado risk is:

$$pU(H_0,W_0)+(1-p)U(H_1,W_1) \tag{1}$$

H_{0s} is defined as health status in the event that a tornado occurs with access to a safe room. The safe room protects health status, thus, $H_{0s} > H_0$. The maximum willingness-to-pay (WTP), *c* solves

$$pU(H_0,W_0)+(1-p)U(H_1,W_1)=pU(H_{0S},W_0-c)+(1-p)U(H_1,W_1-c) \quad (2)$$

For the simplest case, assume that wealth is unaffected by the tornado. Further, suppose that health status is zero in the event of the tornado (i.e. the health outcome is death). The safe room, however, provides complete protection leaving health status the same as in the no-tornado state. Mathematically, $W_1=W_0$, $H_0=0$, and $H_{0s}= H_1$. With these simplifications, equation (2) becomes:

$$(1-p)U(H_1,W_1)=U(H_1,W_1-c) \quad (3)$$

$$F(p,c)=(1-p)U(H_1,W_1)-U(H_1,W_1-c)=0\,. \quad (4)$$

Using the implicit function theorem, we can derive the relationship between maximum willingness-to-pay and the probability of a tornado. So,

$$\frac{\partial c}{\partial p}=-\frac{F_p}{F_c}=\frac{U(H_1,W_1)}{U_W(H_1,W_1-c)}>0\,. \quad (5)$$

Thus, maximum willingness-to-pay for a safe room is increasing in probability, *p*. Now, suppose the perceived reduction in health status due to tornado is some level of harm, but not necessarily death, thus, $H_1 \geq H_{0s} > H_0 \geq 0$. The maximum willingness to pay for this case, c^*, solves

$$pU(H_0,W_0)+(1-p)U(H_1,W_1)=pU(H_{0S},W_0-c^*)+(1-p)U(H_1,W_1-c^*)$$

$$p[U(H_0,W_0)-U(H_{0S},W_0-c^*)]+(1-p)[U(H_1,W_1)-U(H_1,W_1-c^*)]=0 \quad (6)$$

Again, by the implicit function theorem,

$$\frac{\partial c^*}{\partial p}=\frac{-[U(H_0,W_0)-U(H_{0S},W_0-c^*)]+[U(H_1,W_1)-U(H_1,W_1-c^*)]}{pU_W(H_{0S},W_0-c^*)+(1-p)U_W(H_1,W_1-c^*)} \quad (7)$$

$$=\frac{[U(H_1,W_1)-U(H_1,W_1-c^*)]+[U(H_{0S},W_0-c^*)-U(H_0,W_{01})]}{pU_W(H_{0S},W_0-c^*)+(1-p)U_W(H_1,W_1-c^*)}>0 \quad (8)$$

By concavity of U and where U (0,w) = 0, thus, a positive relationship is illustrated between the probability of tornado risk and the maximum willingness to pay. H_1-H_0 is defined as unprotected health loss. In the event of a tornado, the safe room will improve health status up to, but not exceeding the health status in state 1. Further, let θ be the level of protection afforded by the safe room against tornado, where $0<\theta\leq 1$.

$H_{0s} = (1-\theta)\, H_0 + \theta H_1.$ 9)

Trivially, $\partial H_{0s} / \partial H_0 = (1-\theta) \geq 0$ and $1 > (1-\theta) \geq 0.$ (10)

A larger θ implies greater protection. Recall the simplified framework described by equation (3). This is the case where θ = 1. We can examine changes in H_0 for a sense of the level of harm or severity of the tornado. Thus,

$$\frac{\partial c^*}{\partial H_0} = \frac{-p[U_H(H_0,W_0) - U_H(H_{0S},W_0 - c^*)\partial H_{0S}/\partial H_0]}{pU_W(H_{0S},W_0 - c^*) + (1-p)U_W(H_1,W_1 - c^*)}$$
$$= \frac{-p[U_H(H_0,W_0) - (1-\theta)U_H(H_{0S1},W_0 - c^*)]}{pU_W(H_{0S},W_0 - c^*) + (1-p)U_W(H_1,W_1 - c^*)} < 0 \qquad (11)$$

This means that as unprotected health status increases (decreases) within the bounds, $0 \leq H_0 \leq H_1$, willingness-to-pay decreases (increases). Decreasing H_0 relative to H_1 implies greater severity of the loss. Greater severity implies a higher maximum willingness-to-pay. Lastly, substituting $(1-\theta)\, H_0 + \theta H_1$ for H_{0s} into equation (6), we have

$$p[U(H_0,W_0) - U[(1-\theta)H_0 + \theta H_1, W_0 - c^*]] + (1-p)[U(H_1,W_1) - U(H_1,W_1 - c^*)] = 0.$$
$$\frac{\partial c^*}{\partial \theta} = \frac{p[U_H(H_{0S},W_0 - c^*)](H_1 - H_0)}{pU_W(H_{0S},W_0 - c^*) + (1-p)U_W(H_1,W_1 - c^*)} > 0 \qquad (12)$$

Therefore as the ability of the safe room to protect individuals from a possible tornado increases, the higher the maximum willingness to pay for a safe room. To summarize, the simple theoretical model yields three testable implications. They are maximum willingness to pay is:

1. increasing in the probability of the harmful event,
2. increasing in the perceived severity of the loss and
3. increasing in the protective ability of the safe room.

REFERENCES

Bishop, R.C., T.A. Heberlein (1990), *Economic valuation of natural resources: Issues, theory, and applications*, edited by R.L. Johnson and G. V. Johnson, Boulder CO, Westview Press.

Brookshire, D. S., D. L. Coursey (1987), "Measuring the value of a public good: an empirical comparison of elicitation procedures", *American Economic Review,* Vol.77: 554-6.

Brown, S., E. Kruger, and J. Bos (2000), *Injury Update: A Report to Oklahoma Injury Surveillance Participants*, Injury Prevention Service, Oklahoma Department of Health, Oklahoma City, OK.

Camerer C. F., H. Kunreuther (1989), "Decision Processes for Low Probability Events: Policy Implications", *Journal of Policy Analysis and Management*, Vol.8 (4): 565-92.

Churchill, G.A. Jr. (1991), *Marketing Research Methodological Foundations*, Fifth edition, The Dryden Press.

Crocker, T.D., J. F. Shogren (1991), "Preference Learning and Contingent Valuation and Revealed Preference Methodologies: Comparing the Estimates for Quasi-public Goods", *Land Economics*, Vol.72: 80-90.

Crouch, E.A.C., R. Wilson (1982), *Risk/Benefit Analysis*, Cambridge, Balinger.

Dillman, D.A. (1978), *Mail and Telephone Surveys – The Total Design Method*. New York, Wiley.

Donaldson, C., R. Thomas, and D. Togerson (1997), "Validity of Open-ended and Payment Scale Approaches to Eliciting Willingness to Pay", *Applied Economics*, Vol.29: 79-84.

East Bay Seismic Retrofit Survey (1998), University of California, Berkley and University of Pennsylvania.

Ehrlich, I, G. S. Becker (1972), "Market Insurance, Self-insurance and Self-protection." *Journal of Political Economy*, Vol. 80: 623-48.

FEMA Mitigation Directorate (1999), Taking Shelter from the Storm, Building a Safe Room Inside Your House.

Fischer, G.W., M.G. Morgan, B. Fischoff, I. Nair, and L.B. Lave (1991), "What Risks Are People Concerned About?", *Risk Analysis*, Vol.11 (2): 303-14.

Fischoff, B., S. Watson, and C. Hope (1984), "Defining Risk", *Policy Sciences*, Vol.17: 123-139.

Hammitt, J. K (1990), "Risk Perceptions and Food Choice: An Exploratory Analysis of Organic-versus Conventional-produce Buyers", *Risk Analysis*, Vol.10 (3): 367-74.

Harless, D., C. Camerer (1994), "The Predictive Utility of Generalized Expected Utility Theories", *Econometrica* Vol.62: 1251-89.

Hasher, L., R.T. Zacks (1984), *Automatic Processing of Fundamental Information*, American Psychologist.

Kunreuther, H. (1976), "Limited Knowledge and Insurance Protection", *Public Policy* Vol.29 (2): 227-61.

Kunreuther, H. (1978), *Disaster Insurance Protection*, Public Policy Lessons, John Wiley, New York.

Kunreuther, H. (1996), "Mitigating Disaster Losses Through Insurance", *Journal of Risk and Uncertainty*, Vol.12 (2/3): 171-87.

Mansfield, C. (1998), "A Consistent Method for Calibrating Contingent Value Survey Data", *Southern Economic Journal*, Vol.64 (3): 665-81.

McClelland, G.H., W.D. Schulze, and B. Hurd (1990), "The Effect of Risk Beliefs on Property Values: A Case Study of a Hazardous Waste Site", *Risk Analysis*, Vol.10 (4): 485-97.

McDaniels, T.L., M.S. Kamlet, and G.W. Fischer (1992), "Risk Perception and the Value of Safety", *Risk Analysis*, Vol.12 (4): 495-503.

Mitchell, R. and R.T. Carson (1989), *Using Surveys to Value Public Goods: The Contingent Valuation Method*, Resources for the Future, Washington, DC.

Randall, A. (1993), "Passive-use values and Contingent Valuation – Valid for Damage Assessment", *Choices*, Vol.2: 12-15.

Schubert, R., M. Brown, M. Gysler, and H.W. Brachinger (1999), "Financial Decision-making: Are Women Really More Risk-averse?", *American Economic Review,* Vol.89 (2): 381-86.

Singh, H., M. Thayer (1992), "Impact of Seat Belt Use on Driving Behavior", *Economic Inquiry,* Vol.30: 649-658.

Slovic, P., N. Kraus, and V.T. Covello (1990), "What Should We Know About Making Risk Comparisons?", *Risk Analysis,* Vol.10 (3): 389-92.

Slovic, P. (1987), "Perception of Risk", *Science*, Vol.236: 280-85.

Slovic, P., B. Fischoff, and S. Lichtenstein (1980), *Facts and Fears: Understanding Perceived Risk. Societal Risk Assessments: How Safe is Safe Enough?* Edited by Richard C. Schwing and Walter Albers, Jr. Plenum Press, New York.

Smith, V.K. (1986), "Benefit Analysis for Natural Hazards", *Risk Analysis,* Vol.6: 325-34.

Smith, V.K., and W. Devousges (1987), "An Empirical Analysis of the Economic Value of Risk Changes, *Journal of Political Economy,* Vol.95: 1.

Smith, V.K., W.H. Desvousges, and A.M. Freeman III (1985), *Valuing Changes in Hazardous Waste Risks: A Contingent Valuation Analysis*, Research Triangle Institute, Research Triangle Park, North Carolina.

South Florida Mitigation Baseline Survey (1998), DCA, International Hurricane Center, Institute for Public Opinion Research.

Underwood, B.J. (1971), "Recognition Memory" In H.H. Kendler and J.T. Spence, 313-335, Appleton-Century-Crofts, New York.

Viscusi, W.K., W. N. Evans (1990), "Utility Functions that Depend on Health Status: Estimates and Economic Implications", *American Economic Review,* Vol.80 (3): 353-74.

ACKNOWLEDGEMENTS

This work was performed under the Department of Commerce NIST/TTU Cooperative Agreement Award 70NANB8H0059.

In: Economics and the Wind
Editors: B. T. Ewing, et. al., pp. 105-113
ISBN: 1-59454-280-5
©2005 Nova Science Publishers, Inc.

Chapter 9

THE MARKET FOR TORNADO PROTECTION: MARKET AND POLICY RESPONSES FOLLOWING THE MAY 1999 OKLAHOMA TORNADOES

William L. Ridley and Daniel Sutter
Department of Economics, University of Oklahoma, Norman, OK, USA
Kevin M. Simmons
Department of Business and Economics, Austin College, Sherman, TX, USA

INTRODUCTION

The past six years have witnessed the emergence of a market for tornado protection. Engineers have made significant progress over the past several decades in the design of shelters to protect residents and building techniques to reduce wind damage to structures. The basic principles behind the design of modern shelters have been recognized for almost thirty years (Kiesling and Goolsby, 1974). The current market demand for shelters began following a feature on saferoom design at the Wind Engineering Research Center at Texas Tech on NBC *Dateline* in 1997, following the Jarrell, Texas F5 tornado (Kiesling, 2003). The Federal Emergency Management Agency (FEMA) decided to emphasize saferooms as part of their National Mitigation Strategy and in 1998 issued the first edition of "Taking Shelter From the Storm: Building a Saferoom Inside Your House". The May 3, 1999 Oklahoma City F5 tornado stimulated even greater interest in tornado protection and a year later the National Storm Shelter Association was formed to help assure the quality of shelter construction. The Institute for Business and Home Safety includes both shelters and wind resistant construction in their Fortified Homes program. In 2003 DuPont introduced a saferoom product built from Kevlar and promoted by an extensive television and radio advertising campaign featuring NASCAR star Jeff Gordon. FEMA estimates that since 1998 over 300,000 shelters and saferooms have been built nationally (Patton, 2003a).

We examine in this chapter the response of policy makers and the market in providing tornado protection in Oklahoma following the May 3, 1999 tornadoes. The F5 tornado which struck the Oklahoma City metropolitan area that day produced the highest death toll of any tornado in the past twenty years and the most damage of any tornado in U.S. history (Brooks and Doswell, 2001 & 2002). The storms also brought to public attention to the low market penetration of tornado shelters even at the heart of Tornado Alley. Only one home struck by the F5 Oklahoma City tornado had an above ground saferoom and only 16 percent of residents surveyed by the state of Oklahoma reported surviving the storm in a shelter of any type (Brown et al. 2000). Consequently the response in Oklahoma provides an interesting and relevant case study. We detail developments related to both tornado shelters and tornado resistant construction, and consider the provision of shelters for residents of both permanent and mobile homes. We provide a progress report on the status of the market for tornado protection in Oklahoma.

POLICIES

There have been three major policies related to tornado shelters in Oklahoma since May 1999. The first was the Oklahoma Saferoom Initiative funded by the FEMA and the Oklahoma Department of Civil Emergency Management (ODCEM) beginning in June 1999. The Initiative provided $2,000 rebates to residents installing an above ground saferoom or below ground storm shelter. The program proceeded in three phases. Phase 1 of the program was open to home owners whose homes suffered 50% or more damage on May 3rd, while Phase 2 was for homeowners whose homes suffered less than 50% damage that day. All residents statewide were eligible in Phase 3 of the program, with rebates awarded to these applicants on a funds available basis. Residents had to apply for the program by September 30, 1999 and complete installation by November 2000. Shelters had to be built to the specifications described in FEMA (1999). Over 14,000 Oklahomans applied under the program, with 11,000 applicants in Phase 3 alone. The Phase 3 application rate to the Initiative, which best illustrates demand for tornado shelters, was 1.48% for the state as a whole, ranging from .27% in McCurtain County to 5.80% in McClain County. The Phase 3 application rate was positively related to the county tornado rate measured both over the last fifty years and the prior three years (Merrell, Simmons and Sutter, 2002).

The second tornado safety policy measure was State Question 696, a property tax credit measure approved by voters in November 2002. The legislation allows homeowners to receive a property tax exemption for constructing a saferoom in their house. The measure exempts a shelter of up to 100 square feet in a residence, and remains in effect until the home is sold. The measure (which received little publicity prior to the election) won 66 percent of the vote statewide and a majority of the vote in every county. The exemption can apply retrospectively to shelters constructed in 2002. We have no data at this point to determine the impact this tax break will have on shelter construction. The tax exemption is likely to be small for most homes relative to the cost of a saferoom; for a 1500 square foot home with a 100 square foot saferoom and an annual property tax assessment of $1,000, the exemption would amount to $67 annually. With a 5% real discount rate the present value of the exemption over twenty years is $877, while a saferoom is likely to cost in excess of $4,000 (FEMA 1999).

A third major policy response is a second statewide saferoom rebate program. The program was announced during the summer of 2003 and involves a $3 million Federal grant to fund rebates of 75 percent of the cost of a shelter, up to a maximum of $2,000 per household. First priority in the program will be given to residents whose homes were damaged or destroyed in the May 2003 tornadoes. Rebates will then be given to residents affected in the May 3, 1999 tornadoes who installed a shelter before December 31, 2000. Remaining funds will be distributed to applicants across the state. Residents have until October 31, 2003 to register for the program. Program details can be found on the ODCEM's website at www.odcem.state.ok.us/public/saferoom-pro.htm.

Rebate programs similar to the Oklahoma Saferoom Initiative have been implemented in other parts of Oklahoma for residential shelters. Logan County and the city of Lawton have offered homeowners $1,500 rebates for the installation of an approved shelter. Lawton has recently received an additional $1,000,000 federal grant for a new program in 2003 which will enable the city to provide rebates for an additional 500 shelters, or 1.5 percent of the single family homes in Comanche County in the 2000 Census. Housing count totals used in this paper were obtained from the Census Bureau's American Factfinder website for the 2000 Census contained in the SF-3 file at http://factfinder.census.gov. To date the saferoom grant programs in the state have not targeted mobile home parks.

The construction of tornado shelters in public schools has also received attention from policy makers. The ODCEM has established a program to make grants of $300,000 to $600,000 to school districts for the construction of saferooms in schools. Currently 80 school districts across the state have applied for this program.

TORNADO SHELTERS

To examine the rate of shelter installation since May 1999, we obtained records on the number of building permits for tornado shelters issued by five communities in central Oklahoma: Oklahoma City, Norman, Moore, Del City and Midwest City. Table 1 reports the number of permits issued each year between 1999 and 2002 as well as the four-year total. Shelters installed in both new homes and retrofitted homes require permits, although for above ground saferooms in newly constructed homes the details will be contained in the permit for the home and not a separate permit. Table 1 reports the totals for separate shelter permits and thus understates the total number of shelters constructed over the four years. To provide perspective, Table 1 also reports the number of single family housing units in each city in the 2000 Census and the number of building permits for new, privately owned single family homes issued over the same four year period. The permit totals indicate that shelters have made a significant inroad in central Oklahoma. Storm shelter permits as a percentage of single-family homes range from 4.35% in Moore to less than 1% in Norman. As of May 8, 2003 Moore had records of about 750 shelters in the city, so the number of above ground shelters built since 1999 did not exceed 150. Shelter permits as a percentage of new home construction range from 10.0% in Norman to 68.4% in Midwest City. The path of the May 3rd F5 tornado explains the differences in the rate of shelter installation across communities; the tornado did not strike Norman and only a small part of Oklahoma City, so these cities had fewer homes eligible for rebates in Phases 1 and 2 of the Oklahoma Saferoom Initiative and lower rates of shelter installation. Midwest City is an older community with less new construction, which is why shelters comprise such a high percentage of new construction in this community. The annual totals indicate a decline in the rate of shelter installation. A portion of the decline is a natural result of the expiration of the Saferoom Initiative rebates. In addition, shelters are durable products and once purchased, residents do not have to purchase a new shelter until they move. In equilibrium with a durable product only the portion of shelters wearing out will need to be replaced, so the slowing of new installation is consistent with the establishment of equilibrium in the shelter market.

Table 1. Building Permits for Tornado Shelters, 1999-2002

Year	Oklahoma City	Norman	Moore	Del City	Midwest City
1999	465	NA	36	48	NA
2000	1140	86	187	154	297
2001	481	67	89	51	60
2002	184	62	45	3	20
Total	2270	215	597	256	377
Single Family Homes, 2000	147,902	24,816	13,728	7,845	17,278
Shelters as % of Homes	1.53%	.87%	4.35%	3.26%	2.18%
Building Permits, 1999-2002	10,281	2,152	1,498	NA	551
Shelters as % of Permits	22.1%	10.0%	39.9%	NA	68.4%

Note: The total for Midwest City is for 1999 and 2000. Moore reported 240 permits in August 2002 based on a review of previously filed permits, so we include this in the total but not any given year.

The rate of shelter purchase reported in Table 1 might strike the reader as low, since few Oklahomans have purchased shelters. Households will purchase a shelter if the value they place on safety is sufficiently high. The value of the shelter will also depend on the probability of a tornado, which is low. Merrell, Simmons and Sutter (2003) have calculated the cost per fatality avoided for tornado shelters in permanent homes and find that the value exceeds the range of values of safety revealed in labor market studies. Based on this comparison, relatively few households living in permanent houses will probably place a high enough value on safety to want to purchase tornado shelters. Tornado shelters represent a safety investment that only a minority of residents is likely to purchase in the near future.

The availability of shelters for residents who wish to protect themselves provides an alternative measure of the performance of the market. One simple measure of availability is the number of companies and contractors offering installation of shelters. We have tracked the number of contractors listed under the Storm Shelters heading in the Oklahoma City and Tulsa Southwestern Bell Yellow Pages. Table 2 reports the number of companies listed annually in the Oklahoma City Yellow Pages. The number of contractors has increased from 8 in August 1998 before the May 3rd tornadoes to 35 in 2003. In addition, there were 21 contractors listed under the Storm Shelters heading in the 2002 Tulsa Yellow Pages. Clearly many contractors perceive an opportunity to market storm shelters.

Table 2. Oklahoma City Storm Shelter Contractors, 1998-2003

Year	Number
1998	8
1999	29
2000	36
2001	41
2002	36
2003	35

The ability of residents to have a shelter installed in a new home is another element of availability. Once residents choose a location and a homebuilder and floor plan, they may then inquire about adding a shelter or saferoom. Homebuyers who cannot add a shelter to the home they have selected might be unlikely to search to find another builder where they can build a home with a shelter. The Central Oklahoma Home Builders Association as well as several home builders contacted by the authors all indicated a willingness to accommodate buyers willing to pay extra for a shelter, although the builders typically subcontract shelter installation to an independent contractor. Homeowners may also be able to include the amount of the shelter in the financing of the home. One builder of upscale homes in the Oklahoma City area, Greenway Group, includes a saferoom, marketed as a multi-purpose room (a security vault for valuable papers, a wine cellar) in their model homes. Michael Holt, president of Greenway Group, reports receiving considerable positive feedback from prospective buyers on the saferoom.

An active market for tornado shelters will include a resale market. Shelters are a durable, immovable capital improvement to property. With a sufficient demand for shelters, homes equipped with shelters should sell at a premium; that is, a home with a storm shelter should sell for slightly more, controlling for size, age, location and other factors affecting price. While Simmons et al. (2002) found a positive housing price premium for hurricane shelters for coastal property on the Gulf of Mexico in Texas, to our knowledge, researchers have not yet examined whether a premium for tornado shelters exists in home prices. As of early 2003, however, the Oklahoma City and Norman realtors' Multiple Listing Services did not track whether homes for sale include a storm shelter, which suggests that either few buyers inquire about shelters when looking for a house or that few homes offered for sale have shelters. The lack of a resale market for shelters is not surprising at this point since residents started purchasing shelters in sizable numbers only four years ago, so few homes with the new shelters may have been resold yet.

Mobile Homes

Tornadoes pose a particular hazard for residents of mobile homes. Brooks and Doswell (2002) estimate that the fatality rate for residents of mobile homes is 10-15 times higher than residents of permanent homes. Merrell, Simmons and Sutter (2003) also find that the cost per fatality avoided for shelters in mobile homes is about one tenth that for permanent homes. Installation of shelters for mobile homes requires more coordination than for single-family homes. Residents of an owner-occupied single family home need only obtain a building permit and hire a contractor to install a below ground shelter in their yard; these residents can protect themselves if they choose. By contrast, a higher proportion of mobile homes are rental properties, and many are located in mobile home parks where residents do not own the lot. Once installed, underground shelters cannot easily be moved, so residents might not wish to install a shelter at their current residence even if the park allows individual shelters. The magnitude of the tornado threat to mobile homes has led to proposals for regulation requiring the construction of shelters in mobile home parks (Golden and Snow 1991).

Mobile home park operators could though take the initiative to supply storm shelters for residents. Some mobile home parks offer a number of amenities to their residents such as exercise rooms, swimming pools and laundry facilities, and there is no reason storm shelters would not be offered. In fact, a group shelter might well offer a lower cost per resident than individual shelter units. A number of mobile home parks in Oklahoma do indeed offer shelters as an amenity. Examination of listings in the August 2002 Southwestern Bell Yellow Pages revealed that the ads for 12 of 96 mobile home parks mentioned storm shelters or cellars as an amenity for residents. The parks featuring shelters contacted by the authors all had sufficient shelter capacity for all of their residents. More than half of the parks with shelters installed their shelters prior to 1999, so mobile home operators have been aware of the value of offering protection from tornadoes as an amenity to residents for some time. We also examined listings under the Mobile Home Parks heading in the 2002 Tulsa Southwestern Bell Yellow Pages; four of 67 parks advertising in this category mentioned storm shelters in their ads. Fewer parks in Tulsa advertise shelter availability, which is notable given that Tulsa is a FEMA Project Impact community and Oklahoma City is not. Plausibly the difference in rates may be the result of the May 3 tornado striking the Oklahoma City area.

Tornado Resistant Construction

Tornado shelters are designed to protect lives. Although no building design will protect homes from an F5 tornado, better construction techniques can reduce damage from weaker tornadoes. The estimated wind speeds for an F1 tornado, for instance, are in the range of 73 to 112 miles per hour, which is within wind gust requirements in many building codes. And the majority of tornadoes are relatively weak F0 or F1 tornadoes; between 1950 and 1999 74.3% of tornadoes in the Storm Prediction Center's national tornado archive rated on the F-scale were F0 or F1 tornadoes. Thus improved building techniques have the potential to substantially reduce tornado property damage.

A number of building techniques exist which could allow homes to survive weak tornadoes, notably anchoring roofs to walls and walls to the foundation (Golden and Snow, 1991). Although evidence on the cost effectiveness of such construction techniques against tornado risks is sparse, several studies have examined the cost effectiveness of improved building techniques in hurricane prone regions. Stewart, Rosowsky and Huang (2003) find that improved construction is likely cost effective at least along the coast in the southeastern United States. Lavelle, Vickery and Twisdale (2003) find that improved roof connections would efficiently mitigate hurricane damages in Hawaii. In addition, failure to build to then-existing building codes is believed to have increased property losses from Hurricane Andrew by 25% (Platt, 1998; Stewart, Rosowsky and Huang, 2003). The Florida state legislature has mandated that insurers provide actuarially reasonable discounts for policy holders who install mitigation features on their buildings (Khanduri, 2003).

One Oklahoma City builder, Home Creations, adopted wind resistant construction techniques after May 3rd. Home Creations' president Jalal Farzaneh decided after seeing the devastation wrought by these storms that he wanted to build homes that could protect residents from tornadoes. Discussions with construction engineers at the University of Oklahoma led him to include anchor bolts and tornado straps in the design of their new homes. Anchor bolts are cemented into the slab of the home while tornado straps combined with Oriented Strand Board (OSB) sheathing in the walls help keep roofs from being blown off during weak tornadoes. The company has been one of the fastest growing homebuilders in Oklahoma City over past several years, averaging 50% growth per year since 1999. The company advertises tornado safety at their model homes and also featured their building techniques in a television commercial. Potential homebuyers have been very enthusiastic about the design and perceive the improved design as a safety feature as well as a damage loss reduction measure. Mr. Farzaneh believes that half of his company's sales growth since 1999 is due to their tornado resistant construction. The company estimates that the cost of the construction features is $400, and includes wind resistant construction as a part of its list price. Note that insurance premium discounts are not currently available for anchor bolts and tornado straps in Oklahoma, so purchase here reflects homebuyers' own value of tornado safety.

CONCLUSION

Market adoption of new safety devices often proceeds more slowly than some policy makers desire. Consideration of the information a household requires to decide to purchase a tornado shelter provides some insight on the delay. A household would have to consider the following questions. Do tornadoes pose enough of a risk to warrant safety expenditures? Is there a product on the market that can actually reduce the risk of injury or death? Is the contractor chosen to install the shelter going to properly install a shelter that meets engineering standards? We live in a world with many risks, and businesses are not above trying to exploit consumer fears by exaggerating risks or overstating the capacity of a product to offer protection from a threat. Once households determine that the risk is substantial and protection is possible, the problem of quality assurance remains – making sure that the shelters purchased meet sufficient engineering specifications and are properly installed. Mitigation of natural hazards would proceed much more smoothly if information about risks and protection options could be costlessly and credibly conveyed to the public, but this is not possible, and comparing the performance of actual markets to such a standard would be to commit the nirvana fallacy (Demsetz, 1969).

Evaluating the performance of a market is a complicated proposition. People's preferences are subjective, and economists lack any direct means of measuring or observing preferences. We can always rationalize any household's purchase of tornado protection by assuming they place a sufficiently high value on safety, and can similarly explain a decision not to purchase protection by assuming the household places a sufficiently low value on safety. Thus we cannot calculate the number of households for which the expected benefits of a tornado shelter exceed the cost, and so we cannot categorically state whether too many or too few households have purchased tornado shelters.

Instead we have used the availability of tornado safety options to residents as a measure of the performance of the market: Are residents aware of the availability of protection so that those who wish to protect themselves can do so? Do residents seeking protection face excessive difficulties in purchasing shelters? The policy and market responses since May 1999 can be judged favorably according to this standard. Public awareness of the availability of tornado shelters has increased markedly. The Oklahoma Saferoom Initiative was extremely effective in making residents aware of tornado shelters. The Initiative provided rebates for fewer than one percent of the homes in the state and thus clearly was not intended to equip all homes with shelters. But the 14,000 applicants to the program decided to protect themselves, and for each applicant likely several other households seriously examined possible shelter purchase. Encouraging signs in the market are the increase in the number of contractors installing shelters, the supply of community shelters by mobile home park operators, and homebuilders employing wind resistant construction techniques.

Market adoption of automobile air bags provides an illustrative benchmark to keep in mind when considering tornado protection. Although Allstate was convinced of the potential of air bags in 1972, in 1988 only two percent of new cars in the U. S. were equipped with driver side air bags (Mannering and Winston 1995, p. 265). Consumer adoption accelerated quickly after that, even prior to regulation requiring their installation. Mannering and Winston (1995, p. 278) conclude that the market worked well in the case of air bags:

> To be sure, people will endlessly debate whether air bags could or should have been introduced earlier. Nonetheless, because consumers needed time to learn about air bags' performance in actual accidents, automakers were right to make this feature available only gradually. As such, there should be no doubt that ... the market for air bags worked efficiently.

The early returns suggest that the market for tornado safety is functioning well. The May 8, 2003 F4 tornado in Moore and Oklahoma City followed a path very close to the May 3, 1999 F5 tornado, and represents the first field test of storm shelters. The significance of this field test cannot be underestimated, given the considerable concern with assuring the quality of shelters supplied by market contractors (Kiesling, 2003). Patton (2003b) reports how a number of families in Moore survived the May 8th tornado in shelters constructed after the May 3rd tornado. Market demand should respond accordingly as residents see family and neighbors protected by shelters.

REFERENCES

Brown, S., E. Kruger, and J. Bos (2000), "Investigation of Deaths and Injuries Resulting from the May 3, 1999 Tornadoes." *Injury Update*, Oklahoma State Department of Health.

Brooks, Harold E., and Charles A. Doswell III. (2001), "Normalized Damage from Major Tornadoes in the United States: 1890-1999." *Weather and Forecasting*, Vol.16:168-176.

Brooks, Harold E., and Charles A. Doswell III. (2002), "Deaths in the 3 May 1999 Oklahoma City Tornado from a Historical Perspective." *Weather and Forecasting*, Vol.17:354-361.

Demsetz, Harold, (1969), "Information and Efficiency: Another Viewpoint." *Journal of Law and Economics*, Vol.10:1-22.

Federal Emergency Management Agency (1998), *Taking Shelter from the Storm: Building a Safe Room Inside Your House*, FEMA publication #320, 1st edition.

Golden, Joseph H., and Christopher R. Adams (2000), "The Tornado Problem: Forecast, Warning, and Response." *Natural Hazards Review*, Vol.1(2):107-118.

Khanduri, Ahul C. (2003), "Catastrophe Modeling and Wind Storm Loss Mitigation." *11th International Conference on Wind Engineering*, Preprints, Vol.2:2275-2283.

Kiesling, Ernst W., and David W. Goolsby (1974), "In-home Shelters from Extreme Winds." *Civil Engineering*, Vol.44(9):105-107.

Kiesling, Ernst W. (2003). "Comparisons of Storm Shelter Design Guides." *11th International Conference on Wind Engineering*, Preprints, Vol.2:2905-2911.

Lavelle, Francis M., Peter J. Vickery, and Lawrence A. Twisdale (2003), "Hurricane Mitigation Cost/Benefit Analysis for Hawaii." *11th International Conference on Wind Engineering*, Preprints, Vol.2:1639-1646.

Mannering, Fred, and Clifford Winston (1995), "Automobile Air Bags in the 1990s: Market Failure Market Efficiency?" *Journal of Law and Economics*, Vol.38:265-279.

Merrell, David, Kevin M. Simmons, and Daniel Sutter (2003), "The Determinants of Tornado Casualties and the Benefits of Tornado Shelters." Unpublished paper, Department of Economics, University of Oklahoma.

Patton, Ann (2003a), "Grassroots Homeland Security." *Natural Hazards Review*, Vol.27(5):1-3.

Patton, Ann (2003b), "Surviving the Storm: Sheltering in the May 2003 Tornadoes in Moore, Oklahoma." Quick Response Report #163, Natural Hazards Research and Applications Center, University of Colorado. Available on line at www.colorado.edu/hazards/qr/qr163/qr163.html

Platt, Rutherford H. (1999), *Disasters and Democracy: The Politics of Extreme Natural Events*, Island Press, Washington DC.

Simmons, Kevin M., Jamie Brown Kruse, and Douglas A. Smith (2002), "Valuing Mitigation: Real Estate Market Response to Hurricane Loss Measures." *Southern Economic Journal*, Vol.68(3):660-671.

Stewart, Mark G., David V. Rosowsky, and Zhigang Huang (2003), "Hurricane Risk and Economic Viability of Strengthened Construction." *Natural Hazards Review*, Vol.4:12-19.

ACKNOWLEDGEMENTS

We would like to thank Jennifer Nett in Del City, Galen Kitch and Kathy McDaniel in Moore, Kathy Dykes in Midwest City, Julia Yoon in Norman, and Bob Sweet in Oklahoma City for supplying us with shelter permit records. Connie Dill of the ODCEM provided us with details on the Logan County and Lawton rebate programs and the school shelter grant program.

In: Economics and the Wind
Editors: B. T. Ewing, et. al., pp. 115-123

ISBN: 1-59454-280-5
©2005 Nova Science Publishers, Inc.

Chapter 10

IMPACTS OF INSURANCE DEDUCTIBLES AND HURRICANE DAMAGE PERCEPTIONS ON MITIGATION CHOICES

Robert T. Burrus, Jr., Christopher F. Dumas and J. Edward Graham, Jr.
Department of Economics and Finance
University of North Carolina at Wilmington, NC, USA

INTRODUCTION

Advances in hurricane surveillance and early warning technology reduce threats to human life, but tropical weather systems still cause billions of dollars in property damage. Recent patterns of increasing coastal development exacerbate these damages. To reduce potential hurricane losses, the insurance industry and government policymakers provide subsidized insurance and encourage homeowners to purchase structural mitigation.

Many experts conclude that structural mitigation is, indeed, beneficial for the homeowner. Simmons, Kruse, and Smith (2002) find that home values on a Gulf Coast barrier island increase as structural integrity increases. They suggest that the purchase of storm blinds is cost-effective as home values are increased by an amount greater than the cost of installed storm shutters "under very modest assumptions on discounting and depreciation." Kleindorfer and Kunreuther (1999) show that roof reinforcements reduce insurer exposure in the event of a hurricane and that homeowners are "slightly better off" with these defenses.

While these researchers conclude that mitigation has benefits, homeowners do not, in general, mitigate beyond existing building codes (Camerer and Kunreuther, 1989; Kunreuther, 1996; Petak, 1998). Examining this issue, Kunreuther (1996) suggests that homeowners may assign a probability of zero to low-probability, catastrophic events. As well, individual homeowners may fail to consider the destructive nature of a low-probability event. For example, a homeowner facing a 1% probability catastrophic event causing \$50,000 in damage should expect \$500 (.01 x \$50,000) in losses in the average year. A fully-informed risk-neutral homeowner would be willing to pay up to $500 annually for mitigation devices to alleviate these losses. But, if homeowners ignore this expectation, they may not purchase mitigation even if the price is below $500.

Camerer and Kunreuther (1989) suggest that homeowners do not protect against catastrophic events because "ignorance is bliss." Ignoring a potential disaster gives homeowners a (false) sense of security while preparation makes homeowners acknowledge and dread the potential for a hurricane strike. This argument is supported by Petak (1998), who finds that memories of hurricane damage fade quickly.

Other research indicates the availability of insurance undermines the incentive to purchase structural mitigation (Kunreuther and Kleffner, 1992). Burrus, Dumas, and Graham (2002) conclude that subsidized insurance through state wind pools reduces the benefit of mitigation. In fact, they conclude that if deductibles are lowered below a certain threshold, mitigation purchases are not cost-effective. Policymaker and insurer goals of subsidized insurance and mitigation may not be simultaneously feasible.

This study seeks to extend work of Kunreuther (1996), Kunreuther and Camerer (1989), and Burrus, Dumas, and Graham (2002) with an examination of factors influencing mitigation purchases. In particular, we seek to discover whether homeowner perceptions of expected damages and changes in wind insurance offerings impact an individual homeowner's decision to purchase mitigation. To test these premises, survey data were collected from coastal N.C. homeowners.

We describe the survey in the next section. Following the survey description, a model is developed to test whether expected damages and changes in insurance offerings impact hurricane mitigation decisions. The model's results are then provided. The final section concludes the paper.

DATA

A telephone survey of 336 homeowners living in three coastal, hurricane-prone North Carolina counties: (Brunswick, New Hanover, and Pender) provides the data for this study. The survey was conducted after Hurricane Floyd struck North Carolina, but before the Hurricane Isabell strike. A "homeowner" owns (i.e., does not rent) the house and is also the individual in the home making decisions regarding hurricane preparations. The survey collects demographic data as well as information about the extent of existing mitigation, homeowners' subjective hurricane strike probabilities, subjective information about the damages that homeowners anticipate in the event of a hurricane, and whether or not respondents have been impacted by government programs related to hurricanes. Of the 336 homeowners, 291 provided enough information to be included in the data set.

Income and home value questions were posed as categorical questions. Using the midpoint of the income and home value categories, the average homeowner income and the average home value were close to $50,000 and $135,000, respectively. Fifty-two respondents did not answer the income question. Their income categories were estimated using age, education, race, and gender data. As well, forty-one respondents did not answer the home value question. Their home values were estimated using education, miles from the ocean, and the age of the house. Fifty-nine percent of respondents were female. The average respondent had 14 years of education.

The homeowners were asked whether their homes had features to protect against hurricane winds. Almost half of the respondents reported the existence of roof reinforcements in the attic, 29 percent reported having storm resistant window coverings, 17 percent reported having door coverings, and 10 percent reported having reinforced garage doors. Simmons, Kruse, and Smith (2002) also found that approximately 30 percent of homes in an unnamed gulf coast city were equipped with storm shutters. Next, homeowners were asked whether their homes had features designed to protect against floodwaters. Thirty-three percent, 74 percent, and 13 percent of respondents reported their homes being built on fill dirt, on a crawl space, or on pilings, respectively. Twenty eight percent of respondents reported that their outdoor appliances were raised. The typical home was equipped with 2.5 of the eight possible mitigation features.

Homeowners on average estimated that a category 3 hurricane (defined as a storm with wind speeds between 111 to 130 miles per hour and a storm surge from 9 to 12 feet) would do damage equal to about 10 percent of the value of the home. Since the average home value was approximately $135,000, the average homeowner anticipates $13,500 in damage from a category 3 hurricane. Homeowners also responded that the average annual likelihood of a category 3 hurricane strike is 0.39. Interestingly, homeowners overestimate category 3 strike probabilities. The National Weather Service category 3 annual strike probability for the survey region is around 0.005. Thus, on average, a homeowner's expected annual damages from a category 3 hurricane are approximately $5,250.

Also reported were perceptions of government programs designed to provide either hurricane recovery assistance or hurricane damage prevention information. Fifty-four percent reported a positive attitude toward such government programs. Thirteen percent of the survey sample reported attendance at FEMA's regional Project Impact Hurricane Information Expo or some other hurricane damage seminar.

The demand for mitigation was elicited by asking homeowners whether they would buy, at a given price, a set of home improvements that would prevent all damage from a Category 3 hurricane but would provide no protection against stronger hurricanes. Most defensive measures are rated to protect against no more than a category 3 hurricane. The set of improvements that would protect against a category 3 hurricanes would be roughly equivalent to anchoring rafters to wall top plates, reinforcing the wall sheeting attachment to the bottom plate/mud sill, and installing angle brace anchors between the bottom plate/mud sill and footings and plywood coverings for windows and doors (Burrus, Dumas, and Graham, 2002). One of three possible prices ($1,500, $3,000, and $6,000) was selected at random for each survey respondent. Approximately one-third of respondents (n = 95 out of 291) were asked whether they would pay $1,500 for the home improvements, a second group (n = 95) were asked whether they would pay $3,000 for the improvements, and a final set (n = 101) were asked whether they would pay $6,000 for the improvements. Fourteen, 20, and 16 respondents indicated that they would buy the improvements for $1,500, $3,000, and $6,000, respectively. This counter-intuitive response to price is discussed in the results section.

If respondents answered that they would not pay for the improvements, they were then asked whether they would buy the improvements if their "insurance deductibles were increased to five times their current levels." Seventy percent of survey respondents have wind damage insurance as part of their homeowner's policy or as a separate rider. Of the seventy percent with wind insurance, seventy-seven percent could recall their wind insurance deductible. Of these, the average deductible was \$500. Thirty-five percent of survey respondents have flood damage insurance. Of the thirty-five percent with flood insurance, seventy percent could recall their flood insurance deductible. Of these, the average flood insurance deductible was \$556. Hence, an increase in deductibles to "five times current levels" would reflect an increase in the average deductible from around \$500 to \$2,500. Twenty-four, 33, and 30 respondents indicated that they would buy the improvements for \$1,500, \$3,000, and \$6,000, respectively, at the higher deductible level.

If respondents answered that they would not pay for the improvements with the increased deductibles, they were asked if they would buy the improvements if insurance were unavailable. Twenty-six, 40, and 34 respondents indicated that they would buy the improvements for \$1,500, \$3,000, and \$6,000, respectively, if insurance were unavailable (assuming that homeowners answering that they would purchase the improvements before the increase in deductibles or after the increase in deductibles would also purchase the improvements if insurance were unavailable).

MODEL

Examining selected determinants of mitigation purchase behavior, the following equation is estimated using a random-effects, panel data probit model:

$$\text{MIT} = \beta_0 + \beta_1(\text{PRICE}) + \beta_2(\text{INCOME}) + \beta_3(\text{DEDUC}) + \beta_4(\text{NOINS}) + \beta_5(\text{EXPDAM}) + \beta_6(\text{INDEX}) + \beta_7(\text{SEM}) + \beta_8(\text{PERGOVT}) + \beta_8(\text{FEMALE}) + e,$$

where variable names and definitions are summarized in Table 1.

We consider two specifications of the basic model. In the first specification, the dependent variable *MIT* is coded as a binary variable, taking on the value 1 if the answer is "yes" and 0 if the answer is "no" or "don't know". In the second specification, MIT is coded as an ordered variable taking the value 2 if the answers is "yes", 1 if the answer is "don't know" and 0 if the answer is "no". Groothuis and Whitehead (2002) find that "don't know" responses are similar to "no" responses in willingness to pay studies and are similar to a middle response in willingness to accept studies. The first specification is estimated using a binary probit model, while the later specification is estimated using an ordered probit model. Since each respondent was asked 3 mitigation decision questions, the data set is a panel, and the total number of observations of *MIT* is 873.

The *Price* variable is coded as \$1,500, \$3,000 or \$6,000. The law of demand states that an increase in the price of mitigation will decrease the quantity demanded of mitigation, *ceteris paribus*; thus, we anticipate a negative sign for the *Price* coefficient. We believe that mitigation is a normal good; that is, a positive coefficient estimate on *Income* is expected. *DEDUC* is a dummy variable taking the value 1 when deductibles are increased to 5 times the original level. *NOINS* is a binary variable taking the value 1 when no insurance is available. We expect that the probability of purchasing mitigation increases as a homeowner's insurance options are less desirable.

Table 1. Variable Names and Definitions

MIT	1="Yes" respondent purchases mitigation; 0 = other - OR- 2="Yes" respondent purchases mitigation; 1 = "Don't Know"; 0 = "No"
PRICE	Price of mitigation (takes on the values $1,500, $3,000, or $6,000)
INCOME	Homeowner income: categories are $0 - $10,000; 10,001 - 15,000; 15,001 - 20,000; 20,001 - 25,000; 25,001 - 30,000; 30,001 - 40,000; 40,001 - 50,000; 50,001 - 60,000; 60,001 - 75,000; 75,001 - 150,000; above $150,000. Incomes are coded as the midpoint of the income categories.
DEDUC	1=deductible at 5 times original level; 0=otherwise
NOINS	1=no insurance available; 0=otherwise
EXPDAM	Perceived annual strike probability for a category 3 hurricane * damage done by a category 3 hurricane as a percentage of the value of the home * home value
INDEX	The number of the following features the home is equipped with: roof reinforcements, window coverings, door coverings, garage door coverings, raised on fill dirt, raised on crawl space, raised on pilings, and raised outdoor appliances.
SEM	1=homeowner has previously attended a hurricane seminar; 0=otherwise
PERGOV	Attitude toward government assistance. 1=very positive or somewhat positive; 0=other
FEMALE	1=homeowner is female; 0=homeowner is male

EXPDAM is a composite variable reflecting the homeowner's expected hurricane damage from category 3 hurricanes. *EXPDAM* is equal to the homeowner's estimate of the annual strike probability of a category 3 hurricane, multiplied by the homeowner's subjective estimate of the percent damage his or home would suffer in the event of a category 3 strike, multiplied by the value of the owner's home. As *EXPDAM* increases, we anticipate that the probability of purchasing mitigation increases. *Index* is a variable denoting the number of existing mitigation improvements reported by the homeowner. These improvements include structural reinforcements for the roof, windows, doors, and garage doors to protect against wind damage, and home improvements that offer some protection against flood damage, including raising the home on fill dirt, the presence of a crawl space, raising the house on pilings, and raising outdoor appliances. We anticipate that owners with high INDEX values are less likely to purchase the additional mitigation improvements mentioned in the survey.

Two variables capture the impact of government programs on mitigation purchase behavior. *SEM* is a dummy variable taking the value 1 if the homeowner has attended a hurricane damage seminar. Attending a seminar is expected to increase the probability of purchasing mitigation. *PERGOVT* is a dummy denoting homeowners' attitudes toward government hurricane assistance programs. We hypothesize that owners who believe that government programs will help pay for any damages they incur are less likely to purchase mitigation. The factor *Female* is adopted to reveal differences across genders in mitigation purchases.

RESULTS

Coefficient estimates for the probit model are first presented in Table 2. A chi-squared test indicates that the independent variables jointly explain a significant portion of the variance in the dependent variable.

Table 2. Probit and Ordered Probit Results

Variable	Probit (Yes=1, Other =0)				Ordered Probit (Yes=2, Don't Know=1, No=0)			
	Coeff.	b/St.Er.	Coeff.	b/St.Er.	Coeff.	b/St.Er.	Coefficient	b/St.Er.
Constant	-17.97452	-3.610*	-6.795918	-3.193*	-2.607036	-5.272*	-1.817971	-3.787
PRICE	0.001361	2.929*	-0.000596	-2.679*	0.000008	0.140	-0.000170	-1.917†
PRICEDUM			-2.760942	-2.894*			-0.785871	-1.926†
INCOME	0.000091	3.595*	0.000056	3.316*	0.000021	6.261*	0.000020	5.932*
DEDUC	6.462073	3.600*	4.874810	3.500*	1.521625	6.103*	1.516879	6.466*
NOINS	8.219774	3.354*	6.388083	3.193*	2.011632	6.317*	2.009433	5.529*
EXPDAM	0.000076	1.491	0.000045	1.579	0.000011	1.425	-0.000014	-0.740
INDEX	-0.659392	-1.971*	-0.388715	-1.861†	-0.155682	-2.133*	-0.057742	-0.835
SEM	0.268704	0.294	-3.490703	-2.854*	-0.817214	-2.647*	-2.861834	-7.359*
PERGOVT	0.834554	1.771†	4.206659	2.980*	-0.187624	-0.809	-0.207155	-0.884
FEMALE	-4.781795	-3.414*	-4.949388	-3.525*	0.327652	1.422	0.487450	1.879†
LL	-280.689		-278.585		-522.342		-521.647	
Restricted LL	-486.227		-482.625		-771.029		-768.046	
Chi	411.0754		408.0789		497.373		492.7988	
% Correct	71.25%		69.53%		54.87%		53.84%	
McFadden R2	0.42272		0.42277		0.322539		0.320813	

* (†) denotes significant at 5% (10%) level.

The coefficient estimates on Income, *DEDUC*, *NOINS*, and *Index* are statistically significant (at the 5% level) with signs in the expected directions. The coefficient on EXPDAM is positive, as expected, but insignificant. The coefficient estimate on *PERGOVT* is unexpectedly positive and significant at the 10% level. The influence of SEM is positive, as expected, but insignificant. The coefficient on *Female* is negative and significant at the 5% level, a result similar to those found by Kruse and Simmons (2004) and Ozdemir (2004).

The coefficient on *Price* is positive and significant, an unexpected result inconsistent with the law of demand. The source of the unexpected sign on *Price* can be found in the descriptive statistics. Although more respondents were willing to purchase the mitigation improvements at a price of \$3,000 compared to the number willing to purchase at \$6,000 (as expected), it was also the case that more respondents were willing to purchase the mitigation improvements for \$3,000 than were willing to purchase for \$1,500 (an unexpected result). Apparently, the influence of purchase decisions inconsistent with the law of demand outweighed the influence of purchase decisions consistent with the law of demand in the estimation of the PRICE coefficient.

A possible explanation of the inconsistent behavior may be that respondents believed that the \$1,500 mitigation improvements were of inferior quality. Burrus, Dumas, and Graham (2002) found that the price of mitigation improvements sufficient to protect a home against Category 3 hurricane wind speeds is approximately \$3,000-\$5,000. If homeowner estimates of mitigation costs are similar to those of Burrus, Dumas, and Graham, then homeowners may not believe that mitigation improvements costing $1,500 are of comparable quality.

In an attempt to isolate the respondents who received a price of $1,500, a dummy variable (*PRICEDUM*) was added to the probit model. *PRICEDUM* takes on the value 1 if the respondent received a price of $1,500 and 0 otherwise. The coefficient estimates for the new model are reported in column 4 of Table 2. In the new model, the coefficient estimates on *Price* and *PRICEDUM* are negative and significant indicating that there was a difference in the cohort that received a price of $1,500 that is not captured by the other independent variables. Again, differences in the perceived quality of the improvements across price categories may be the explanation. Other model results remained largely unchanged by the addition of the *PRICEDUM* variable, with the exception that the coefficient estimate on SEM becomes negative and significant, indicating that individuals attending government sponsored hurricane awareness seminars are somewhat less likely to purchase mitigation (even after controlling for existing mitigation). Perhaps these respondents were sufficiently educated about hurricane mitigation devices that our failure to explicitly indicate which mitigation devices would be used to reduce damages to zero in a category 3 hurricane raised suspicions (In the survey, we called the improvements simply a set of home improvements that would prevent all damage from cat 3 hurricanes. This limitation was imposed to limit the length of the survey question).

The sixth and eighth columns of Table 2 present results from the ordered probit model specifications, where "don't know" answers are treated as a category between "no" (I wouldn't purchase mitigation) answers and "yes" (I would purchase mitigation) answers. The second ordered probit model includes *PRICEDUM*. Chi-squared statistics indicate that the variables in each model are jointly significant.

Results for the ordered probit model specifications generally support the findings from the binary probit models; coefficient estimates for *DEDUC* and *NOINS* remain positive and significant in both models, while the estimate on *EXPDAM* is not significant in either model. However, in both ordered probit specifications, the coefficient signs for *Female* and *PERGOVT*, which were significant in the binary probit specifications, are reversed and insignificant (except for *Female* in the final model). The switch in the sign of the coefficient estimate for female may be explained by considering that, of the 108 "don't know" responses which were coded as "no" in the probit models, 75 were from females. The ordered probit model reveals uncertainty in female mitigation choice rather than an unfavorable attitude toward mitigation. The change in sign and significance of the coefficient estimate for the *PERGOVT* variable indicates that accounting for "don't know" responses reduces the estimate of the negative influence of government assistance programs on mitigation purchases.

Concluding Comments

The primary goal of this paper is to investigate the impacts of insurance deductibles and hurricane damage expectations on homeowners' structural mitigation purchase decisions. The National Flood Insurance Program and the Florida Windstorm Underwriters Association currently write policies giving premium reductions for mitigation purchases. Burrus, Dumas and Graham (2002) found that mitigation purchase behavior may be more sensitive to increases in insurance deductible levels than to decreases in insurance premium levels. Mitigation devices must reduce damages to a level below the insurance deductible for mitigation to provide financial benefits, and higher deductibles make mitigation purchases more attractive. Survey results indicate that increased insurance deductibles do increase the probability of structural mitigation purchases. If anything, mitigation purchases are even more sensitive to deductive levels than indicated by Burrus, Dumas and Graham.

Increases in subjective expected hurricane damage do not appear to significantly impact mitigation decisions. Survey results indicate that homeowners overestimate the strike probabilities of severe hurricanes. However, results indicate that homeowners likely underestimate the damage that would be caused by a severe hurricane strike. In combination, the effect of overestimating strike probabilities outweighs the effect of underestimating damage, such that homeowners overestimate expected damage. Even so, survey results indicate that homeowners' damage expectations have little influence on mitigation purchase behavior. Indeed, even though homeowners reported average annual expected damage of $5,250 from category 3 hurricanes alone, many were unwilling to purchase a package of mitigation measures that would protect them from category 3 damage for a one-time cost of $3,000. Apparently, homeowners either do not understand the implications of their strike probability and damage estimates for expected damages, or they do not have confidence that mitigation measures will perform as advertised. Assuming that the problem lies with expected damages, an interesting question for future research would be: If homeowners were confronted with the average annual expected damage of $5,250 implied by their subjective probability and damage estimates, would they revise their probability and damage estimates, or would they change their decision regarding mitigation purchases?

We find also that the impact of mitigation price on mitigation purchases appears to vary – increasing the price of mitigation from low to moderate levels appears to increase purchases (perhaps because homeowners associates low prices with poor quality), while increasing price from moderate to high levels appears to decrease purchases (as would be expected). Larger household income increases the probability of purchasing mitigation, while higher levels of pre-existing, installed mitigation decrease the probability of further mitigation purchases. There is mixed evidence that gender and expectations of government disaster assistance affect mitigation purchases. Females may be somewhat less likely to purchase mitigation, and expectations of government assistance may somewhat decrease mitigation purchases. Although the evidence is mixed, it appears that hurricane seminar attendance may slightly decrease the likelihood of mitigation purchases, though the reason remains a question for future research.

REFERENCES

Burrus, Robert T., Christopher F. Dumas and J. Edward Graham (2002), "*Catastrophic Risk and Wealth-Maximizing Choices for the Homeowner*", Financial Services Review, Vol. 11: 327-340.

Groothuis, Peter A. and John C. Whitehead (2002), "Does "don't know" Mean No? Analysis of "don't know" Responses in Dichotomous Choice Contingent Valuation Questions", *Applied Economics,* Vol. 34: 1953-1940.

Kleindorfer, Paul R. and Howard C. Kunreuther (1999), "The Complementary Roles of Mitigation and Insurance in Managing Catastrophic Risks", *Risk Analysis,* Vol. 19: 727-738.

Kruse, Jamie Brown and Kevin M. Simmons (2004), "Risk Mitigation: Individual and Market Behavior", *Economics and Wind,* B. T. Ewing and J. B. Kruse, eds. Nova Science Publishing.

Kunreuther, Howard (1996), "Mitigation Disaster Losses Through Insurance", *Journal of Risk and Uncertainty,* Vol. 12: 171-187.

Kunreuther, Howard and Anne E. Kleffner (1992), "Should Earthquake Mitigation Measures Be Voluntary or Required?", *Journal of Regulatory Economics,* Vol. 4: 321-333.

Ozdemir, Ozlem (2004), "*Risk Perception and the Value of Safe Rooms as a Protective Measure*" Economics and Wind, B. T. Ewing and J. B. Kruse, eds. Nova Science Publishing.

Petak, William (1998), Mitigation and Insurance. Paying the Price: *The Status and Role of Insurance Against Natural Disasters in the United States,* eds. Howard Kunreuther and Richard J. Roth. Washington, D.C., Joseph Henry Press.

Simmons, Kevin M., Jamie Brown Kruse, and Douglas A. Smith (2002), "Valuing Mitigation: Real Estate Market Response to Hurricane Loss Reduction Measures" *Southern Economic Journal,* Vol.68: 660-671.

In: Economics and the Wind
Editors: B. T. Ewing, et. al., pp. 125-138
ISBN: 1-59454-280-5
©2005 Nova Science Publishers, Inc.

Chapter 11

HURRICANE RISK PERCEPTIONS AND PREPAREDNESS

John C. Whitehead
Department of Economics, Appalachian State University, Boone, NC

INTRODUCTION

Preparedness is one component of effective hurricane risk mitigation. Emergency managers attempt to persuade residents of coastal zones to watch weather reports closely, develop and rehearse evacuation plans, store necessary supplies, and prepare property when storms threaten. Many coastal zone residents do not follow these recommended guidelines, even when recent experience suggests that the benefits of preparation exceed the costs. Understanding the factors that encourage these behaviors is an important step toward motivating coastal zone residents to become better prepared and minimize the losses from hurricanes. Toward this end we explore the relationship between wind and flood risk perceptions and hurricane preparedness.

Measures of objective and subjective risk factors are among the most important predictors of evacuation and other mitigating behavior during hurricanes (Baker, 1991). Those who do not feel safe staying home tend to evacuate (Dow and Cutter, 1997). Mobile home residents are more likely to evacuate than other housing residents (Baker, 1991; Whitehead et al., 2000). Storm intensity (Whitehead et al., 2000) and actual damages (Riad, Norris, and Ruback, 1999) are also factors in evacuation behavior. The purchase of mitigating goods is another type of mitigating behavior. Simmons and Kruse (2000) find that coastal residents value houses with hurricane shutters greater than inland residents. Ozdemir and Kruse (2000) find that the purchase of tornado shelters is based on risk perceptions.

In this paper we measure wind and flood risk perceptions and five determinants of hurricane preparedness in surveys of North Carolina coastal residents conducted after hurricane Bonnie (1998) and hurricanes Dennis and Floyd (1999). These data allow an analysis of changes in risk perceptions and preparedness and their interrelationship. We explore a two-stage model. In the first stage, objective risk factors, hurricane experience, and demographics are determinants of risk perceptions. In the second stage, risk perceptions, hurricane experience, and demographics are the determinants of hurricane preparedness.

In the rest of the paper we describe the surveys and data. Then we use multivariate regression models to analyze the determinants of risk perception and preparedness. Finally we discuss our results and offer some conclusions.

THE SURVEYS

During August of 1998 hurricane Bonnie approached the North Carolina coast prompting evacuations of all eight coastal counties. Hurricane Bonnie made landfall on the coast of North Carolina, near Cape Fear, 20 miles south of Wilmington (Avila, 1998). At landfall hurricane Bonnie was a low category 3 storm and quickly diminished to a category 1 storm on the Saffir-Simpson Hurricane Scale (Tropical Prediction Center, 1999). During the next two days a weakening hurricane Bonnie made its way up the entire North Carolina coast. Much of coastal North Carolina experienced hurricane Bonnie as a tropical storm.

During January 1999 we conducted a telephone survey of North Carolina residents who were affected by hurricane Bonnie in the summer of 1998. The survey used a random digit dial sample of households in the eight North Carolina ocean counties: Brunswick, Carteret, Currituck, Dare, Hyde, New Hanover, Onslow, and Pender. Of the households contacted, 76% completed the interview. The data has 1063 complete and partially complete cases.

During August of 1999, hurricane Dennis approached the North Carolina coast as a category 1 storm, missed the coast, stalled off the Outer Banks for two days, and then landed on the northeast North Carolina coast and quickly lost hurricane intensity (Beven, 2000). Again, portions of the entire North Carolina coast received evacuation orders. Less than one month later, hurricane Floyd traveled north along the Atlantic coast as a strong category 4 storm, weakened as it reached North Carolina, landed near Wilmington as a category 3 storm, and left the state the next day (Pasch, Kimberlain, and Stewart, 2000).

During January 2000 we attempted to contact the same member of the household that we contacted after hurricane Bonnie. Of the 1063 survey respondents, 66 had moved out of the sample counties, 20 had a non-working number, 99 had disconnected numbers, 16 had changed their number, and 29 numbers had become either a business, government, organization, or institute number. Subtracting these unavailable respondents from the total leaves 826 potential contacts. Of the potential contacts, 542 interviews were completed with another 23 interviews partially completed. These 565 contacts represent a response rate of 68% from the hurricane Bonnie survey respondents and an overall 49% response rate from the hurricane Bonnie sample. We focus on respondents to both surveys ($n = 533$).

We performed a multivariate regression analysis to determine who was more likely to respond to the follow-up survey. The major factor explaining whether recontacted respondents agreed to participate in the follow-up survey is whether the respondent evacuated for hurricane Bonnie ($p = .01$). The overall evacuation rate for hurricane Bonnie was 26%. The hurricane Bonnie evacuation rate for the subsample of resurvey respondents is 22% and 31% for the subsample of nonrespondents. Length of time at residence increases the probability of resurvey response ($p = .01$), a typical result for panel surveys. Non-respondents had lived at their residence an average of 9 years at the time of the Bonnie survey. Respondents had lived at their residence an average of 12 years.

DEPENDENT VARIABLES

Risk Perceptions

Following the conceptual model two sets of dependent variables are considered. In the first stage of the model the dependent variables are hurricane wind and risk perceptions. Hurricane wind risk perception is elicited with the question:

> "Now consider the risks from wind damage from a hurricane. In your opinion, was the home where you lived at the time of Hurricane [name] located in a high-risk site, a medium risk site, or a low-risk site?"

A similar question was asked to elicit flood risk perceptions:

> "Now consider the risks from coastal flooding from a hurricane. In your opinion, was the home where you lived at the time of Hurricane [name] located in a high-risk site, a medium risk site, or a low-risk site?"

Respondents were allowed to interpret the three-response categories, high, medium, and low, in their own way.

After hurricane Bonnie (1998), 46% and 34% of respondents perceived that they lived in a medium and high wind risk home. Following hurricanes Dennis and Floyd (1999), respondents revised their wind risk perceptions downward with 45% and 30% considering their home medium and high risk. The difference across surveys is statistically significant at the $p = .10$ level (χ^2=5.00[2 df]). After hurricane Bonnie, 26% and 14% of respondents thought they lived in a medium and high flood risk home. Following hurricanes Dennis and Floyd, respondents revised their flood risk perceptions downward with 23% and 12% considering their home low, medium and high risk. However, the differences across surveys are not statistically significant (χ^2=2.55[2 df]). Flood risk perceptions are significantly lower than wind risk perceptions in the first (χ^2=90.64[4 df]) and second (χ^2=80.34[4 df]) surveys.

Considering the interpersonal changes in risk perception, 49% and 41% of respondents changed their wind and flood risk perception from the first to the second survey. Nineteen percent of all respondents revised their wind risk perception up (i.e., from low to medium or high, from medium to high) and 29% revised their wind risk perception down. Seventeen percent of all respondents revised their flood risk perception up and 23% revised their flood risk perception down. When considering the interpersonal differences, changes in risk perceptions are significantly different at the $p = .01$ level for wind risk (χ^2=73.37[4 df]) and flood risk (χ^2=85.85[4 df]).

Hurricane Preparedness

In the second stage of the conceptual model the dependent variables are measures of hurricane preparedness. Preparedness is measured by whether the respondent follows the five steps of the North Carolina Division of Emergency Management's recommended steps of hurricane storm preparation: whether the household (1) has an evacuation plan, (2) rehearses the evacuation plan, (3) prepares their property in advance of a storm, (4) stores supplies, and (5) watches weather reports closely. The existence of an evacuation plan is elicited with the question:

> *"Which of the following recommended steps of Hurricane Storm Preparation does your household follow? Does your family have a Hurricane Evacuation Plan?"*

Respondents who answered yes were then asked: "Do you rehearse your Hurricane Evacuation Plan?" Other questions are "Do you prepare your property in advance of a storm?" "Do you store up to 2 weeks of supplies in your home?" and "Do you watch or listen to weather reports closely?"

Forty-six percent of the sample had an evacuation plan after hurricane Bonnie (1998) and 56% had an evacuation plan after hurricanes Dennis and Floyd (1999). The increase in evacuation plans is statistically significant at the p = .01 level (χ^2=10.94[1 df]). Of those respondents who had an evacuation plan, 39% (1998) and 34% (1999) rehearsed their plan. For those who had an evacuation plan in both years (n = 172), 43% did not rehearse in either year, 20% rehearsed in both years, 19% rehearsed only after hurricane Bonnie (1998), and 17% rehearsed only after hurricanes Dennis and Floyd (1999).

Seventy-one respondents had an evacuation plan after hurricane Bonnie (1998) but not after hurricanes Dennis and Floyd (1999). One hundred twenty-five respondents had an evacuation plan in 1999 but not in 1998. Of those who had an evacuation plan in either year, 26% (1998) and 27% (1999) rehearsed the plan. There is no statistical difference in rehearsals across time (χ^2=0.34[1 df]).

Most respondents store supplies and prepare their property in advance of a storm while almost all respondents watch weather reports closely. Sixty-nine percent (1998) and 61% (1999) store two weeks of supplies. This difference is statistically significant at the p = .01 level (χ^2=7.97[1 df]). Ninety-two percent (1998) and 89% (1999) of respondents prepare their property. This difference is statistically significant at the p = .10 level (χ^2=2.83[1 df]). Ninety-eight percent (1998) and 96% (1999) of respondents watch weather reports closely. This difference is not statistically significant (χ^2=2.53[1 df]).

INDEPENDENT VARIABLES

Objective Risk

We consider several objective measures of risk as factors potentially affecting risk perceptions and hurricane preparedness. Variables that measure objective risk are *hurricane experience, property damage, mobile home, shutters, island residence, storm surge zone*, and *flood plain*. Property damage is equal to one if the respondent suffered property damage and zero otherwise. Property damage is expected to increase both wind and flood risk perceptions. Mobile home is equal to one if the respondent lived in a mobile home and zero otherwise. Mobile home is expected to increase wind risk perceptions.

Shutters is equal to one if the respondent had installed storm shutters on their home and zero otherwise. The shutters variable is expected to increase wind risk perception if the respondents in high-risk areas are those who install the shutters. However, shutters could have the opposite effect if respondents feel that shutters completely mitigate against risk. Storm surge zone is equal to one if the respondent lives in a storm surge zone and zero otherwise. Flood plain is equal to one if the respondent lives in the 100-year flood plain and zero otherwise. Storm surge zone and flood plain are expected to increase flood risk perception.

Hurricane experience is a measure of objective risk and is captured by a dummy variable equal to zero for the hurricane Bonnie (1998) data and one for the hurricanes Dennis and Floyd (1999) data. The effect of hurricane experience on perceived risk may be either positive or negative. If experience with hurricanes suggests that hurricanes are mild weather events, hurricane experience might lead respondents to adopt low perceptions of risk. If experience suggests that hurricanes are severe weather events, hurricane experience might increase risk perceptions.

Demographics

Demographic variables include *pets*, *homeowner*, *apartment*, *white*, *female*, *age*, *education*, and *income*. Pets is equal to one if the respondent owns at least one pet and zero otherwise. Similarly, homeowner is equal to one if the respondent owns their home, apartment is equal to one if the respondent lives in an apartment, townhouse, or condominium, white is equal to one if the respondent is white, and female is equal to one if the respondent is female. Age is the age of the respondent. Education is the number of years of schooling. Income is the 1998 household income of the respondent (in thousands).

County dummy variables are also included. *Brunswick*, *Carteret*, *Onslow*, and *Pender* are equal to one if the respondent lives in those counties and zero otherwise. *Outer Banks* is equal to one if the respondent lives in the "Outer Banks" counties of Currituck, Dare, or Hyde Counties and zero otherwise. New Hanover County is the omitted variable. We have no a priori expectations concerning the county dummy variables.

Data Summary

Most of the variables are similar in the two surveys (Table 1). Thirty-four percent of the sample suffered property damage during hurricane Bonnie (1998) and 33% suffered property damage during hurricanes Dennis and Floyd (1999). However, these numbers mask significant differences in the households that suffered property damage. Forty-eight percent of the sample did not suffer damage in either storm season. Eighteen percent suffered property damage in 1999 but not 1998. Nineteen percent suffered property damage in 1998 but not 1999. Only 15% suffered damage in both storms.

Table 1. Independent Variables

	Bonnie (1998)		Dennis/Floyd (1999)	
	Mean	**Std.Dev.**	**Mean**	**Std.Dev.**
Property Damage	0.34	0.47	0.33	0.47
Mobile Home	0.13	0.34	0.13	0.33
Shutters	0.17	0.38	0.16	0.36
Island	0.14	0.35	0.12	0.32
Storm surge zone	0.19	0.39	0.19	0.39
Pets	0.66	0.47	0.66	0.47
Homeowner	0.81	0.39	0.83	0.38
Apartment	0.08	0.27	0.08	0.26
White	0.85	0.35	0.85	0.35
Female	0.60	0.49	0.60	0.49
Age	47.85	16.45	47.85	16.45
Education	13.71	2.17	13.71	2.17
Income	42.91	30.53	42.91	30.53
Outer Banks	0.11	0.32	0.11	0.32
Brunswick	0.12	0.32	0.12	0.32
Carteret	0.15	0.36	0.16	0.36
Onslow	0.28	0.45	0.28	0.45
Pender	0.09	0.29	0.09	0.29

From the hurricane Bonnie (1998) survey, 13% of the sample lived in mobile homes, 17% have storm shutters, 14% lived on an island, 19% lived in a storm surge zone, and 22% lived on a flood plain. Each of these characteristics is slightly lower after hurricanes Dennis and Floyd (1999). Almost two-thirds of the sample owns a pet in both surveys. Eighty-one percent and 83% of the sample are homeowners in the first and second surveys. Eight percent of the sample lives in an apartment, townhouse, or condominium in both surveys.

Eighty-five percent of the sample is white and 60% is female. The average age is 48 years, the average education level is 14 years, and the average household income is $43 thousand.

EMPIRICAL MODEL

We estimate the factors that affect the wind and flood risk perceptions using the ordered probit model (Greene, 1999)

$$y_i^* = \beta' X_i + e_i \tag{1}$$

where y_i^* is the unobserved latent risk perception variables, $i = 1, \ldots, n$, β is a vector of parameters, X_i is a vector of independent variables and the error term, e_i, is distributed normally with zero mean and variance equal to σ^2. The latent dependent variable is measured by the ordinal dependent variables. With $m = 3$ risk choices the dependent variables are coded $y = 0, \ldots, m-1$. The ordered probit model uses the same structure as the basic probit model with a censoring parameter, μ,

$$
\begin{aligned}
y &= 0 \quad \textit{if } y^* \leq 0 \\
y &= 1 \quad \textit{if } 0 < y^* \leq \mu \\
y &= 2 \quad \textit{if } \mu \leq y^*
\end{aligned}
\tag{2}
$$

where y = 0 is low risk, y = 1 is medium risk, and y = 2 is high risk. The ordered probit model estimates the probability of the outcome variable using the normal distribution

$$
\begin{aligned}
\Pi(y=0) &= \Phi(-\beta' X_i) \\
\Pi(y=1) &= \Phi(\mu - \beta' X_i) - \Phi(-\beta' X_i) \\
\Pi(y=2) &= 1 - \Phi(\mu - \beta' X_i)
\end{aligned}
\tag{3}
$$

where Φ is the standard normal distribution function.

Since we have multiple observations on both risk variables (i.e., measures of risk perceptions in the first and second surveys) we treat the data as a panel. The random effects ordered probit model is a panel data extension of the ordered probit model where the error term accounts for the correlation across respondents

$$y_{it}^* = \beta' X_{it} + e_{it} \tag{4}$$

where $t = 1, 2$ time periods (i.e., observations for each respondent). The error term, e_{it}, is distributed normally and is composed of two parts, $v_{it} + u_i$, where v_{it} is the normally distributed random error with mean zero and variance, σ_v^2, u_i is the error common to each individual with mean zero and variance, σ_u^2, and $\sigma_e^2 = \sigma_v^2 + \sigma_u^2$. The correlation in error terms, $\rho = \sigma_u^2/\sigma_e^2$, is increasing in the contribution of the individual error to the total error and is a measure of the appropriateness of the random effects specification.

The determinants of hurricane preparedness are estimated with the binary probit model (Greene, 1999). The probit model is similar to the random effects probit, equation (1), except the latent dependent variable is measured by the dummy variable

$$
\begin{aligned}
y &= 0 \quad \textit{if } y^* \leq 0 \\
y &= 1 \quad \textit{if } y^* > 0
\end{aligned}
\tag{5}
$$

where y = 1 if the respondent engaged in evacuation preparation and y = 0 otherwise. The probit model estimates the probability of the outcome variable with the normal distribution

$$\Pi(y=1) = \Phi(\beta' X_i) \tag{6}$$

The random effects probit model, which is similar to equation (4) but with only two outcomes, is used for the panel data. Each of the probit models is estimated with the LIMDEP statistical software (Greene, 1998).

Empirical Results

Risk Perceptions

The hurricane Bonnie (1998) and hurricanes Dennis and Floyd (1999) wind risk models are statistically significant according to the model χ^2 value (Table 2). In the hurricane Bonnie model we find that property damage, mobile home and island residence have positive effects on perceived wind risk. Residents who live in a storm surge zone and the 100-year flood plain perceive higher wind risks. These variables likely distinguish between those who live near the water and are exposed to hurricane wind damage and those who live in the inland portions of each county. Those who live in the Outer Banks counties, Onslow and Pender counties perceive higher wind risks than New Hanover County residents.

Table 2. Ordered Probit Models of Wind Risk Perception

	Bonnie (1998)		Dennis/Floyd (1999)		Panel	
	Coeff.	**t-ratio**	**Coeff.**	**t-ratio**	**Coeff.**	**t-ratio**
Constant	-0.207	-0.47	0.009	0.02	-0.029	-0.07
Property Damage	0.392	3.67	0.259	2.34	0.344	4.04
Mobile Home	0.392	2.49	0.084	0.53	0.279	2.01
Shutters	-0.015	-0.12	-0.022	-0.16	-0.032	-0.28
Island	0.377	2.29	0.295	1.77	0.387	2.66
Storm surge zone	0.403	2.83	0.212	1.58	0.348	2.93
Flood Plain	0.222	1.75	0.234	1.87	0.217	2.12
Pets	-0.062	-0.54	0.186	1.66	0.089	0.85
Homeowner	0.147	0.97	-0.208	-1.35	0.011	0.08
Apartment	0.215	1.05	-0.163	-0.83	0.110	0.65
White	0.059	0.38	0.038	0.25	0.035	0.24
Female	-0.079	-0.76	-0.148	-1.45	-0.138	-1.41
Age	-0.002	-0.67	-0.000	-0.04	-0.001	-0.35
Education	0.032	1.23	0.025	1.02	0.033	1.33
Income	0.003	1.56	0.003	1.55	0.003	2.10
Outer Banks	0.380	1.89	0.176	0.93	0.337	1.74
Brunswick	0.154	0.88	0.190	1.08	0.239	1.53
Carteret	0.227	1.37	0.203	1.24	0.268	1.73
Onslow	0.301	2.13	0.021	0.15	0.187	1.42
Pender	0.430	2.32	0.398	2.00	0.497	2.54
Property Damage (1998)			0.077	0.71		
Hurricane Experience					-0.168	-2.29
□	1.350	18.70	1.252	18.24	1.552	22.43
□					0.67	8.92
□□	65.18		46.25		135.58	
Sample Size	533		533		533	
Time Periods	1		1		2	

We find different determinants of wind risk perception in the hurricane Dennis and Floyd (1999) model. The determinants of risk are the property damages, island, flood plain, pets, and Pender County variables. We also include a lagged property damage variable, the coefficient of which is not statistically significant. Surprisingly, those who live in mobile homes perceive the same wind risks as those who live in a fixed structure. Closer inspection of the relationship between wind risk and mobile home supports this result. A significantly greater number of mobile home residents perceive high wind risks than others after hurricane Bonnie (χ^2=6.06[2 df]). However, there is no statistically significant difference in wind risk perceptions between the two groups after hurricanes Dennis and Floyd (χ^2=0.11[2 df]).

The random effects probit model constrains all coefficients to be equal across the years of the survey. The measure of correlation across time periods, ρ, is significantly different from zero, indicating that the random effects specification is appropriate. In this model all of the determinants of wind risk perception are the same as those in the hurricane Bonnie (1998) model except for the Onslow dummy variable. In addition, those with higher incomes and those in Carteret County perceive higher wind risks. The hurricane experience dummy variable measures the additional experience acquired from hurricanes Dennis and Floyd. The effect of hurricane experience is negative indicating that wind risk perceptions are significantly lower after hurricanes Dennis and Floyd when holding the other independent variables constant.

Each of the flood risk models are statistically significant according to the model χ^2 value (Table 3). In the hurricane Bonnie (1998) model we find that property damage, storm shutters, storm surge zone, flood plain residence, and Outer Banks variables have positive effects on perceived risk. Older respondents have lower perceived flood risks.

Table 3. Ordered Probit Models of Flood Risk Perception

	Bonnie (1998)		Dennis/Floyd (1999)		Panel	
	Coeff.	t-ratio	Coeff.	t-ratio	Coeff.	t-ratio
Constant	-0.003	-0.01	0.239	0.47	0.251	0.56
Property Damage	0.264	2.24	0.157	1.25	0.215	2.17
Mobile Home	-0.083	-0.51	-0.067	-0.36	-0.067	-0.43
Shutters	0.237	1.70	-0.169	-1.10	0.094	0.72
Island	0.242	1.46	0.440	2.39	0.360	2.49
Storm surge zone	0.906	6.31	0.766	5.20	0.914	7.38
Flood Plain	0.339	2.46	0.718	5.06	0.561	5.10
Homeowner	-0.075	-0.59	-0.231	-1.74	-0.110	-0.95
Apartment	-0.035	-0.21	-0.403	-2.19	-0.217	-1.44
Pets	0.099	0.40	-0.374	-1.30	-0.073	-0.35
White	-0.066	-0.41	0.163	1.00	0.018	0.12
Female	0.119	1.00	-0.003	-0.02	0.057	0.52
Age	-0.007	-2.13	-0.009	-2.38	-0.009	-2.63
Education	-0.020	-0.72	-0.020	-0.68	-0.024	-0.94
Income	-0.001	-0.40	-0.002	-1.07	-0.001	-0.83
Outer Banks	0.319	1.66	0.179	0.81	0.318	1.70
Brunswick	-0.157	-0.73	0.005	0.02	-0.119	-0.63
Carteret	0.209	1.10	0.085	0.44	0.151	0.87
Onslow	0.036	0.22	-0.034	-0.20	-0.013	-0.08
Pender	0.090	0.42	0.120	0.51	0.059	0.29
Property Damage (1998)			0.451	3.66		
Hurricane Experience					-0.127	-1.53
□	0.963	12.31	0.981	12.06	1.141	14.99
□					0.67	6.45
□□	105.39		135.94		233.92	
Sample Size	533		533		533	
Periods	1		1		2	

In the hurricanes Dennis and Floyd (1999) model we find that lagged, but not current, property damage has a positive effect on flood risk. The current property damage coefficient is also insignificant in a model that does not include the lagged property damage variable. As in the hurricane Bonnie model, the storm surge zone, flood plain and age variables have statistically significant effects on flood risk. In addition, island residents perceive higher flood risks. Homeowners perceive lower flood risks than renters and apartment dwellers perceive lower flood risks than those in single-family homes.

In the panel data model, the correlation in errors across time periods is significantly different from zero, indicating that the random effects specification is appropriate. Property damage, island, storm surge zone, flood plain and Outer Banks residents perceive higher flood risks than others. Older respondents perceive lower risks. When the determinants of flood risks are held constant there is no difference in risk perceptions across time.

Hurricane Preparedness

The probit models for four of the hurricane preparedness activities are presented in Tables 4-7. Since almost all respondents watch weather reports closely, determinants of this measure of preparedness are not analyzed. In the individual models we test for whether perceived wind and flood risk are predictors of evacuation preparedness and include the demographic variables as control variables. In the random effects probit models we also test the effects of hurricane experience. Each of the probit models, except one, is statistically significant. In the random effects probit models the ρ statistics are statistically significant indicating that the panel data specification is appropriate.

In the hurricane Bonnie (1998) evacuation plan model, wind risk perception increases the likelihood that a household will have an evacuation plan (Table 4). Flood risk perception has no effect. Other results are that white and female respondents are more likely to have an evacuation plan. In the hurricanes Dennis and Floyd (1999) model, wind risk has a positive effect on whether the respondent has an evacuation plan. In the panel model, wind risk, white, female, and education each contribute to explaining whether the household has an evacuation plan. With hurricane experience, respondents are more likely to have an evacuation plan.

Table 4. Probit Models of Hurricane Preparedness: Evacuation Plan

	Bonnie (1998)		Dennis/Floyd (1999)		Panel	
	Coeff.	t-ratio	Coeff.	t-ratio	Coeff.	t-ratio
Constant	-1.348	-3.12	-0.710	-1.67	-1.469	-3.31
Wind Risk	0.162	1.96	0.222	2.78	0.223	3.09
Flood Risk	0.088	1.08	0.056	0.66	0.076	1.03
White	0.269	1.68	0.152	0.96	0.267	1.70
Female	0.220	1.93	0.156	1.36	0.238	2.03
Age	0.003	0.84	-0.005	-1.47	-0.001	-0.39
Education	0.032	1.18	0.044	1.62	0.049	1.77
Income	0.001	0.74	0.0002	0.09	0.001	0.57
Hurricane Experience					0.362	4.10
ρ					0.396	6.39
$\chi 2$	17.71		19.40		78.74	
Sample Size	533		533		533	
Periods	1		1		2	

In the evacuation plan rehearsal models we include only respondents who had an evacuation plan in either year (Table 5). In the hurricane Bonnie model, flood risk perception increases the likelihood that a household will rehearse their evacuation plan and wind risk perception has no effect. Older respondents and those with more education are more likely to rehearse. None of the coefficients in the hurricanes Dennis and Floyd (1999) model are statistically significant. In the panel model, increasing perceived flood risk increases the likelihood that a household will rehearse their evacuation plan and wind risk has no effect. Other results are that older respondents are more likely to rehearse their evacuation plan. Those with greater income are less likely to rehearse their plan.

Table 5. Probit Models of Hurricane Preparedness: Rehearse the Plan

	Bonnie (1998)		**Dennis/Floyd (1999)**		**Panel**	
	Coeff.	**t-ratio**	**Coeff.**	**t-ratio**	**Coeff.**	**t-ratio**
Constant	-2.401	-3.94	-0.017	-0.03	-1.307	-2.50
Wind Risk	-0.013	-0.12	0.028	0.28	0.004	0.04
Flood Risk	0.190	1.84	0.084	0.82	0.147	1.71
White	-0.035	-0.16	-0.282	-1.38	-0.185	-1.04
Female	-0.094	-0.63	-0.113	-0.77	-0.114	-0.92
Age	0.015	3.17	0.001	0.23	0.008	2.07
Education	0.087	2.32	-0.013	-0.35	0.038	1.18
Income	-0.004	-1.59	-0.005	-1.90	-0.005	-2.19
Hurricane Experience					0.083	0.78
ρ					0.192	2.05
$\chi 2$	18.78		8.30		22.20	
Sample Size	368		368		368	
Periods	1		1		2	

Wind and flood risk perceptions have no effect on whether respondents store two weeks of supplies (Table 6). Older respondents are more likely to store supplies in the hurricane Bonnie (1998) model. Respondents with higher incomes are less likely to store supplies in the hurricanes Dennis and Floyd (1999) model. In the panel model, older respondents are more likely to store supplies. Respondents with higher educations and incomes are less likely to store supplies. With hurricane experience respondents are less likely to store supplies.

Table 6. Probit Models of Hurricane Preparedness: Store Supplies

	Bonnie (1998)		**Dennis/Floyd (1999)**		**Panel**	
	Coeff.	**t-ratio**	**Coeff.**	**t-ratio**	**Coeff.**	**t-ratio**
Constant	0.825	1.847	0.740	1.734	1.119	2.48
Wind Risk	0.023	0.266	0.066	0.820	0.074	0.97
Flood Risk	-0.007	-0.079	-0.010	-0.122	-0.016	-0.21
White	-0.078	-0.465	0.070	0.436	0.002	0.01
Female	0.132	1.119	-0.155	-1.342	-0.023	-0.19
Age	0.007	1.922	0.004	1.167	0.007	1.95
Education	-0.042	-1.492	-0.036	-1.325	-0.050	-1.80
Income	-0.002	-1.136	-0.004	-2.169	-0.004	-2.18
Hurricane Experience					-0.285	-3.16
ρ					0.393	6.06
$\chi 2$	12.65		12.86		60.66	
Sample Size	533		533		533	
Periods	1		1		2	

In the hurricane Bonnie (1998) prepare property model, white and higher income respondents are more likely to prepare their property (Table 7). In the hurricanes Dennis and Floyd (1999) model, those who perceive higher wind risks and white respondents are more likely to prepare their property. In the panel model respondents who perceive higher wind risks are more likely to prepare their property in advance of a storm. White and higher income respondents are also more likely to prepare property. With hurricane experience respondents are less likely to prepare their property.

Table 7. Probit Models of Hurricane Preparedness: Prepare Property

	Bonnie (1998)		Dennis/Floyd (1999)		Panel	
	Coeff.	t-ratio	Coeff.	t-ratio	Coeff.	t-ratio
Constant	0.773	1.21	0.137	0.246	0.774	1.07
Wind Risk	0.132	1.06	0.255	2.221	0.261	1.78
Flood Risk	-0.025	-0.20	-0.041	-0.342	-0.072	-0.45
White	0.522	2.65	0.790	4.365	0.992	3.98
Female	0.166	0.96	-0.201	-1.228	-0.073	-0.35
Age	0.002	0.40	-0.003	-0.746	-0.002	-0.32
Education	-0.043	-1.00	0.039	1.037	0.013	0.26
Income	0.014	2.95	0.0004	0.159	0.007	1.94
Time (=1 if 1999)					-0.257	-1.65
ρ					0.547	5.86
$\chi 2$	23.57		32.18		73.80	
Sample Size	533		533		533	
Periods	1		1		2	

CONCLUSIONS

We find that respondents perceive slightly higher wind and flood risks after hurricane Bonnie (1998) than after hurricanes Dennis and Floyd (1999). The reduction in risk perceptions may be due to the misleading effects of hurricane Floyd, which approached North Carolina as a category 4 storm but landed as a category 2 storm on the ocean-bordering counties producing less wind than expected. The rain-induced flooding from hurricanes Dennis and Floyd occurred primarily in the inland coastal plain counties. This experience may have led coastal North Carolina residents to revise their perceived wind and flood risks downward.

Some of the determinants of risk are similar across both types of risk. Those who face the highest risks from hurricanes, residents of islands, storm surge zones, and flood plains, are more likely to perceive greater wind and flood risks. Those who have incurred property damages perceive greater wind and flood risks. We also find differences in risk perception across the type of risk. Mobile home owners perceive higher wind risks but not flood risks. Females perceive lower wind risks. Those who are older perceive lower flood risks. Those with higher incomes perceive greater wind risk but not flood risk. This result may be due to the higher potential economic damages from wind in high-income neighborhoods. We find some geographic differences in wind and flood risk perception.

We find that risk perceptions differ across storm season. Demographic and geographic factors influence risk perceptions after hurricane Bonnie (1998) but not after hurricanes

Dennis and Floyd (1999). One area of concern is that mobile home owners perceive the same risks from wind as those in fixed structures after experiencing hurricanes Dennis and Floyd. Again, this downward reduction in risk perceptions may be due to the misleading effects of hurricane Floyd. Homeowners and apartment dwellers perceive lower risks in 1999 but not in 1998. Another finding is that the property damage that occurred in 1998 increases flood risk perceptions in 1999, but current property damage does not. This result perhaps reflects the greater flooding in the ocean-bordering counties after hurricane Bonnie relative to flooding after hurricanes Dennis and Floyd.

In terms of evacuation planning respondents are better prepared for evacuation after hurricanes Dennis and Floyd (1999) than before. Somewhat surprisingly, respondents are less well prepared for a hurricane in terms of preparing property and storing supplies after hurricanes Dennis and Floyd than before. Perceived wind and flood risks are factors that are considered when preparing for a hurricane. However, these results are not stable over time. Also, the effect of demographic variables on hurricane preparedness changes over time.

Several of these findings should be of concern to emergency managers. The first is that risk perceptions are not stable over time. Perceived hurricane risks are lower after the experiences of two hurricanes in 1999. Perhaps, hurricane risk perceptions decrease when negative impacts from hurricanes are less than expected. The converse may also be true. Risk perceptions may increase when negative impacts are greater than expected.

Second, hurricane preparedness is not stable over time. Respondents are better prepared for evacuation but less prepared for weathering a storm in their home and protecting their home from a storm after experiencing hurricanes Dennis and Floyd. These contrasting results may be consistent. If respondents are more likely to evacuate after hurricanes Dennis and Floyd they may consider property preparation and supply storage to be less important mitigation activities.

Third, objective measures of risk, those that do not change over time, are taken into account when forming hurricane risk perceptions. Those at the most risk, those in mobile homes and those who suffer property damage, perceive lower risks than are warranted.

These results have policy implications. Hurricane preparedness is important for effective risk mitigation. Since reductions in perceived risk lead to lower levels of hurricane preparedness, better risk communication methods are needed to improve preparedness. Coastal residents may experience storms that weaken as they approach the coast or upon landing where hurricane damage and mortality is less than expected. At these times, residents should be better informed that not all major storms weaken as they approach the coast. As in many risk communication problems, however, the information is readily available to those who choose to seek it. Therefore, incentives that lead to the consumption of the risk information are needed.

REFERENCES

Avila, Lixion A. (1998) *Preliminary Report, Hurricane Bonnie 19-30 August 1998*, National Hurricane Center, *http://www.nhc.noaa.gov/1998bonnie.html*, October.

Baker, Earl J. (1991), and "Hurricane Evacuation Behavior," *International Journal of Mass Emergencies and Disasters*, Vol.9: 287-310.

Beven, Jack (2000), *Preliminary Report: Hurricane Dennis 24 August – 7 September 1999,* National Hurricane Center, http://www.nhc.noaa.gov/1999dennis_text.html, January.

Dow, Kirstin, and Susan L. Cutter (1997), "Crying Wolf: Repeat Responses to Hurricane Evacuation Orders," *Coastal Management*, Vol.26: 237-251.

Greene, William H. (1998), *LIMDEP Version 7.0 User's Manual,* Revised Edition, Econometric Software, Inc. Plainview, New York.

Greene, William H. (1999), *Econometric Analysis*, Third Edition, Prentice Hall, Upper Saddle River, New Jersey.

Ozdemir, Ozlem and Jamie Brown Kruse, (2000), *Relationship between Risk Perception and Willingness-to-Pay for Low Probability, High Consequence Risk: A Survey, Discussion Paper 2000-04*, Department of Economics and Geography, Texas Tech University.

Pasch, Richard J., Todd B. Kimberlain, and Stacy R. Stewart (2000), *Preliminary Report: Hurricane Floyd, 7– 17 September 1999.* National Hurricane Center, *http://www.nhc.noaa.gov/1999floyd_text.html*, January.

Riad, Jasmin K., Fran H. Norris, and R. Barry Ruback, (1999), "Predicting Evacuation in Two Major Disasters: Risk Perception, Social Influence, and Access to Resources," *Journal of Applied Social Psychology*, Vol.29: 918-934.

Simmons, Kevin M. and Jamie Brown Kruse (2000), "Market Value of Mitigation and Perceived Risk: Empirical Results," *Journal of Economics*, Vol.26: 41-51.

Tropical Prediction Center (1999), *The Saffir-Simpson Hurricane Scale*. National Hurricane Center, *http://www.nhc.noaa.gov/aboutsshs.html*, July 14.

Whitehead, John C., Bob Edwards, Marieke Van Willigen, John Maiolo, Ken Wilson, and Kevin Smith (2000), "Heading for Higher Ground: Factors Affecting Real and Hypothetical Hurricane Evacuation Behavior," *Environmental Hazards*, Vol.2: 133-142.

In: Economics and the Wind
Editors: B. T. Ewing, et. al., pp. 139-148
ISBN: 1-59454-280-5
©2005 Nova Science Publishers, Inc.

Chapter 12

VALUING SAFE ROOMS IN HURRICANE PRONE REGIONS

John R. Crooker
Department of Economics and Finance, Central Missouri State University, Warrensburg, MO
Jamie Brown Kruse
Wind Science and Engineering Research Center, Texas Tech University, Lubbock, TX, and Director of the Center for Natural Hazards Mitigation, East Carolina University, Greenville, NC

INTRODUCTION

There is scientific evidence that suggests Atlantic hurricane activity rotates in 40-60 year cycles, with this period divided roughly in half between low and high activity seasons (Gray at al, 1996). This is particularly relevant to the current time as some feel we are ending a 20-30 year period of historically low hurricane activity (Landsea, 1999; Fitzpatrick, 1999). Perhaps illustrating this shift in hurricane activity, the 4-year period 1995-1998 unleashed a record of 33 hurricanes in the Atlantic Ocean.

A compounding factor that increases the potential for hurricane damages is the rapid growth in U.S. population along coastlines (Fitzpatrick, 1999; Maiolo et al, 1999). Certainly, larger populations in hurricane-threatened regions will lead to higher costs if a hurricane incident occurs. There are also several subtle features that have the potential for exacting significant costs as a result of hurricane threats.

First, the growing population will impose a much greater burden on evacuation resources. This factor alone creates the potential for prohibitively long clearance times in several highly populated coastal cities. In recent years, the standard response to threatening storm events was to evacuate the region. In many areas, this approach is no longer viable because of inadequate ability to evacuate the populace when a hurricane threat appears (Hampson, 2001).

Another subtle feature of the growing population is that many new permanent coastline residents have no experience with hurricanes. This implies preparedness and responses in high stress situations may not coincide with that of experienced and informed decision-makers (Whitehead, 2001; Fitzpatrick, 1999). For example, ill-prepared residents may opt to evacuate too late and find themselves cut-off from evacuation routes due to storm surges and freshwater floods (Fitzpatrick, 1999).

Also troubling is the notion that individuals' risk perceptions (and ultimately hurricane preparedness) is non-stable over time (Whitehead, 2001). This empirical result suggests that officials in charge of issuing hurricane warnings and evacuation orders will have difficulty anticipating how households will respond to information they disseminate. Moreover, the response to previous evacuation orders and storm warnings cannot be relied on to predict how the populace will react to the same information in a later storm event.

In light of these factors many coastal regions must become less reliant upon evacuation as the dominant philosophy in storm events. The focus of this investigation is to assess the value of safe rooms during hurricanes and tropical storms. The safe rooms are potentially valuable because they foster a notion of lessened dependence on evacuation and greater preparedness. Certainly, the owner of a safe room receives the direct benefit in avoiding wind damage to his person and immediate property. In addition to this direct benefit, safe rooms provide external benefit to the region through lessened demand on evacuation resources. Thus, safe rooms may offer a solution to the problem of reducing clearance times in highly populated areas.

The remainder of this paper is divided into three sections. The next section provides a review of the literature; the next section demonstrates the value of safe rooms in various scenarios based on past empirical studies; and the final section presents our conclusions.

Review of the Literature

In this section, we explore studies related to safe room performance, hurricane wind damage, hurricane flood damage, evacuation costs, risk perceptions, clearance times, and non-evacuation alternatives in storm events. All of these topics are relevant to our valuation of safe rooms in hurricane-prone regions.

Most past studies regarding the value of safe rooms have concentrated on their use in areas with a significant tornado threat. These values are largely driven by the direct benefit that accrues to the owner of the safe room (Ozdemir and Kruse, 2000; Kruse and Simmons, 2001). Engineering performance data suggest safe rooms are adequate to the wind speeds associated with powerful hurricanes at landfall (Tertell et al.,1999). This suggests safe rooms can protect occupants from wind damage in hurricane conditions.

The remaining concern is protection from storm surges and other hurricane related flooding. Yet, *in situ* (or vertical evacuation) has been a storm surge avoidance strategy for some time (Simpson and Riehl, 1981). High rise apartment complexes, business buildings and schools have satisfied engineering performance tests to satisfy hurricane certification status for both wind and flood avoidance. More stringent building codes in Texas, which increased construction costs between 10-20%, have improved durability of structures under hurricane conditions (Simpson and Riehl, 1981). Other cities have experienced similar successes by updating building codes. Occupants of homes that are safe from flooding due to storm surge can look to safe rooms for protection from wind and resultant rain damage which is the primary threat. Those that cannot eliminate the flood threat have only the option to evacuate.

Evacuation costs during recent hurricanes in North Carolina have been estimated to be $323 per household (Whitehead, 2001). This value comes from a series of telephone survey efforts administered by scientists at East Carolina University following major hurricane events in North Carolina. This cost includes direct expenses such as hotels, dining out, etc. Also, the researchers imputed indirect expenses such as lost earnings associated with the decision to evacuate. These costs are immediately avoided if there is adequate wind and flood protection in the home. Moreover, scientists and emergency planners have argued that in many coastal regions, individuals mistakenly view evacuation as their primary or only choice (Fitzpatrick, 1999). As a result of this attitude, inadequate preparations are being taken. If a hurricane makes landfall in these highly populated regions, congestion from over-evacuation would inhibit clearance of evacuation arteries with catastrophic results (Fitzpatrick, 1999). Thus, households in these regions are undervaluing the indirect benefits of safe rooms as well. There is a thread of literature suggesting a tendency for an individual to misperceive risk. We highlight this tendency below. Certainly, the ability to avoid exposure to health damaging events is valuable to households (Tietenberg, 2000; Hamilton and Viscusi, 1999). We argue that safe rooms provide such an indirect benefit and thus should be considered when valuing safe rooms.

In our present analysis, we suggest large indirect values to the general region accompany widespread adoption of safe rooms. This is an indirect value for safe rooms as the benefits do not accrue directly to the owner. Rather, as more households prepare for hurricane events with safe rooms, there is a lessened need for evacuation resources. By reducing congestion, existing routes can evacuate more people in a given amount of time ultimately reducing clearance times. This is spillover benefit to those in flood prone regions that have no alternative but to evacuate. Also, with fewer people evacuating, the necessary distance to travel to find suitable lodging accommodations, etc. diminishes and so do evacuation costs. Moreover, safe room adoption additionally implies that there is greater community preparedness for hurricane events. This means the psychological trauma associated with this stressful event is reduced as well. The size of these external benefits generated by widespread safe room adoption will likely differ by geographic characteristics and will be considered in the next section. In regions where current clearance times are not adequate in storm events, we suggest safe rooms have significant values. Estimates by Fitzpatrick (1999) indicate that many metropolitan areas require two days to achieve clearance evacuations. Given our limited ability to predict hurricane tracks accurately, it is not likely that adequate warnings could be given to achieve clearance in these areas.

The literature on risk perceptions suggests troubling news for the state of hurricane preparedness and evacuation choices. Past studies in hurricane and non-hurricane applications demonstrate a preponderance of evidence suggesting risk perceptions tend to be formed poorly (Kunreuther, 1976; Kunreuther, 1978; Smith, 1986; and Whitehead, 2001). Whitehead (2001) found that individuals became less well prepared for hurricanes after Hurricanes Dennis and Floyd in 1999.

Whitehead hypothesizes that when hurricanes fall short of expectations, individuals rate downward the potential of future hurricane events. This suggests that households take this experience as illustrative of future hurricane activity. Recent hurricane activity in North Carolina was characterized by powerful hurricanes that diminished rapidly to weak hurricanes or tropical storm status as they made landfall (Avila, 1998; Beven, 2000; and Whitehead, 2001).

Past economic studies have found that individuals place between $1.6-5 million on the value of their life (Tietenberg, 2000). These studies place value on life by examining individual choices involving risk avoidance. The 2000 East Carolina University study found that 52.3% of those that evacuated indicated the most important reason for evacuation was the threat to themselves and their families. For the purposes of this investigation, we will conservatively take 50% of the $1.6 million low end value for human life. We project that for a typical household of 2.4 occupants an approximate value of household life is $1.92 million. Taking 50% indicates that only about half of the evacuators do so out of primary concern for household life. Effectively, this assumption places no weight on the life values of the other half of evacuators. While unrealistic, we find this to be appropriate to truly establish a conservative value for safe rooms. Thus, we will proceed as if a hurricane event that threatens household life puts at risk the equivalent of $1.92 million in wealth for the representative household. Only in regions where high congestion makes complete evacuation improbable should these values be considered.

In the following section, we examine the value of safe rooms in three stylistic scenarios. Also, tables are presented that relate hurricane likelihoods with subsequent safe room values. We impute values based on the information discussed above in related studies. While we do not suggest these are the finest safe room values researchers may glean, we do suggest the values provide an important first attempt to establish what these values might be.

THE VALUE OF SAFE ROOMS IN HURRICANE-PRONE REGIONS

Our focus now is on the value of safe rooms in hurricane-prone regions. Due to the nature of hurricanes, these values are dependent upon the probability that a hurricane will make landfall in the vicinity, the potential for storm surge and freshwater floods, and the ability to evacuate. For illustrative purposes, we consider a historical case and individuals' demonstrated propensity to evacuate. Next, we consider a moderately populated coastal area and stylized evacuation tendencies.

Empirical Example

Densely Populated Coastal Areas likely possess the largest value for safe rooms. A significant value stems from the *public good* aspect of safe rooms. That is, if households with minimal flood risk have access to a safe room, the strain on evacuation resources is reduced. With less congested evacuation routes, clearance times improve. With shorter clearance times, public officials can delay the call for evacuation until more accurate landfall predictions arrive. The ability to hold for more accurate storm track predictions also reduces the number of costly unnecessary evacuations.

Federal Emergency Management Agency (FEMA) officials have seriously questioned the ability of many coastal metropolitan areas to achieve clearance given current dependence on evacuation routes (Hampson, 2001). For a category 4 hurricane, it is estimated to require 50-60 hours to evacuate Ft. Myers, Florida or New Orleans, Louisiana. Miami/Fort Lauderdale and West Palm Beach, Florida. would require between 30 and 39 hours. The cities like Myrtle

Beach, South Carolina; Long Island, New York; and Savannah, Georgia would require 20-29 hours. These time requirements are unrealistic given the current ability to forecast and predict changes in hurricane tracks.

According to a recent U.S. Weather Research Program Implementation Plan regarding a hurricane landfall, the best opportunities to improve hurricane warnings in the U.S. is to increase warning lead-time to 24 hours and beyond (Executive Summary, 2000). Also, the National Hurricane Center provides likely storm surge information from Sea, Lake and Overland Surge from Hurricanes (SLOSH) models with about 12 hours of lead-time. For the densely populated cities mentioned above, a lead-time of 12 hours is not adequate to prevent significant loss of life.

Recent media reports have chronicled the inability of existing evacuation options to achieve clearance after evacuation orders have been given. For example, Hurricane Floyd prompted 3 million people (more than three times the expected number) to jam evacuation routes attempting to clear areas from southern Florida to South Carolina (Hampson, 2001). Reportedly, cars lined up for literally hundreds of miles on many interstates. Fortunately for these evacuators, the hurricane tracked northeast and did not make landfall in their vicinity. Had the hurricane made landfall in this region, (a significant likelihood) the estimated loss of life would have been in the thousands with many of those attempting to evacuate directly in harms way. Another media report described the scene on the interstate highways as "something from a B grade monster movie. Panicked people flee from some impending doom only to put themselves in a position of complete helplessness unprotected from high winds, blowing debris and potential freshwater floods." (Larson, 1998)

We argue that in these circumstances, safe room values are substantial. We will decompose the safe room values into private and public values for a Hurricane Bonnie scenario. The private values accrue to the owner of the safe room and are present provided the homeowner is not in a storm surge area or flood plain (Figure 1 maps potential areas affected by storm surges with the SLOSH model simulations). Largely, these benefits are the savings from not evacuating, which as we discussed above are approximately \$323 (Whitehead, 2001), and as well as avoiding potential calamity on congested interstates. In densely populated areas, we will assume that 1 in 300 evacuators find peril on evacuation routes when hurricanes do make landfall in the region. The 1 in 300 ratio was assumed based on FEMA official statements from the July 5, 2000 USA Today article that Hurricane Bonnie had the potential to take 10,000 lives of evacuators in the Southern Florida and South Carolina vicinity. Estimates indicate that 3 million people from these regions evacuated. Given the stated goal of the hurricane warning system of maintaining no more than a 3 to 1 over-warning ratio, we may infer the probability given a warning has been issued of a hurricane making landfall in the region is 0.25. Thus, the expected private benefit from a safe room conditional on a hurricane warning in the region is \$323+0.25(1/300)x\$1,920,000 = \$1,923. The dominant value (83%) of private benefit in densely populated hurricane prone areas comes from avoiding peril on the evacuation route. If we aggregate for 2 million people out of flood prone regions, we find the potential for safe rooms to provide \$3.8 billion worth of private benefit. Finally, note that this value is conditional upon a hurricane warning being issued in the region.

To calculate the public value of safe room, we assume that there is a sufficient number of safe rooms adopted to permit timely evacuations even in densely populated coastal areas. Thus, the expected public benefit of widespread safe room adoption conditional on a hurricane warning in the region is 1,000,000(0.25)(1/300)$1,920,000=$1,600,000,000. That is, $1.6 Billion is the aggregate public good benefit of widespread adoption given a hurricane warning. Note that this value stems from the benefit to those in flood plains that may now evacuate without route congestion risks due to widespread safe room adoption.

Total benefit of widespread safe room adoption in a hurricane warning environment similar to the one that existed during Hurricane Bonnie is $5.4 Billion. If we factor this across 2 million safe rooms this indicates that each safe room has a value of $2,723 in the event of a hurricane warning. It likely would not require the full adoption of 2 million safe rooms to achieve the indicated benefit. However, in keeping with the spirit of a conservative estimate for each safe room, we take the larger figure which diminishes the per unit value. In light of better or more accurate information, it is appropriate to make the substitution in this calculation.

To determine the unconditional expected value of a safe room from a category 4 hurricane, we would need to determine the probability of a category 4 hurricane *warning* in the area. Note that we need the probability of a warning and not the probability of a hurricane making landfall. Certainly, we anticipate the probability of a warning being issued is significantly higher than that of hurrricane actually making landfall. In assessing the probability of this warning, we should keep in mind the tendency for hurricane warning officials to warn the public one level beyond the existing storm intensity (USWRP, Executive Summary, 2000). Multiplying the probability that this warning will occur by the conditional expected value gives us the unconditional expected value of a safe room from a category 4 hurricane. Note that this value would be the category 4 value only. We would need to add the category 1-3 values to determine the full value of the safe rooms in this area.

If the probability of a category 4 warning was 1%, the unconditional value of a safe room is $27.23. Now, if we assume that there are no evacuation congestion problems from lessor warnings, we can form table 1 below. Note that we need the probability of a warning and not the probability of a hurricane making landfall. Certainly, we anticipate the probability of a warning being issued is significantly higher than that of a hurricane actually making landfall. Hence, unconditional safe room annual values range from $59 to $101.

Table 1. Annualized Safe-room Values in Highly Populated Regions

			Hurricane Warning Probabilities			
		Total Annual Value ($)	W ($)	X ($)	Y ($)	Z ($)
Evacuation Probabilities	A	101	54	27	14	7
	B	84	45	22	11	6
	C	67	36	18	9	4
	D	59	31	16	8	4

Each row of table 1 supposes a different likelihood of evacuation by the household, with row D (detailed specifically below), characterizing the lowest likelihood of evacuation. The columns of table 1 suppose various probabilities of warnings by hurricane category. Assuming a discrete distribution of hurricane warning probabilities for a hurricane season, we may sum the values for a row to derive the annual safe room value for the stated evacuation likelihood (as done in table 1 above). The hurricane warning probabilities for group W assume the probability of a category 1 warning is 10%, category 2 is 5%, category 3 is 2.5% and category 4 is 1.25%. Group X assumes the probability of a category 1 warning is 5%, category 2 is 2.5%, category 3 is 1.25% and category 4 is 0.63%. Groups Y and Z are similarly defined. Evacuation Probabilities Group A assumes the household evacuation propensity in the absence of a safe room is 30% in a category 1 warning, 50% in a category 2 warning, 70% in a category 3 warning and 90% in a category 4 warning. Group B assumes the household evacuation propensity in the absence of a safe room is 20% in a category 1 warning, 40% in a category 2 warning, 60% in a category 3 warning and 80% in a category 4 warning. Group's C and D are similarly defined with the exception that Group D assumes the household evacuation propensity in the absence of a safe room in a category 1 warning is 5%.

Moderately Populated Coastal Region

In a moderately populated coastal region, the private good and public good values of safe rooms are considerably less. Fundamentally, this is because the act of evacuating is a better substitute as there is a smaller or insignificant risk of health threatening events during the process of evacuation. The value of a safe room in a category 1 hurricane warning is: the probability of a category 1 hurricane warning multiplied by the probability the household would evacuate had no safe room been available multiplied by $323 (the recouped value from not evacuating). Similarly, the value of a safe room in a category 2 hurricane warning is: the probability of a category 2 hurricane warning multiplied by the probability the household would evacuate had no safe room been available multiplied by $323 (the recouped value from not evacuating). After calculating these conditional expected values of safe rooms in the various hurricane warning categories, the full value of the safe room in a moderately populated coastal region would be calculated by summing the values calculated immediately above. Table 2 below indicates these values for illustrative probabilities of hurricane warnings and evacuation propensities.

Table 2. Annualized Safe-room Values in Moderately Populated Regions

		Hurricane Warning Probabilities				
		Total Annual Value($)	W ($)	X ($)	Y ($)	Z ($)
Evacuation Probabilities	A	51	27	14	7	3
	B	39	21	10	5	3
	C	28	15	7	4	2
	D	22	12	6	3	1

Hurricane Warning Probabilities W, X, Y and Z are consistent with our use in the presentation of Table 1 as are the Evacuation Probabilities A, B, C, and D. Table 2 demonstrates that when evacuation is a close substitute to a safe room, safe room values are significantly lower. The range of values for safe rooms is $22-$51 per year. This is about half the value calculated for safe rooms in highly populated coastal regions. Again, our calculations suggest that most gains from safe rooms would come in highly populated areas.

CONCLUSIONS

The goal of this investigation was to assign an approximate value for a safe room in hurricane prone regions. For many reasons this is an arduous task. For example, research has noted that individuals' propensity to evacuate and risk perceptions are non-stable (Whitehead, 2001). However, by inferring safe room values and in the absence of better information, we assumed behavior would resemble past decisions. While this is not appropriate, there do not seem to be any better alternatives given existing data. This indicates the need for additional research on the evacuation decisions of households in hurricane events.

We calculate that in densely populated coastal areas, safe rooms provide an annual value of \$59 to \$101 per unit. Recall that the value of life estimates used in these calculations are about half the lower-bound found in many studies. In less populated coastal areas, safe rooms provide an annual value of \$22 to \$51 per unit. There are also significant public good values associated with safe rooms in highly populated coastal areas. This suggests a role for government is warranted to ensure the proper provision of the public good aspect of safe rooms.

This research looked at the fundamental value of safe rooms in hurricane prone regions. The study does not consider the costs of implementing safe rooms in the household. Essentially, comparing the costs to the benefit would determine if private households are likely to install safe rooms. In the event that our estimated annual private safe room values exceed the annual costs, we would expect households to begin installing safe rooms. We also note that past studies indicate that hurricane mitigation devices have been found to increase home values in real estate markets by more than 5% (Simmons, Kruse and Smith, 2002). This suggests wider adoption of safe rooms is possible.

In the event that safe rooms are not adopted in these areas, it may be because households do not understand the availability of safe rooms. Another possibility is that households do not perceive the benefits and costs appropriately. In either case, this suggests additional study regarding safe room adoption in hurricane prone regions is appropriate.

REFERENCES

Avila, L., and R. Pasch, "Another active Atlantic hurricane season," *Weatherwise,* 50, 36-40, 1997.

Beven, J. L. II, "*A study of three hybrid storms*," Preprints: 22th Conference on Hurricanes and Tropical Meteorology, American Meteorological Society, Ft. Collins, CO, 1997.

Day, D.C. and Kunreuther, H., *The Economics of Natural Disasters: Implications for Federal Policy*, Free Press, New York, 1969.

Fitzpatrick, P. J., *Natural Disasters, hurricanes: a reference handbook*, ABC-CLIO, Santa Barbara, Calif., 1999.

Hamilton, J.T. and W. K. Viscusi, "*Calculating Risks: The Spatial and Political Dimensions of Hazardous Waste Policy.*" M.I.T. Press, Cambridge, MA, 1999.

Hampson, Rick, "So many people—and no where left to run," *USA Today*, Tuesday, July 5, 2001.

Kunreuther, H., *Disaster Insurance Protection: Public Policy Lessons*, Wiley, New York, 1978.

Kruse, J. B. and K. M. Simmons, "*Report on Saferoom Investment*," Report to the Department of Commerce, Windstorm Mitigation Initiative, 2001.

Larson, E., "Waiting for Hurricane X," *Science*, 158 (10), 1998.

Landsea, C., "*Hurricanes, Typhoons, and Tropical Cyclones*," Federal Emergency Management Agency, 1999.

Maiolo, J. R., Delia, A., Whitehead, J.C., Edwards, B., Wilson, K., VanWillgen, M., Williams, C., and Meekins, M., "*A Socioeconomic Hurricane Evacuation Impact Analysis and a Hurricane Evacuation Impact Assessment Tool (Methodology) for Coastal North Carolina: A Case Study of Hurricane Bonnie*" for the North Carolina Division of Emergency Management, July, 1999.

Ozdemir, O, and J. B. Kruse, "*Risk Perception and the Value of Safety: In-residence Storm Shelters in Tornado-Prone Areas*," Report to the Department of Commerce, Windstorm Mitigation Initiative, 2000.

Simmons, K. M. and J. B. Kruse, "Market Value of Mitigation and Perceived Risk: Empirical Results," *Journal of Economics*, 26, 41-51, 2000.

Simpson, R.H. and H. Riehl, *The Hurricane and its Impact,* Baton Rouge, LA, LSU Press, 1981.

Smith, E., "Atlantic and East Coast Hurricanes 1900-1998: A Frequency and Intensity Study for the 21st Century," *Columbia Earthscape*, 80 (12), 1999.

Smith, S.K. and McCarty, C., "Demographic Effects of Natural Disasters: A Case Study of Hurricane Andrew," *Demography* 33, 265-275, 1996.

Tertell, P., C. Oliver, E. Kiesling, K. Mehta, R. Carter, W. Coulbourne, J. Crandell and J. Hoopingarner, "*Taking Shelter From the Storm: building a safe room inside your house*," Federal Emergency Management Agency, 1999.

Tietenberg, T., *Environmental and Natural Resource Economics,* Addison-Wesley, 5th edition, 2000.

U. S. Weather Research Program, "USWRP Implementation Plan—Hurricane Landfall," *Executive Summary*, Draft September 21, 2000.

Whitehead, J. C., "*Risk Perceptions and Hurricane Preparedness*," unpublished manuscript, November, 2001.

ACKNOWLEDGEMENTS

This work was performed under the Department of Commerce NIST/TTU Cooperative Agreement Award 70NANB8H0059.

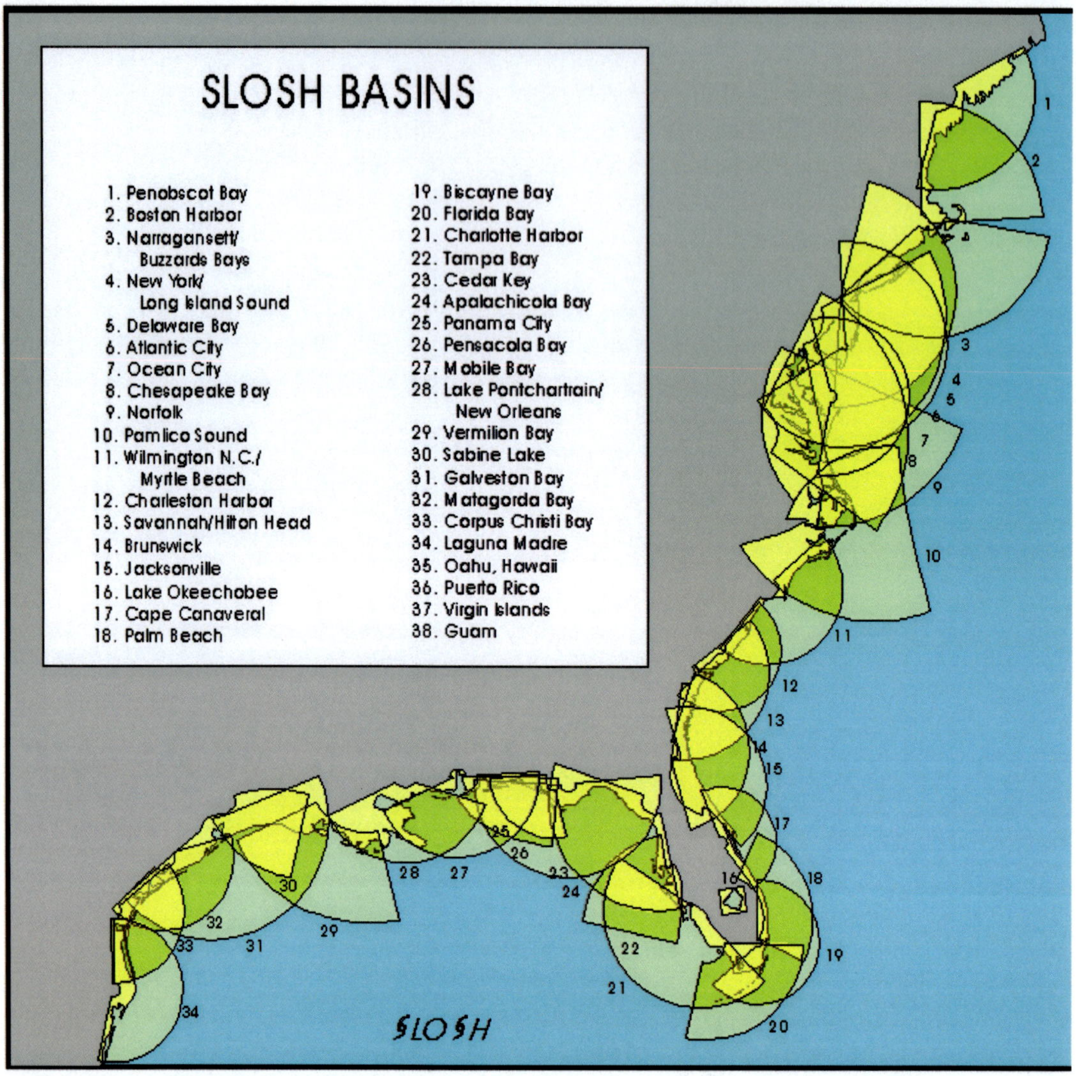

Figure 1. Slosh Basins on the Atlantic and Gulf Coast.

In: Economics and the Wind
Editors: B. T. Ewing, et. al., pp. 149-158
ISBN: 1-59454-280-5
©2005 Nova Science Publishers, Inc.

Chapter 13

NATURAL HAZARDS, FATALITY RATES AND SOCIETAL VULNERABILITY

Nicole Cornell Sadowski and Daniel Sutter
Department of Economics, University of Oklahoma, Norman, OK, USA

INTRODUCTION

The costs of natural hazards and disasters have risen dramatically in the United States over the past several decades. The costliest natural disasters in U.S. history, the Northridge Earthquake and Hurricane Andrew, have occurred within the last dozen years, and seven of the ten worst have occurred since 1989. Average annual losses from all natural hazards have increased from $20 million per million residents in 1975 to $1 billion per million residents in 1994 (in constant 1994 dollars; Mileti, 1999 p.67). The rising cost of natural disasters and the potential for catastrophes with costs in excess of $20 billion, threaten the financial viability of insurance companies and force insurers to turn to reinsurance. The world reinsurance market was slow to recover from the massive losses of Hurricane Andrew and the Northridge and Kobe earthquakes, which occurred all within two and a half years. The slow recovery led to calls for the U.S. government to subsidize reinsurance.

Researchers have explored the causes of rising costs of natural hazards. The escalating costs seem ironic given the considerable investments made – through engineering, meteorology and seismology – to make hazards less deadly. Fatalities from many hazards have indeed been falling. For instance, the annual tornado fatality rate fell from 1.8 per million in 1925 to .11 per million in 2000 (Brooks and Doswell, 2000) and the annual hurricane fatality rate fell from .5 per million people in the 1950s to .05 in the 1990s. Dennis Mileti, after reviewing the costs of natural hazards, concluded, "While fatalities in developed countries have steadily decreased by 75 percent during the past 50 years, economic losses are rapidly increasing." (Mileti, 1999 p.101)

A number of explanations have been advanced for increasing damages, including an increase in the frequency of weather extremes, often attributed to global warming. Note that the frequency of landfalling hurricanes has not been increasing, as Katz (2002) demonstrates and as Table 1 illustrates. Recent research has established that damages for numerous hazards are not rising when normalized increases in population and wealth as well as inflation (Pielke and Landsea, 1998; Brooks and Doswell, 2001; Changnon, 2001; Katz, 2002). Thus the increase in hazard damages is a product of increasing societal vulnerability, that is, more people and property in hazard prone areas. Researchers have consequently explored possible explanations for increasing vulnerability. Low probability event bias is one explanation, the tendency for people to ignore low probability events on the assumption that such unlikely events "won't happen to me" (Camerer and Kunreuther, 1989). Government subsidization of insurance, infrastructure investments, and post-disaster relief also encourages living in hazard prone areas (Platt, 1998; Mileti, 1999). A wealthier nation can also afford greater losses from hazards, so an income effect could result in greater use of hazard prone areas.

Table 1. Landfalling U.S. Hurricane by Safir-Simpson Category by Decade

Decade	Category					Total
	1	2	3	4	5	
1940s	5	8	7	1	0	21
1950s	4	1	8	2	0	15
1960s	4	5	3	2	1	15
1970s	6	2	4	0	0	12
1980s	8	2	4	1	0	15
1990s	5	6	4	1	0	16

We offer another explanation here – the very reduction in the lethality of natural hazards. By lowering the full price of living in hazard prone areas, advances in meteorology and engineering and which allow timely evacuation and construction of more durable buildings save lives but also increase the population of the hazard area. We test this hypothesis for the case of hurricanes. Improved forecasts and evacuations have reduced the fatality rate from hurricanes but have done little to reduce the damage to structures along the coast. We estimate a time-varying measure of hurricane lethality using a data set of all landfalling hurricanes in the continental U.S. between 1940 and 2000. We then use this measure of hurricane lethality as an explanatory variable in a regression of the determinants of population change in coastal counties along the Atlantic and Gulf coasts, and find that a reduction in hurricane lethality increases population growth, ceteris paribus.

The remainder of this chapter is organized as follows. The next section elaborates on how a reduction in the lethality of hazards increases the at-risk population and damages if and when a catastrophe occurs. The third section presents the first stage of analysis, an investigation of the determinants of fatalities from a landfalling hurricane. Section four then uses the time-varying estimate of the lethality of hurricanes to analyze the determinants of population growth in counties along the Atlantic and Gulf coasts of the United States. We find that a reduction in the fatality rate for hurricanes produces a statistically significant increase in coastal county populations over the next decade, consistent with our hypothesis. The final section concludes.

Hazard Risks and the Choice to Live in a Hazard-Prone Region

The proposition that a reduction in the lethality of natural hazards could increase their potential damages appears on first glance paradoxical, particularly to noneconomists. Rational residents though should consider the full cost of living (or vacationing) in a locale in making a decision about where to live (or vacation). The expected utility model of choice predicts that people will consider all of the good and bad features, amenity and disamenity values, of the locale. Natural hazards are one such amenity, although by not means the only amenity. People should consider the expected costs of natural hazards in deciding to live in a flood plain, or near a fault line, or on a hurricane exposed coast. The expected cost of the hazard includes the risk to life and limb. Reducing the lethality of the hazard lowers the full cost to residents of living in a vulnerable area.

The following example illustrates our point. Imagine a coastal island with beautiful beaches and a fabulous ocean view. The island would be a prime venue for coastal living or vacationing except that devastating hurricanes can strike the island at any time of the year. Suppose initially that hurricanes cannot be forecast, so residents can be caught by surprise on the island and face great peril at any time. With no warnings people cannot live or vacation on the island without bearing the risk of death or injury from a hurricane. Few people may be willing to risk death by residing or visiting the island under these circumstances; indeed, if the frequency of hurricanes is sufficiently high, the island may well remain uninhabited. If uninhabited, a hurricane clearly will not cause any property damage when striking the island. Now consider the impact of the development of hurricane tracking and forecasting, which allows residents and visitors time to flee the island in advance of any approaching hurricane.

The population of the island will undoubtedly increase as many people who have long wanted to live or vacation on the island now are willing to do so because they will not be killed or injured by a hurricane. Note that our example could be made less stark and more realistic in several ways without affecting the point. Hurricanes occur only during a pretty well defined season, so only a portion of the year will residents face this risk. Nonetheless, if vacationer will not visit during the hurricane season, rentals through the remainder of the year may not be sufficient to support development of the island.

Although the effect of improved forecasts and warnings and technology for any hazard is never so dramatic, a reduction in the probability of death from a hazard reduces the full cost of living in the hazard prone area. People on the margin when contemplating living in the hazard area will move in when the hazard becomes less lethal, increasing societal vulnerability.

Whether the increase in societal vulnerability increases damages depends on the exact way in which the hazard becomes less dangerous. Three different mechanisms can be distinguished. First, a hazard could be made less dangerous by reducing the probability or severity of the hazard. For instance, weather modification might reduce the frequency of damaging hailstorms, while removing underbrush can reduce the severity of wild fires. Second, engineering could allow strengthening of structures in the hazard area could be strengthened, as with earthquake resistant buildings and elevating homes located on a flood plain. Third, the at-risk population may be better able to take cover or evacuate the hazard path, thus reducing the probability of fatality or injury conditional on the hazard occurring. A reduction in lethality through any of these mechanisms increases the at-risk population, but only in the third case is damage definitely predicted to increase. In the first two cases the at-risk population increases but expected damages per household or person falls, offsetting an increase in population and leaving the effect on total damages indeterminate. In the third case the probability of the hazard and thus expected damage per household is unchanged, so the increase in population increases damages. We believe that reductions in hurricane lethality fit the third category due to more timely and effective warnings and evacuations. But we are testing in this paper only whether a reduction in lethality increases the at-risk population, so any of the three mechanisms yields the effect for which we test.

Do people consider natural hazards and other natural amenities in making location decisions? Low probability – high consequence event bias, as described by Camerer and Kunreuther (1989) suggests that the expected utility model may not apply to natural hazards. Low probability event bias suggests that people may treat the low probability of hurricanes and earthquakes and tornadoes as a zero probability – they think and act as if such events "won't happen to me." If low probability event bias is pervasive, a reduction in the probability of death or injury due to the hazards should not increase societal vulnerability, because people already ignore the risk, so a less lethal hazard should not make people feel safer. Yet prior research has produced evidence that people do consider natural hazards and amenities. Labor market studies find that wages across different cities depend on weather conditions. Roback (1982), for example, finds that heating degree days in winter, total snowfall, and the number of cloudy days are disamenities while clear days are amenities. Moore provides a survey of other evidence on the amenity values provided by weather (1998, pp.90-95). A study in Los Angeles found housing price premia for areas of the city with higher air quality (Brookshire et al. 1982). Brookshire et al. (1985) found that homes in California in state designated special seismic zones – near fault lines and thus at a particular risk from earthquakes – sold at a discount compared to homes at a safer distance. Beron et al. (1997) found that the discount for special seismic zones declined after the 1989 Loma Prieta earthquake, which was not as devastating as many expected for an earthquake of that magnitude.

Improvements in safety lower the expected cost of dangerous or reckless activity. The resulting increase in recklessness is really just a consequence of the law of demand. One of the first studies to find evidence of offsetting behavior was Peltzman's (1975) study of auto fatalities following the automobile safety regulations of the 1960s. The behavior proposed here is related to moral hazard in insurance, in which insurance against a loss reduces the return to effort to avoid the loss, although not exactly equivalent since moral hazard requires that effort by the insured party to avoid a loss be difficult to observe.

THE DETERMINANTS OF HURRICANE FATALITIES

We wish to test the effect of changes in the lethality of hurricanes on the population of coastal counties. Improved forecasts, better preparation and evacuation, and improved engineering all should reduce the expected number of deaths from a given hurricane, but this prediction holds only ceteris paribus, that is, holding the strength and location of the hurricane constant. Consequently we cannot simply use the number of persons killed in the last hurricane or the last ten hurricanes as a measure of lethality. Note that Sobel and Nesbitt (2002) for instance use the fatality rate in the past 100 races as a measure of lethality in NASCAR races, but we must control for differences in hurricanes. Thus we first estimate a regression model of hurricane fatalities in order to produce a time varying estimate of lethality. We then use this measure as a dependent variable in a regression model of coastal county population growth.

We employ a data set of all landfalling hurricanes in the continental United States between 1940 and 2000, as recorded in the National Hurricane Center's (NHC) hurricane archive, a total of 94 storms (http://www.nhc.gov/pastall.shtml). We model the number of persons killed by a hurricane as follows:

Fatalities = f(Category, Density, D40, D50, D60, D70, D80).

Our dependent variable is the number of person directly killed by the hurricane, which excludes by convention deaths due to inland flooding. The direct fatalities occur along the coast and are typically the result of storm surge and hurricane winds.

Our control variables are as follows. Category is the rating of the hurricane on the Safir-Simpson hurricane intensity scale. Hurricanes are rated on an integer scale from "1" a minimal hurricane, to "5", based on sustained wind speed, storm surge and barometric pressure. A "category 1" storm has sustained winds between 74 and 95 miles per hour and a 4-5 foot storm surge, while a "category 5' storm has winds in excess of 155 miles per hour and a storm surge greater than 18 feet (see also the National Hurricane Center's website at www.nhc.noaa.gov/aboutsshs.shtml). By convention, hurricanes are rated based on their strength on the Safir-Simpson scale at time of landfall and storms typically weaken quickly once ashore. Density is the population density in persons per square mile of the counties struck by the hurricane, as reported in the NHC archive. The variable is the mean of the estimated population density of each county in the year of the hurricane based on linear interpolation from the decennial censuses. We expect both Category and Density to be positive determinants of fatalities. D40, D50, D60, D70 and D80 are dummy variables which equal one if the hurricane occurred in the decade of the 1940s, 1950s, 1960s, 1970s or 1980s respectively, or zero otherwise. The 1990s are the omitted category in our regressions, and so the coefficients on the decade dummy variables indicate the effect on fatalities of a hurricane in that decade relative to the 1990s. The decade dummy variables capture the effect of changes in hurricane lethality over time. We expect that hurricanes have become less lethal, so given that the 1990s are the omitted category, we expect positive coefficients for the decade dummies with the magnitude of the coefficients declining over time. Table 1 displays the breakdown of the number hurricanes of different intensities by decade. The decade totals exhibit no trend in the number of landfalling hurricanes over time.

The number of fatalities produced by a hurricane takes on integer values with a high proportion of zeros. The number of fatalities from hurricanes ranged from 0 to 394 with a mean of 24.3 and a median of 3; 23 of the 94 hurricanes fortunately produced no direct fatalities. Our dependent variable is thus a count variable, so we employ a Poisson regression model to estimate fatalities. The Poisson model (Greene, 2000 pp.880-886) assumes that the dependent variable is distributed as a Poisson random variable with the parameter Δ of the distribution dependent on the independent variables of the model. The model is estimated in log-linear form.

Table 2 displays the estimates of our model of hurricane fatalities. As expected, Category and Density are both positive and statistically significant (at better than the one percent level) determinants of expected fatalities. A one category increase in the strength of a hurricane at landfall nearly triples expected fatalities. The decade dummy variables are all statistically significant at the one percent level, except D70, which is significant at only the ten percent level, and all are positive except D80, which is negative. A downward trend in the decade dummy variables is evident, even though the coefficients are not ordered monotonically. The reduction is also quantitatively large; expected fatalities from a hurricane in the 1990s would be over 60 percent lower than the comparable hurricane in the 1940s. Note that we cannot with this model determine the cause of the reduction in fatalities, that is, whether improved forecasts, more effective evacuations or better engineering have made hurricanes less deadly.

Table 2. Poisson Regression of Hurricane Fatalities

Independent Variable	Estimate	Standard Error	95% Interval	Confidence
Category	1.081†	.0255	1.031	1.131
Density	.000718†	.0000	.0006	.0008
D40	.9937†	.0912	.08149	1.173
D50	1.354†	.0844	1.181	1.528
D60	.4865†	.0965	.2974	.6757
D70	.2145*	.1270	-.0344	.4634
D80	-.4082†	.1286	-.6602	-.1562
Intercept	-.6580†	.1130	-.8794	-.4366

Note: Number of observations = 93. † and * indicate significance at the 1% and 10% levels respectively.

THE DETERMINANTS OF COASTAL COUNTY GROWTH

We next estimate a model of population growth in coastal counties. Our data set is a panel of decennial population changes in 146 counties in 15 states along the Atlantic and Gulf of Mexico coasts between 1950 and 2000, for a total of 730 observations. We employ two dependent variables, the change in the number of persons living in the county during the decade, ΔPop, and the percentage change in the county population during the decade, %ΔPop. The first variable captures society's total vulnerability while the second variable indicates the proportional change in vulnerability.

We estimate the following model of county population change:

ΔPopulation = f(Lethality, InitialPop, Area, Density, Hit, ProbHurricane, USPopulation, State).

Our independent variable of interest is Lethality, which is based on our time varying measure of hurricane fatalities estimated in the previous section. A reduction in hurricane lethality should increase coastal populations, but only with a lag as it will take time for people to recognize that hurricanes have become less deadly and then decide to move. We use the dummy variable for the previous decade as the lethality variable for the current decade, so for population growth between 1960 and 1970, Lethality is the coefficient of D50 from Table 2.

Our other control variables are as follows. InitialPop is the population of the county at the start of the decade. A more populated county might be more likely to grow faster since the large initial population indicates that the county possesses considerable positive amenities. But crowding is a disamenity, so InitialPop could have a negative sign. Area is the land area of the county in square miles; a larger county has more land to accommodate new residents, holding constant the initial population. Thus we expect a positive sign for area. Density is the population density of the county in thousands of persons per square mile at the start of the decade. This captures whether the county is already highly populated at the start of the period and is included in place of InitialPop and Area in the percentage growth regression. Again this variable could have either a positive or negative sign depending on whether the amenity value of the county outweighs crowding. Hit is a dummy variable, which equals "1" if the county was struck by a hurricane during the decade of the observation. A hurricane will damage existing homes, businesses and infrastructure, and the diversion of resources to reconstruction might reduce county growth, so we expect a negative sign for Hit. A current hurricane could also affect residents' (or potential residents') perception of hurricane risk as well, which would also slow growth. ProbHurricane is the annual probability of a major hurricane (1 rated "category 3" or higher on the Safir-Simpson scale) striking the county, as reported in Sheets and Williams (2001). A higher probability of a hurricane increases expected hurricane damage, provided that residents pay the full cost of damage through higher insurance premiums or out-of-pocket after a loss, which implies a negative sign for this variable. But this measure, which does not change for a county over time, might be correlated with other characteristics affecting the desirability of the county. USPopulation is the U.S. population in millions at the start of the decade. The model is also estimated with state dummy variables; Florida, for instance, equals '1" for counties located in Florida, and "0" otherwise. The state dummy variables capture differences in the desirability of different states' coastlines as well as any state policies like insurance subsidies or land use regulations which inhibit or encourage coastal development. Virginia is the omitted state (last alphabetically of the 15 coastal states) so the coefficients on the state variables indicate the effect relative to Virginia.

Table 3 presents our regression results, which employ White's heteroskedasticity-consistent standard errors. For each model Lethality has a negative and significant coefficient, indicating that reductions in hurricane fatalities have indeed increased population growth. Note that in the ΔPop model Lethality is significant at only the ten percent level, but is significant at the one percent level in the %ΔPop model. The impact of the reduction in lethality is quantitatively large as well; the reduction in lethality between the 1950s and 1990s increased population by almost 17,000 persons, and increased the growth rate by about .4%. Overall the model performs much better for ΔPop than %ΔPop as indicated by the adjusted R^2. Of the other control variables, note that Hit has a negative sign in both specifications but is not significant, so counties did not grow significantly slower in a decade in which they were struck by a hurricane. InitialPop and Area are positive and significant determinants of ΔPop but Density is insignificant in the specification for %ΔPop. The state fixed effects are not reported, and no consistent pattern of significance emerged for any state across the two specifications. Indeed, no state dummy variable was significant at even the ten percent level in the %ΔPop specification.

Table 3. Determinants of Coastal County Population Growth

Independent Variable	Change in Population	Percentage Change in Population
Intercept	61000*	1.94†
	(2.00)	(2.84)
Lethality	-12500*	-.288†
	(1.86)	(2.95)
Initial Population	.116†	
	(5.43)	
Area	31.6†	
	(4.48)	
Density		-.0177
		(1.14)
U.S. Population	-356*	-.00736†
	(2.67)	(3.04)
Prob Hurricane	11200†	.02183
	(4.57)	(1.48)
Hit	-1880	-.04327
	(.40)	(1.52)
Adjusted R^2	.443	.0704

Note: Number of observations = 730. Absolute t-statistics based on White's heteroskedasicity-consistent standard errors in parentheses. * and † indicate significance at the 10% and 1% levels respectively. Both models also include state fixed effects, which are not reported here.

CONCLUSIONS

Previous research has established that rising damages from natural hazards are largely due to increased societal vulnerability; that is, damages for many hazards have not increased when normalized for changes in population, wealth and inflation. An explanation for increasing damages for these natural hazards then must address increasing population and wealth in hazard prone areas. We have offered a seemingly paradoxical cause for increasing vulnerability, the investments by society to reduce the lethality of hazards. The probability of being killed or injured is part of the full price of living in a hazard prone area, and so as a hazard becomes less deadly the law of demand implies that more people should live in the hazard-prone area. We tested this proposition for hurricanes. A reduction in the lethality of hurricanes, as estimated in a regression analysis of fatalities from landfalling hurricanes in the continental U.S., increases population growth in Atlantic and Gulf coast counties, everything else equal. Elsewhere we apply the method used here to show that reductions in hurricane lethality increase damages as well (Sadowski and Sutter, 2003). As Mileti (1999) argues, natural hazards interact with the built environment in a complicated manner. Our analysis here illustrates one dimension of the complexity.

An extension would test whether the relationship between lethality and societal vulnerability for other hazards and in other countries. Note that for different hazards, if reductions in lethality are due to engineering or reducing the severity of the hazard, damages may not necessarily increase. Also note that we do not claim that reduced lethality is the only or even largest cause of increased vulnerability, rather a source that has not been previously emphasized.

Our results do not establish that society is worse off as hazards become less deadly. The total impact of the hazard on society even if increased use of hazard prone areas increases property damages from hazards. The inability to use a hazard prone area due to the risk to life and limb is part of the full cost of natural hazards, though rarely included in any tallies. As long as residents of the hazard area bear the full-expected cost of property damage, reducing the lethality of the hazard makes society better off even though conventionally measured hazard losses rise.

Improvements, which make hazards less deadly, can, however, increase the cost to society of policies, which subsidize living in hazard prone areas. Suppose policies effectively subsidize half the property damage from hurricanes. Residents (or vacationers) bear the full cost of being killed or injured in a hurricane, so if hurricanes are sufficiently deadly, few people may choose to take advantage of the subsidy to live on the coast. A discounted ticket on the Titanic, after all, would not have been a very good deal. As hurricanes become less deadly, the subsidy will induce more people to live or vacation on the coast. In this case a reduction in hazard lethality can raise the full cost to society of natural hazards. Although reductions in lethality seemingly are an improvement, the fallacy of the second best cautions that safer hazards may make society worse off if subsidies are in place.

REFERENCES

Brooks, Harold E. and Charles A. Doswell III, (2002), "Deaths in the 3 May 1999 Oklahoma City Tornado from a Historical Perspective", *Weather and Forecasting,* Vol.17: 354-361.

Camerer, Colin F. and Howard Kunreuther (1989), "Decision Processes for Low Probability Events: Policy Implications", *Journal of Policy Analysis and Management,* Vol.8 (4): 565-592.

Changnon, Stanley A. and Geoffrey J.D. Hewings (2001), "Losses from Weather Extremes in the United States", *Natural Hazards Review,* Vol.2 (3): 113-123.

Greene, William H. (2000), *Econometric Analysis*, 4th edition, Prentice Hall, Upper Saddle River NJ.

Katz, Richard W. (2002), "Stochastic Modeling of Hurricane Damage", *Journal of Applied Meteorology*, Vol.41: 754-761.

Mileti, Dennis S. (1999), *Disasters by Design*, Joseph Henry Press, Washington DC.

Moore, Thomas Gale (1998), *Climate of Fear*, Cato Institute, Washington DC.

Peltzman, Sam (1975) "The Effects of Automobile Safety Regulation", *Journal of Political Economy*, Vol.83 (4): 677-725.

Pielke Jr., Roger A. and Christopher W. Landsea (1998), "Normalized Hurricane Damages in the United States, 1925-1995" *Weather and Forecasting*, Vol.13: 621-631.

Platt, Rutherford H. (1999), *Disasters and Democracy: The Politics of Extreme Natural Events*, Island Press, Washington DC.

Roback, Jennifer (1982), "Wages, Rents and the Quality of Life", *Journal of Political Economy*, Vol.90 (6):1257-1279.

Sadowski, Nicole Cornell and Daniel Sutter (2003), "Hurricane Fatalities and Hurricane Damages: Do Declining Death Tolls Increase Damages?" *Working Paper, Department of Economics, University of Oklahoma.*

Sheets, Bob and Jack Williams (2001), *Hurricane Watch: Forecasting the Deadliest Storms on Earth,* Vintage Books.

Sobel, Russell S. and Todd M. Nesbitt (2002), "Automobile Safety and the Incentive to Drive Recklessly: Evidence from NASCAR", *Working Paper, Department of Economics, West Virginia University.*

In: Economics and the Wind
Editors: B. T. Ewing, et. al., pp. 159-177

ISBN: 1-59454-280-5
©2005 Nova Science Publishers, Inc.

Chapter 14

GUIDELINES FOR THE UNIFORM DEFINITION, IDENTIFICATION, AND MEASUREMENT OF ECONOMIC DAMAGES FROM NATURAL HAZARD EVENTS

Charles W. Howe
Environment and Behavior Program,
Institute of Behavioral Science, University of Colorado at Boulder, Boulder, CO, USA
Harold C. Cochrane
Hazards Assessment Lab, Colorado State University, Fort Collins, CO, USA

ABSTRACT

This brief set of guidelines has been distilled from a larger project entitled *Uniform Framework and Measurement Guidelines for Damages from Natural and Related Manmade Hazards,* funded by NSF Grant CES-8717115. That project also produced the more extensive *Natural Hazard Damage Handbook,* authored by Howe, Cochrane, Bunin, and Kling, dated August 1991 and available from NTIS; an updated *Natural Hazards Data Resources Directory,* available from the Natural Hazards Research and Applications Information Center, University of Colorado; and a user questionnaire, *Assessing Damages from Natural and Manmade Hazards: A Survey of User Practices and Needs.*

It is our hope that these guidelines will be helpful to those who are faced with the difficult tasks of field estimation and to the international effort to establish a global disaster data base for the International Decade for Natural Disaster Reduction. The authors express their appreciation to Jane E. Bunin of Natural Science Associates, Inc. and Robert W. Kling of Colorado State University, our colleagues in writing the handbook and whose materials underlie sections on damages to natural capital and damages to historical monuments, respectively.

We also want to thank Dr. Eleonora Sabadell, Director of the Natural and Manmade Hazards Mitigation Program of NSF, who encouraged this work and provided advice throughout the project. Only the authors are responsible for remaining shortcomings.

INTRODUCTION

This set of guidelines is intended as a primer for personnel responsible for the identification and measurement of damages from natural hazard events. The writing style, orientation, and level of detail were shaped in part by the results of a user survey in the U.S. that indicated a majority of those gathering and using damage data were trained in engineering or a related technical fields. The respondents generally felt that insufficient budgets and the complex nature of loss measurement methods limit their ability to gather and make better use of damage data. A sizable majority indicated that they were involved in flood hazard assessments.

The need for such guidelines arises from the ad hoc measures that are often presented to the public as "damages" or impacts of natural hazard events. The problems with existing damage data can be illustrated by quotes from studies of the quality of U.S. flood damage data carried out by Thomas P. Grazulis regarding the documentation of national annual flood losses:

> The most widely quoted overall "loss" numbers are from the [National Weather Service,] Office of Hydrology... . There is currently no plan of attack or any set of guidelines for filing, refining, or using that data base. Numbers of varying quality are inserted with no reference as to where they came from or exactly what "loss" was estimated or measured. This data base is a curious combination of intelligent, well-meaning and hard working people being given minimal time to maintain a poorly conceived system with unsubstantiated data on a low priority basis. I haven't found anyone within the flood research community [who] actually believes the NWS numbers (Memo to NSF Advisory Committee, February 2, 1989).

Thus, it is important to establish a standard set of definitions of and measurement methods for natural hazard damages and to create institutional frameworks that have the capability and resources to follow such guidelines.

THE DEFINITION OF NATURAL HAZARD DAMAGES

Impacts

At a purely physical level, we speak of the *impacts* of a natural hazard event: an impact is any measurable physical change in geological, ecological, atmospheric, or human systems attributable to that event. Among the impacts of a flood are changes in alluvial materials in the valley; changes in the numbers and types of the various plants and animals; permanent shifts in the direction, volume, or velocity of water flows; physical destruction of crops and livestock; changes in buildings; losses of human life; and deferral or abandonment of production processes. What principle underlies the identification and measurement of these impacts? It is the *with-without principle:*

> We seek to identify and measure all changes between the system as it evolves *with* the natural hazard event having taken place and as it would have evolved *without* the occurrence of the natural hazard event.

It must be noted that this principle does *not* mean identifying and measuring a set of variables at points in time before and after the event. Changes attributable to the event can be dynamic and continue over time, so that the "with-without" difference must be cumulatively measured by monitoring the system over time. In addition, the *continuation of changes* that were occurring prior to the event must be measured. For example, assume that annual corn production in the Wabash River Valley in the year preceding a flood amounted to one million tons. In the year of the flood, corn production amounted to 500,000 tons. Is the change of 500,000 tons attributable to the flood? Not necessarily, for there might have been a downtrend (or uptrend) in corn production due to market or climatic factors that would have reduced production to 750,000 tons even in the absence of a flood. Then only a loss of 250,000 tons can be attributed to the flood.

If we carefully apply the with-without principle to a system affected by a natural hazard event, we can identify and (in principle) measure the impacts of that event. Yet, even minor natural hazard events have innumerable impacts. We are concerned with those impacts that involve changes in human well-being (i.e., changes in values).

Values and Policy

Value changes are more complex than physical impacts. *Values* are rates at which individuals or groups are willing to trade off one thing for another. For example, suppose investigation has shown that reducing the ocean catch of tuna by one million tons per year would allow the dolphin population to increase by one million. One could interpret this scientific information to say that the cost of one more dolphin in the permanent population is one ton of tuna foregone. That is still not a value statement. However, the statement that human society *would be willing* to give up one ton of tuna to raise the dolphin population by one is a value statement. In this case, the combination of physical data and human values imply that a policy decision to decrease tuna fishing and allow the dolphin population to increase would be desirable.

Economic values have been classified into two groups: 1) use values, and 2) non-use values. An object or service has use value if it *is directly* involved in interactions with individuals. A sandwich has use value to a hungry person, while a painting has use value to people even though the painting is not consumed in the process. Use value is manifested in peoples' *willingness to pay* to acquire or access the object. Data on use values usually come from market prices, but also can be derived from surveys of peoples' willingness to pay.

Non-use values represent concern for the continued existence of assets and environmental conditions (e.g., fertile soil or clean water) in situations where the person or group valuing the asset is not actually using the asset. Such values are especially important in assessing damages to natural areas and historical monuments or artifacts. Some of these non-use values can be estimated in terms of the relevant public's willingness to pay for preservation (see Mitchell and Carson, 1989; Krutilla and Fisher, 1975; Greenley, Walsh, and Young, 1982).

Natural hazard policy questions always involve tradeoffs among values. For example, flood policy seeks answers to the questions:

1. What are the benefits (values gained) and costs (values given up) of various programs of flood control?
2. Who gains and who loses from each?
3. In the light of both, which alternative should be undertaken?

Hazard damage measurement is part of the hazard policy process because it measures the *loss of values* caused by natural hazard events, some of which could be avoided through mitigation programs. Hazard damages are thus losses of human-centered use and non-use values that result from natural hazard events.

Estimating Damage Values

Some impacts have values directly associated with them. A loss of 1,000 tons of grain due to a windstorm usually will have a *market value* determined by the market price of grain. Market prices usually are the best value measure, but sometimes they require adjustment. Data on damages often are drawn from the accounting records of businesses, units of government, and the national income accounts. To be incorporated in these systems, natural *hazard* impacts must be reducible to monetary values. Private accounting systems record and monitor asset values and revenues and costs. National income accounting as practiced in the United States produces such common economic measures as gross domestic product, personal income, consumption, and savings, but omits many environmental and social values and costs. National income accounting does not maintain records of the values of stocks of public and private assets, although it does record the amount of private asset depreciation to permit calculation of net (as opposed to gross) domestic product. These national accounting concepts have been extended down to multi-state regions (regional accounting) and to the state level (e.g., gross state product, state personal income, and state disposable income). Large-scale natural hazard events can have significant impacts on these highly aggregated measures.

Many dimensions of the environment are valued directly or indirectly by the population. For example, water pollution increases cities' and industries' water intake costs while also destroying recreational fishing and aesthetic enjoyment. This broadening of policy-relevant environmental and social values has led to:

1. methods to extend monetary valuation to environmental goods and services that have no explicit market value (e.g., recreation on public land, health and aesthetic values from cleaner air, and existence values);
2. the development of environmental and social indicators to record changes for which economic values seem inappropriate; and
3. the development of multiple-objective evaluation procedures into which both economic values and non-economic impacts could be fit.

Multiple-objective planning and evaluation, developed during the late 1960s and early 1970s through the work of the U.S. Water Resources Council and its consultants (Principles and Standards for Planning Water and Related Land Resources, *Federal Register* 38, 174, September 10), recognized this widening set of economic, environmental, and social values by providing decision makers and the public with data on market economic values, non-market economic values (e.g., monetized value of non-priced recreation, values of health improvements, and existence values), as well as environmental and social indicators. Decision makers then choose "weights" to be placed on each of these variables to rank policy alternatives. In this way, the policy process can deal with both monetized values and non-monetized impacts. It remains the responsibility of technical personnel to provide the best damage data allowed by time and budgets and, if important damages are not being considered, to call them to their superiors' attention.

The discussion to date has been cast in terms of damages physically linked to a natural hazard event, even though they may occur over some period of time. Other damages occur indirectly as a result of natural hazard events. For example, suppose a flood prevents the planting of a crop on river bottom land. At the farm level, the direct damage would be measured by the net income the farm would have realized from the crop: sales value less the value of all inputs and harvesting cost. In addition, there may be *secondary* damages to the suppliers of farm inputs and processors of agricultural output. They may lose profit or wage incomes. Since there is greater uncertainty about these damages, very conservative estimates should be used. The reader can consult the *Natural Hazard Damage Handbook (1991),* Bendavid *(1972),* or Pleeter *(1980)* for appropriate methods.

In sum, natural hazard economic damages are represented by the traditional market and national income measures and asset values and supplemented by relevant non-market values and appropriately measured secondary damages.

The Identification and Measurement of Direct Economic Damages

Monetization of Impacts in the Computation of Damages

In order to monetize (provide dollar values for) physical impacts caused by a natural disaster, market prices most often are used. However, do prices exist for all the assets, commodities, and services that are relevant? When prices do exist, do they reflect the values we want to capture? The following situations are encountered:

1. market prices exist for many assets, commodities, and services in situations where the prices correctly reflect social values;
2. market prices exist, but need to be adjusted to reflect social values correctly;
3. market prices do not exist, but credible methods exist for estimating the prices needed for program or project evaluation; or
4. market prices do not exist, and no general, credible methods for simulating those values exist.

Naturally, analysts (especially economists) differ about where the dividing line should fall between any two of the above situations. How do we know whether or not a price is "right" or whether it needs to be adjusted before being used in damage estimation? This is explained by the roles that prices ideally play in the organization of a well-functioning economic system: prices are intended to indicate to the *user* of a unit of a good or service (producer or consumer) the real cost of making that unit available, while prices should indicate to *a producer* the value placed by society on another unit of output. In competitive economies, markets will encourage production to be extended to levels at which incremental costs just equal incremental social values, with both reflected in market prices.

Under what circumstances do market prices *fail* to reflect the appropriate opportunity cost and/or marginal social value of a commodity? Unfortunately, this failure occurs under many real life circumstances. The agricultural sector-which produces crops, livestock, and dairy products-is usually cited as the ideal manifestation of competition because it contains many relatively small producers and many buyers. Yet *domestic* agricultural prices are severely distorted by price support programs that keep market prices far above marginal social values by directing part of farm output into government storage (usually to be dumped on international markets). Wages may fail to reflect the real cost (opportunity cost) of labor under minimum wage regulations. Prices of products produced by only a few producers who tacitly collude in the setting of prices are likely to exceed producer unit costs and thus overstate real costs to buyers (e.g., airline services, cable TV services, automobiles). Thus, prices may need adjustment before being used to estimate economic damages. In practice, only major distortions can be corrected.

Many lost services and amenities do not have market prices, such as recreation on public lands, improvements in air and water quality, beautiful landscapes and views, and enjoyment of public gardens. In some cases, it is possible to estimate prices (unit values) for such services so they can be included in economic assessment. One major method consists of survey techniques called *contingent valuation methods* that ask people what they would be willing to pay for some non-marketed good (Mitchell and Carson, 1989; Cummings, Brookshire, and Schulze, 1986). Another approach would be the *travel cost method* of valuing recreation (Knetsch, 1972). Placing dollar values on outdoor recreation represents the most frequent application of these methods and has gained general acceptance. The federal courts have accepted values for such amenities estimated by contingent valuation methods (see U.S. Court of Appeals for the D.C. Circuit, July 14, 1989, No. 86-1529), but many public officials still prefer physical description rather than attempting to monetize all costs. Trying to place a value on the loss of human life is one such case.

Conceptual Framework for Identifying and Measuring Direct Economic Damages

The productive resources of society consist of the stocks of accumulated human-made capital (buildings, equipment, inventories, and scientific and technological knowledge), human capital (skills and energy), and natural capital (soil, forests, minerals, water, and environmental conditions). The measurement of direct economic damages centers on six types of effects: 1) damages to human-made capital; 2) interruptions of production processes; 3) identification of economic activities to be monitored over time: 4) damages to historical monuments and historical assets; 5) damages to human capital (i.e., human illness and mortality; and 6) damages to natural capital.

Damages to Human-Made Capital

We turn to the "balance sheet" of assets in the form of human-made capital. The majority of quantifiable losses from natural hazard events occur due to damage to such assets. Human-made assets can be classified as:

- long-lived business and government physical assets,
- business and government inventories of physical goods,
- non-business residential properties, and
- other non-financial personal property.

Financial assets are omitted from damage evaluation since they really represent underlying real asset values and related income flows. For example, if a company's factory is destroyed, the value of the factory is counted but not the decrease in the value of the company's shares on the stock market. It is important to avoid *double counting* financial asset values and the underlying asset and profit values. Thus, financial assets should be omitted from further consideration.

Table 1. Analyzing Damages to Human-Made Capital Assets

Alternative Values for Assets:
- book values (may be outdated),
- depreciated replacement value (appropriate),
- market values of similar assets, or
- insurance and realtor records

Complete Destruction of Long-Lived Assets:
- Will They be Replaced?
- Yes → damages = market value of similar asset
- No → damages = present value of income losses resulting from loss of the asset

Partial Destruction of Long-Lived Assets:
- Will They be Rehabilitated?
- Yes → damages = cost of rehabilitation
- No → damages = present value of income losses over the remaining operating life of the asset

Long-lived assets typically have "book values" in the accounting records of private businesses. Households do not keep asset accounts, but insurance and realtors' records are valuable sources of residential values. Government asset records generally are poor and depreciation accounting is not practiced, so *book* values of government assets are either nonexistent or irrelevant. Long-lived business assets are entered at their purchase price and then depreciated over time according to one of several traditional formulas, with the annual depreciation treated as a business expense and a deduction from the asset value. Because of price level increases over time, most book values are out of date and may even be irrelevant to damage calculations. Modern management accounting (as opposed to financial accounting-frequently several sets of books are kept) updates long-lived asset prices on a "depreciated replacement cost" basis. Table 1 lists some of the major considerations in measuring damages to assets.

If an asset is totally destroyed, the first question is whether or not it will be replaced. If so, the next question is: What will replace it? The replacement could be an asset of similar age and depreciation or a new asset. The theoretically correct measure of damage would be the *change* in present value of anticipated capital outlays. Partial destruction of assets leads to the same question: Will the asset be rehabilitated? One must know what is meant by "rehabilitation," but let us assume the objective is to upgrade the damaged asset to the same productivity and remaining life as the original asset at the time of damage. The cost of such an upgrading appropriately measures the damage. If a partially destroyed asset is not worth rehabilitating but is still worth keeping in operation, the damage will be captured by the *reduction* in the present value of the income stream caused by lesser productivity or a shortened asset life.

The formula for the present value of incomes lost is:

$$PV = L_0 + \frac{L_1}{(1+r)} + \frac{L_2}{(1+r)^2} + \dots \frac{L_T}{(1+r)^T} \qquad (1)$$

where L_0 is income lost in the current year, L_t is the income lost in year t, L_T is the income lost in the last year of the project's expected life, and r is a discount rate-usually the borrowing rate of the governmental unit or business making the computation.

It is not uncommon for government loss estimates to violate these principles. The cost of the Loma Prieta earthquake on the San Francisco and Oakland freeway systems, for example, was stated by transportation authorities to include the costs of seismic upgrading.

It will cost $60 million just to reopen San Francisco's quake damaged freeways, and state highway engineers say it will cost hundreds of millions more to bring them up to safety standards of the 1990s. Caltrans recently told the state Legislature that the post-quake highway network in the Bay Area would require an infusion of $1.7 billio... . Because the 7.1 [temblor] of Oct. 17 remains fresh in the minds of the legislators, Roberts said, "We will be able to finish in four years what prior to the earthquake would have taken forever" (*San Francisco Examiner,* November 21, 1989).

Retrofitting to make freeways and structures *safer is not a* cost of the earthquake. The temporary repairs of $60 million to the Embarcadero, Interstate 880, the Oakland Bay Bridge, and U.S. 101 *are* attributable to the earthquake. The $1.7 billion worth of seismic upgrades *is not.* Since the design changes reflected in higher construction costs are not a product of the earthquake, they should not be counted as a cost of the earthquake. It is appropriate to count only the cost of restoring the freeways to their pre-event condition.

One final point concerns the treatment of land. It is important to distinguish between damage to structures and a possible reduction in the value of building sites. In most areas, the value of real estate depends mostly on location, with building improvements contributing only a part of the property's overall value. Occasionally, damage assessments incorrectly count the *total* market value of land and structures. This is incorrect since the land still has value, although that value may differ from the pre-event value.

Interruptions of Production

Such items as labor services, raw material, and use of equipment are combined to produce goods and services that can be used for consumption, investment, provision of government services, exports to other countries, and other things. *Value added* in a production process is the difference between the market value of the product produced and the market value of inputs purchased from other producers. (This is shown in equation 2). Value added is thus equivalent to the sum of income payments made directly by the firm to human, natural, and human-made capital. When a natural hazard event occurs, production processes are interrupted, resulting in a reduction in these payments over some time. *For natural hazard damages, it is the reduction in value added plus the value of damages to the stocks of capital that constitute the damages to a business firm from the hazard event.* Table 2 presents a breakdown of situations and analytical considerations.

Value added = market value of the product produced, less the value of inputs purchased from other producers= accounting profits plus depreciation expenses, wages and salaries and taxes. (2)

The full value added is really delayed or lost only if the productive resources (e.g., labor and land) are left completely unused (unemployed) during the production interruption. If all or some of these resources find alternative employment during the production interruption, then only the *difference* between the original income payments to these resources and the new temporary income rate is used in calculating lost value-added.

Whether or not interrupted production can be *made up* is an important consideration (Table 2). If it can, then the value added (business net incomes and other factor payments, mostly wage and salary payments) generated by that production is merely delayed. For delays of less than six months, the actual losses will be small.

Table 2. Analyzing Interruptions in Production

Production Processes Frequently Interrupted by Natural Hazard Events

- agricultural production
- commercial fishing
- manufacturing operations
- transportation systems
- service industries (health, recreation, etc.)
- government operations and services

Will interruptions in production be made up?

Yes → damage = present value of *delays* in value added (usually small)

No → damage = loss of total *value added* until resumption of production, adjusted for temporary earnings from other employments of the inputs

Losses of the activities of the government sector (local, county, state, federal, and special districts) are more difficult to monetize since there really is no market for government services. Government services are principally of two types: 1) general administration, maintenance of order, etc., and 2) the provision of services (e.g., education, libraries, recreation, health services, and utilities). Both types of public services are critical to the performance of the economy, and the interruption of these services can have severe impacts on individuals and the other sectors of the economy.

How do we measure the direct economic losses from the interruption of government services? While we can measure *the cost* of government services, it is difficult to measure the *value* of the services as we do for the private sector since there are no charges for many services (general administration, libraries, education, recreation), and the charges for others are frequently unrelated to their costs. National income accounting values government outputs by their costs. Thus, *losses of government services can be valued conservatively as the costs not incurred,* but this is likely to result in a large understatement of lost value.

Some types of government administration expenditures *rise* as a result of natural hazard events, especially for activities that mitigate damages. These increases in government administration and public safety expenditures are *costs* caused by the natural hazard event and should be counted as damages.

It is important to note that if government costs are used as a proxy for the value of lost government services, then lost government *revenue* cannot also be included. To do so would double count impacts.

An Inventory of Economic Activities to be Monitored

The preceding sections have provided guidelines for the measurement of lost real assets that were either damaged or were no longer able to contribute to value added as a result of natural *hazard* events. It is useful to have a checklist of economic activities or sectors that may be impacted by natural hazard events to help in the identification of damages. Such a checklist for commercial and government activities is provided by the U.S. Standard Industrial Classification (SIC), used by all U.S. federal data gathering agencies for the classification of data.

We propose that each agency with responsibility for natural hazard damage data collection construct a subset of the two-digit SIC economic activities that are present in their jurisdiction as a checklist of commercial and government activities that should be monitored for damages. Table 3 presents the two-digit activities, but it may be worthwhile to use the more detailed three- and four-digit categories that can be copied from the SIC manual. While the SIC covers all production activities, it does not have categories for all types of assets (e.g., it has residential construction but no residential units per se).

Table 3. Standard Industrial Classification (Two Digit) of Economic Activities for Purposes of Damage Data Classification

A. Agriculture, Forestry, and Fishing
01. Agricultural Production-Crops
02. Agricultural Production-Livestock
07. Agricultural services
08. Forestry
09. Fishing, Hunting & Trapping

B. Mining
10. Metal Mining
12. Gas Mining
13. Oil and Gas Extraction
14. Nonmetallic Minerals, Except Fuels

C. Construction
15. General Building Contractors
16. Heavy Construction, Excavation Building
17. Special Trade Contractors
36. Electronic and Other Equipment
37. Transportation Equipment
38. Instruments and Related Products
39. Miscellaneous Manufacturing Industries

E. Transportation and Public Utilities
40. Railroad Transportation
41. Local and Interurban Passenger Transit
42. Trucking and Warehousing
43. U.S Postal Service
44. Water Transportation
45. Transportation By Air
46. Pipelines, Except Natural Gas
47. Transportation Services
48. Communication
49. Electric, Gas and Sanitary

F. Wholesale Trade
50. Wholesale Trade-Durable Goods
51. Wholesale Trade-Nondurable Goods

G. Retail Trade
NEC 52. Building Materials and Garden Supplies
53. General Merchandise Stores
54. Food Stores
55. Automotive Dealers and Service Stations
56. Apparel and Accessory Stores
57. Furniture and Home Furnishings
58. Eating and Drinking Places
59. Miscellaneous Retail

H. Finance, Insurance, and Real Estate
60. Depository Institutions
61. Nondepository Institutions
62. Security and Commodity Brokers

D. Manufacturing
20. Food and Kindred Products
21. Tobacco Products
22. Textile Mill Products
23. Apparel and Other Textiles
24. Lumber and Wood Products
25. Furniture and Fixtures
26. Paper and Allied Products
27. Printing and Publishing
28. Chemicals and Allied Products
29. Petroleum and Coal Products
30. Rubber and Miscellaneous Plastics
31. Leather and Leather Products
32. Stone, Clay and Glass Products
33. Primary Metal Industries
34. Fabricated Metal Products
35. Industrial Machinery and Equipment
63. Insurance Carriers
64. Insurance Agents, Brokers, and Services
65. Real Estate
67. Holding and Other Investment Offices

I. Services
70. Hotels and Other Lodging Places
72. Personal Services
73. Business Services
75. Auto repair, Services
76. Miscellaneous Repair Services
78. Motion Pictures
79. Amusement and Recreation
80. Health Services
81. Legal Services
82. Educational Services
83. Social Services
84. Museums, Botanical, Zoological Gardens
86. Membership Organizations
87. Engineering and Management Services
88. Private Households
89. Services,

J. Public Administration
91. Executive, Legislative, and General
92. Justice, Public Orders, and Safety
93. Finance, Taxation and Monetary
94. Administration of Human resources
95. Environmental Quality and Housing
96. Administration of Economics Programs
97. National Security and Int. Affairs

K. Nonclassifiable Establishments
99. Nonclassifiable establishments

The big SIC omission is the *household sector,* including both "household production" and household assets. As already noted, damages to residences and their contents constitute a major form of natural hazard loss and are canvassed by various agencies. In addition, whenever there is significant damage to residences, household production processes are interrupted: food preparation, laundry, provision of rest, relaxation and recreation. The reduction in household value added occasioned by natural hazard events should be included in damages. The problem in valuing household value added is that there is no market test of the value; however, that need not preclude the development of some rules of thumb. An example would be to allow $N per day per adult displaced from his or her residence. Some of this loss is reduced by the provision of emergency services for food and housing. At present there is no accepted standard for valuing loss of household production and amenities, but this should be changed.

The failure to recognize important personal costs and the value of lost leisure is clearly illustrated by the events occurring after the October 17, 1990, Loma Prieta earthquake. The collapse of the Cyprus Structure of Interstate 880, damage to the Embarcadero Freeway, and the temporary closure of the Oakland Bay Bridge disrupted Bay Area traffic patterns for one full month. The resultant daily commuter delays, lasting as much as four hours, were costly to both area firms and their employees, but the costs to commuters have been ignored. Longer commutes consumed more energy, increased risks, and often resulted in frustration and lost family and leisure time. These costs should be monetized and counted as damages.

Damages to Historical Monuments and Historical Assets

Every community, region, and country has certain assets that are valuable in giving that society a sense of historical continuity and cultural identity. Such cultural assets often are unique and irreplaceable, and also have the character of *public goods;* therefore, market prices either are unavailable or inappropriate to use in valuing the assets. Because valuation is difficult, cultural assets often are undervalued or, worse, omitted altogether in a tally of damages from natural hazards.

Society values cultural assets at many levels. Some portion of the population benefits directly from such assets in the way of personal visits or other direct experience; this benefit generates *use value.* Members of society, both direct users and non-users, also attach non-use values to these assets (sometimes subdivided as option, bequest, or existence values). Cultural assets contribute to the integrity and continuity of social identity in a way that enhances the quality of life for all members of society, giving those assets *tradition* or *existence value.* Each component of the value of the benefits generated by cultural assets can be important and must be considered in calculating overall values lost.

Methods for estimating the value of cultural assets are not highly developed. Appraisers can estimate *market values,* but such prices often will understate the full social value of the asset. Therefore, it is necessary to develop proxies for market prices, that is, indirect measures of what people are willing to pay for an asset. One approach is to estimate the *costs* society has shown itself willing to bear for preservation of an asset. In this case, one must be careful to single out the *net value (i.e.,* aggregate willingness to pay less preservation costs) that would be lost by destruction of the asset. Other methods of non-market valuation can be adopted from environmental economics: the *travel cost* method, which is a variation of the opportunity cost method; and the *contingent valuation* method, which uses survey techniques to estimate a population's willingness to pay for an asset.

Damages to Human Capital: Valuing Human Morbidity and Mortality

When an individual is injured or becomes ill due to a natural hazard event, the major impacts take the form of 1) the loss of the individual's productivity in the household, 2) the loss of the individual's productivity in market-related production activities, and 3) the disutility of physical and psychological malaise. As noted earlier, loss of household productivity typically is ignored. Market-related productivity losses will be picked up in terms of losses of value added in business activities. Measures of physical and psychological malaise would be ideally determined by the individual's willingness to pay to avoid discomfort, but this is a difficult task. Thus, *a lower bound* on human discomfort can be taken to be the value of the cost of medical care given to the individual.

Valuing lost lives is a contentious activity. Certainly the protection of human life is the major concern of natural hazards policy. The procedure of capitalizing (calculating the present value of) lost income is now recognized as inadequate. The relevant concept of human life is not that of a particular person after the natural hazard event, but that of an increase in expected life losses before an event. Survey methods to elicit persons' willingness to pay for a reduction in risk, stated as a reduction in the expected number of deaths, are now considered the appropriate measure (e.g., Mitchell and Carson, 1989). In cases where monetized values must be used, values from numerous studies are available. For practical purposes, it should be adequate to report the number of deaths and the locational and socioeconomic characteristics of the victims.

Damages to Natural Capital

Some damages to natural capital (e.g., rivers, lakes, forests, and other natural areas) can be included with the economic damages due to loss of household and market-related productivity. If recreational activities are interrupted or permanently destroyed, or if valuable standing timber is destroyed, survey valuation techniques or market prices can be applied to the physical measures of damage. However, current concern for the environment goes beyond monetized ecosystem damage. This section provides a brief summary of noneconomic measures of changes in ecosystems brought about by natural *hazard* events.

Natural hazard events impact the environment in many ways. A volcanic eruption may pollute the air and cause sedimentation in streams. Tidal surges and tsunamis may contaminate coastal lands and aquifers with salt water. Some of these impacts lead directly to monetizable damages and should be included in the economic assessment section of the multiple-objective appraisal of the event. Other impacts on the environment may not produce discernible damages following the event, but may set in motion subsequent environmental changes that may cause later damages. For example, the collapse of a remote mountain dam following an earthquake may not immediately affect any human activities, but the deposition of rocks, gravel, and silt in adjacent valleys may eventually modify available grazing lands for wild or domestic stock or change flood-flow pathways. Such ecosystem changes need to be recorded, described, and monitored; they can be recounted in the environmental section of the multiple-objective assessment of the natural hazard event and should include economic losses related to the environmental changes.

Assessing ecosystem change can be straightforward if the ecological effects of the natural hazard event are primarily direct effects. However, changes that are delayed, indirect, or cumulative are often of greater importance than direct effects and require assessments that involve predictions of ecosystem behavior. Also, predictions of the pattern and rate of ecological recovery are necessary if mitigation of ecosystem damage is being considered. In other words, both predictions of ecosystem behavior and identification and measurement of direct ecological effects may be important in assessing the impacts of natural hazard events.

Choosing the most applicable spatial scale for observing the landscape greatly impacts the perceived effects of the natural hazard event. At a regional scale, the local loss of a few windblown trees could be negligible; however, at a local scale, the same loss of a few trees could constitute ecological damage if, for example, locally important wildlife habitat is destroyed. The concept is equivalent to taking the appropriate *accounting stance.* A national accounting stance (i.e., large-scale ecological boundaries) could fail to show a locally important effect, while a local accounting stance (i.e., small-scale ecological boundaries) could show a serious impact that is not, however, an impact at the regional scale.

Environmental impacts should be examined in the context of the natural hazard event cycle. The pre-event stage is the long-range planning and preparation stage in which baseline data should be gathered on the characteristics of the ecosystem. These data may also help predict impacts on valued ecosystem components. If predicted impacts are severe enough, it may be necessary to undertake a mitigation strategy to reduce or eliminate undesirable effects or plan a rehabilitation strategy.

In the immediate pre- and post-event stage, the main concern is the preservation of environmental attributes valued by humans, for example, when deciding which locations receive higher priority in containing an oil spill.

In the post-event stage, assessing what damage has occurred to valued ecosystem components is a major task. Assessment involves prediction of indirect, delayed, and cumulative impacts as well as measurement of direct impacts. The assessment should include a prediction of whether natural recovery processes will restore the ecosystem to a state considered desirable by society in an acceptable period of time. (The ecological effects of and recovery from the 1980 eruption of Mt. St. Helens have been the subject of numerous studies that documented the post-event changes that took place.) If damage is severe enough, and the natural recovery process is not satisfactory, rehabilitation strategies must be specified.

Assessment of ecological damage following a disturbance will be considerably more accurate and informative if baseline data have been gathered prior to the event and if monitoring continues during the recovery phase. Checklists should enumerate types of potential impacts and include guidelines for impact identification and evaluation. Within each impact type, particular ecosystem parameters should be listed and measured to indicate the size of the impact. Simple checklists are useful in the early phases of environmental impact assessment. An example of a useful checklist is found in Table 4.

The natural hazard event can also be treated as an experiment, particularly if it created major impacts and their outcome is uncertain. A program to monitor the effects of the event or its mitigation can detect unexpected impacts, which can then be used to adjust future responses (Beanland and Duinker, 1986; Munn, 1985; National Research Council, 1986;

Ward, 1978). Holling (1978) suggested adaptive management, which bases decisions on the need for increased knowledge and includes experimentation designed to increase information about ecological effects.

Recent developments in remote sensing, geographic information systems, and computer modeling provide some powerful methods that will aid us in predicting future impact scenarios and understanding better the contribution that natural *hazard* events make to spatial patterns and landscape mosaics. Geographic information systems (GISs) are modeling systems using computer mapping and data tables to generate layers of information about ecosystems. Models can also produce data predicting ecosystem behavior. Some studies have also used a geographic information system with various species-habitat and spatial-population models.

Both the natural hazard event and the ecosystem need to be measured in the proper context. What is the nature of the disturbance? For example, is it a 100-year flood? Is it a severe crown fire? What is the nature of the ecological system at the site? Is it an old-growth forest? Is it an overgrazed grassland? What existing data are there? In many cases, a field survey will be needed to collect on-site information.

It is important to identify temporal and spatial boundaries early in the environmental assessment. Boundaries are critical to designing the study, interpreting results, predicting effects, and determining impact significance. Response and recovery times must also be considered when planning the time frame of the study. In addition, the observed effects of a natural hazard event can be critically affected by the spatial scale employed to evaluate the landscape.

Continued study of an affected site is necessary to determine whether predictions of the impacts from the event or from human mitigation activities are correct. Such knowledge allows preparation for future events and any needed adjustments (Holling, 1978). Monitoring should continue at least for the recovery period. Monitoring programs need to be well planned so that they use a minimum of time and money and focus on the most valued or least understood components (Beanland and Duinker, 1983).

The ecological damage assessment guidelines are intended to be adaptable to the needs of particular agencies and types of natural hazard events. Past success in evaluating ecological impacts has been poor; therefore, a systematic approach should be taken. There is substantial need for both intra- and interagency coordination in designing environmental evaluations. Impacts should be conceptualized at appropriate scales for managing natural resources; these scales should not necessarily bear relation to the scale of agency jurisdictions. At inappropriate scales important ecological effects, including cumulative impacts, may be missed.

Table 4. Outline of Potentially Useful Field Survey Data (Expanded and Modified from Ward 1978)

Ecosystem Structure (Components)

- *Species composition, abundance, and growth form and stature*-can be measured by looking at ecological density for entire area; density for specific habitat; relative abundance (e.g., number of rabbits seen in x time at y place); normal fluctuations; growth form (e.g., tree, shrub, tall herb, or low herb); and relationship and connectedness to substrate
  - *Feeding relationships among species*
  - *Ecological dominance and key species*-(important in maintaining the particular structure and overall functions of *a* community). Ecological dominance refers to a species that controls a major portion of community energy flow (e.g., high abundance, biomass, or productivity). Key species are species that have strong influences on most other organisms in a community, and, if removed, would drastically change community. Elements can initially be identified by visual identification.
  - *Species diversity*-can be affected by many variables and does not provide an accurate indicator of the health of an ecosystem. Must be careful not to overestimate. Recommend using number of species rather than other measures.
  - *Indicator species and ecological indicators*-used to evaluate prevailing conditions. It is better to use several species than a single species. More reliable to use a more general characteristic or a direct measure than an indicator. Recommend *not* measuring a small species population with high turnover.
  - *Size, shape, and heterogeneity of disturbed areas, and, if more extensive, boundaries of the resources affected by the natural hazard event*
  - *Physical factors,* such as topography

Ecosystem Function (Processes)

- *Productivity equals rate of production of organic matter* - this measure indicates the capacity of a physical system io support life. Should measure total rate or one component. Most commonly measured function is "net primary," which measures gross (total photosynthetic) minus respiratory use. The standing crop or biomass on-site is not equal to productivity, but is acceptable if producers are large and long-lived and immediate consumption of products is minimal.
- *Trophic structure and energy flow* - energy acts in an open system (e.g., solar = input, heat dissipation = output). Goal is only to estimate, to see whole system and biological importance of components. Nutrition relations make up the food web. Recommend grouping species with similar nutritional needs.
- *Nutrient relationships* - occur in a closed system (e.g., pools of nitrogen, phosphorous, etc.). Nutrient concentrations, pathways, and rates of transfer may change due to natural hazard event. These changes may affect species composition.
- *Decomposition processes* - difficult to study, but are important and complex. Temperature and water are important factors. These processes are not usually studied in environmental impact assessments. These processes occur via physical and biological action, with biological actions occurring primarily due to bacteria and fungi. Can either study certain organisms or total activity.
- *Succession and development of communities* - succession is reasonably directional change in species structure of a community over time. Look at population age and size structure and reproductive success of species.
- *Individual species characteristics* (e.g., reproductive strategies, success, and health of organisms)

Other

- *Disturbance event characteristics* (e.g., intensity of the event)
- *Evidence of other or potential natural hazard events*
- *Evidence of or potential for cumulative impacts*
- *Evidence of patterns and rates of recovery*
- *Characteristics of neighboring ecosystems and organisms that may colonize or affect the disturbed area*
- *Evidence of controlling or limiting environmental factors (resource availability) or driving physical/chemical forces on ecosystem.*

Summary

Identifying and measuring directly imposed economic damages are the most important steps in quantifying natural hazard damages. The objective is to monetize the "real" damages that take two main forms: 1) damages to natural, human-made, and human assets, and 2) delays or losses of value added in production processes. Double counting of real damages and their financial reflections (e.g., changes in stock values) must be avoided.

The measure of damage to human-made capital assets is complicated by the irrelevance of most accounting book values. If there is complete destruction and full replacement with new assets is warranted, damages ideally are measured by the depreciated replacement value or the market price of similar used assets.

If assets are damaged and rehabilitation to previous status is warranted because the gain in benefits will exceed costs of rehabilitation, a practical lower bound is the cost of rehabilitation. If no rehabilitation is warranted, then damages must be measured as the present value of the loss of value added.

When production is interrupted by a hazard event because of unavailability of purchased inputs, damage to the production site, or inability to sell the product, it must be determined whether the production has been

permanently lost or just delayed. Value added that is merely delayed but will be made up results in a much lower present value of damages than value added that is permanently lost.

Value added in the public sector (government administration or service activities) that is lost due to a hazard event is generally measured by the cost of the services, since there usually is no market price for such services. When special public sector hazard response services are required by a hazard event, the added costs of these services constitute damages attributable to the event.

The dangers of double counting or over counting damages must be emphasized. A common and incorrect practice is to count the *total* value of production delayed or lost rather than just the value added. Another incorrect example is found in flood damage estimates that contain both lost production and lost incomes from the same production.

A national accounting stance is almost always appropriate. However, local jurisdictions will be interested in past or prospective relief programs that reduce the local incidence of costs. Relief payments and rehabilitation subsidies reduce the damages borne by the locality, but not the real damages.

References

Beanland, Gordon E., and Peter N. Duinker. 1983. *An Ecological Framework for Environmental Impact Assessment in Canada, Halifax, Nova Scotia.* Dalhousie University Institute for Resource and Environmental Studies.

Bendavid, Avrom. 1972. *Regional Economic Analysis for Practitioners.* New York: Praeger Publishers.

Brookshire, D.S., and W.D. Schulze. 1990. *Methods Development for Valuing Hazards Information.* Technical Report Prepared for the United States Geological Survey, Contract No. 14-08-001-17529.

Clark, William C. 1977. "Managing The Unknown," in Robert W. Kates (ed.), *Managing Technological Hazard: Research Needs and Opportunities, pp.* 111-154. Boulder, Colorado: University of Colorado, Institute of Behavioral Science, Program on Technology, Environment and Man, Monograph #2.

Cummings, R.G., D.S. Brookshire, and W.D. Schulze. 1986. *Valuing Environmental Goods: An Assessment of the Contingent Valuation Method.* New York: Rowman and Allenheld.

Friesma, P., J. Caporaso, G. Goldstein, R. Lineberry, and R. McClearly. 1979. *Aftermath: Communities and Natural Disasters.* Beverly Hills: Sage Publications.

Grazulis, Thomas P. 1988. *A Flood Loss Assessment and Data Base.* Report to National Science Foundation Advisory Committee, March 27. NSF Grant No. CES-8709735. 1989 *A Flood Loss Assessment and Data Base.* Report to National Science Foundation Advisory Committee, February 2. NSF Grant No. CES-8709735.

Greenley, Douglas A., Richard G. Walsh, and Robert A. Young. 1982. *Economic Benefits of Improved Water Quality: Public Perception of Option and Preservation Values.* Boulder, Colorado: Westview Press.

Holling, C.S. (ed.) 1978.*Adaptive Environmental Assessment and Management.* New York: John Wiley and Sons.

Howe, Charles W., Harold C. Cochrane, Jane E. Bunin, and Robert W. Kling. 1991. *Natural Hazard Damage Handbook.* National Technical Information Center.

Knetsch, Jack. 1972. *Economics of Water-Based Recreation.* Washington, D.C.: American Geophysical Union.

Krutilla, John V., and Anthony Fisher. 1975.*The Economics of Natural Environments.* Baltimore: Johns Hopkins Press.

Michell, R.C., and R.T. Carson. 1989. *Using Surveys to Value Public Goods: The Contingent Valuation Method.* Washington, D.C.: Resources for the Future.

Munn, R.E. (ed.) 1985. *Environmental Impact Assessment: Principles and Procedures* (Second Edition), SCOPE 5. Chichester: John Wiley and Sons.

Pleeter, Saul. 1980. *Economic Impact Analysis: Methodology and Applications.* Boston and The Hague: Martinus Nijhoff Publishing.

Pryor, L.D. 1988. *Ecological Mismanagement in Natural Disasters,* Commission on Ecology Papers Number 2, International Union for Conservation of Nature and Natural Resources, The Environmentalist 2: Supplement No. 2: 1-14.

Roberts, R. Blaine, Jerome W. Milliman, and Richard W. Ellson. 1982. *Earthquake Predictions: Simulating Their Economic Effects.* Technical Report prepared for NSF under Grant PRF80-19826.

Russell, Clifford S., David G. Arey, and Robert W. Kates. 1970. *Drought and Water Supply: Implications of the Massachusetts Experience for Municipal Planning.* Baltimore: Johns Hopkins University Press for Resources for the Future.

U.S. Department of Commerce, Bureau of the Census. 1989. *National Data Book and Guide to Sources: Statistical Abstract of the United States 1989.* Washington, D.C.: United States Government Printing Office.

Ward, Diana Valiela. 1978. *Biological Environmental Studies: Theory and Methods.* New York: Academic Press.

Water Resources Council. 1979. "Principles and Guidelines: Procedures for Evaluation of National Economic Development, Final Rule," *Federal Register,* 44(242).

Young, Robert A., and S. Lee Gray. 1984. *Regional Models, Welfare Economics and the Evaluation of State Water Plans.* Department of Agricultural and Natural Resource Economics, Colorado State University.

ACKNOWLEDGEMENTS

This article is reprinted with permission from the Program on Environment and Behavior, Institute of Behavioral Science, University of Colorado.

In: Economics and the Wind
Editors: B. T. Ewing, et. al., pp. 179-183

ISBN: 1-59454-280-5
©2005 Nova Science Publishers, Inc.

Chapter 15

ECONOMICS AS A COMPONENT OF A MULTIDISCIPLINARY WIND RESEARCH PROGRAM

Kishor Mehta
Wind Science and Engineering Research
Center, Texas Tech University, Lubbock, Texas Tech University, USA

INTRODUCTION

Due to the increase in population and economic development, especially in coastal areas, our society is increasingly exposed to atmospheric hazards such as hurricanes, tornadoes and severe thunderstorms. Every year these hazards cause many fatalities and injuries, major disruption in community lifelines such as power, communications, transportation and commerce in addition to a large amount of property damage. Nationwide, losses due to atmospheric hazards have increased exponentially over the last decade and could reach more than $50 billion annually in the next decade. The wind environment can be detrimental (eg. windstorms) as well as beneficial for ventilation and wind energy. Since the wind environment will be with us forever, it is crucial that we accomplish fundamental improvement in our understanding of atmospheric phenomena; develop and apply advanced engineering techniques; identify effective policy that is cognizant of underlying economic forces and human behavior. In so doing we have the opportunity to improve the quality of life for the current generation as well as future generations.

WIND RESEARCH AS A MULTIDISCIPLINARY EFFORT

Research on the effects of windstorms encompasses several disciplinary areas of research. The multidisciplinary research is pursued under an umbrella of Wind Science and Engineering (WISE) Research Center at Texas Tech University. In order to produce effective policy tools research thrust areas must include (1) Structural Response and Design concepts, (2) the Atmospheric Boundary Layer and (3) Economics and Risk Management. If we implement public policy that relies on our knowledge in one research thrust area while ignoring the others, the policy will not meet expectations at best or is doomed to failure at worst. This section breaks down and describes research topics within and cutting across these main research thrusts.

Structural Response and Design Concepts

Understanding the complex interaction of turbulent wind in the atmospheric boundary layer with buildings and structures and mitigating the effects of severe winds is the focus of this research thrust. This goal requires an understanding of experimental and computational fluid mechanics, full- and model-scale (wind tunnel) experimental techniques, static and dynamic structural analysis, structural design and building and structure failure mechanisms.

Post-disaster investigations provide the real-life background for research in structural response and design for the extreme wind environment. Damage surveys provide the information for an extensive damage documentation database. Current surveys coupled with the meticulous work of other researchers provide information of the meteorology of the storm, the resulting wind field, windborne debris generation, the effects of debris impact, structural response of buildings and structures, the damage incurred to the civil infrastructure, and estimates of the economic losses resulting from the windstorm.

Protecting life and mitigating property damage from severe wind events demands detailed knowledge of the wind environment and of the inventory of civil infrastructure. Post-disaster surveys provide the crucial source of information on these rare but devastating storms. Several steps are critical in the process: establishing the overall storm path, characterizing the wind and debris environment that impacts structures in the path, and assessing damage to individual structures. There are significant uncertainties in the process. For example, in tornadoes the ground level wind speeds are assessed based on the appearance of damage, which is highly subjective and dependent on the structures in the path, their design, and their quality of construction.

Expert elicitation is used to provide subjective interpretation of the intensities of a tornado. Expert elicitation reduces subjective biases that may occur with an individual's assessment of damage. It is difficult to assess precisely the extent of damage and associated wind speeds because of the large number of uncontrolled variables. A project to refine F-scale for tornado is underway that rates tornado intensity based on an engineering expert elicitation process. If the results are accepted by the National Weather service it will be termed Enhanced Fujita (EF) scale.

Another procedure, Fuzzy Set Theory (FST) has a high potential to incorporate uncertainties in assessment of damage. Fuzzy modeling provides a mathematical foundation for qualitative and subjective assessments. FST accounts for uncertainty and replaces informal and ad-hoc approaches to analyzing imprecise and vague information. Since overall characterization of damage is made with linguistic variables, a fuzzy assessment of the tornado path in terms of F-scale is one way of representing the uncertainties. Examples of uncertainties associated with each building might include maximum wind speeds, duration of the wind loading, quality of construction, cause of failure, characteristics of the debris field and so on.

A major barrier to compiling an adequate database for advanced mathematical and statistical applications is the time-consuming nature of the work. Following a storm assessing damage to individual structures requires a large group of skilled personnel to conduct the survey in a timely manner. Research in remote sensing of damage using satellite imagery, image processing and GIS will overcome the problems of time- and personnel-consuming nature of damage documentation.

Bluff Body Aerodynamics is the study of the flow impinging on buildings and the resulting pressures on surfaces of the structures. In order to predict the structural response of buildings and their components for design, full-scale and model scale experiments are used. The experiments are used to establish point-and-area pressure due to architectural features of low rise buildings such as overhanging eaves and parapet walls. Wind tunnel testing of model scale buildings and structures has been used extensively in wind research. Full scale tests with naturally occurring wind are important to verify results found in the 1/10 to 1/400 scale models used in wind tunnel.. Differences exist between full scale and model scale measurements. Research continues to address and resolve these differences.

Structural Design is the end result of engineering research and risk management. The goal of this research area is to produce economically effective and reliable wind resistant design. Establishment of national standards for wind loads (ASCE-7 National Standard for Wind Loads) has a significant impact on local building codes and resulting construction. The process of producing designs based on sound research reaches its final step with full-scale structural testing. Saferoom designs for residential and public shelter have been produced and tested. Future challenges are to develop wind damage mitigation strategies that are cost effective. On a long term basis structural research will need to develop performance based criteria for design that are compatible with the risks acceptable to developers and owners.

The Atmospheric Boundary Layer

The study of wind-related effects depends on the ability to understand surface winds occurring in nature. Wind, which is movement of air, depends on large scale weather phenomena. Atmospheric scientists around the world continue to pursue research on large weather phenomena by direct and indirect measurements and numerical modeling. Built environment and people are affected primarily by surface winds; these winds at micro-scale can be understood by field measurements and statistical modeling. Surface wind characteristics are important in model scale (wind tunnel) simulations of structural response of buildings and structures.

Field Observation of Boundary Layer Processes

Field efforts are required to build a database of observations for numerical model initialization, validation and verification. Areas of continuing research include surface layer wind fields in hurricanes and observational studies of thunderstorms wind field characteristics and evolution. Portable meteorological instrumented towers and Doppler on Wheels (DOW) radars are used to obtain measurements in landfalling hurricanes and in outflow regions of thunderstorms. Use of several towers permit assessment of spatial and temporal characteristics of wind gusts. The observations can be converted to mathematical/numerical models through statistical procedures.

Mathematical Analysis and Numerical Prediction of Wind Related Phenomenon

Due to inherent challenge of measuring atmospheric wind fields and conditions directly, the use of modeling to depict the characteristics and evolution of the atmosphere is advantageous. Fertile research areas for this type of analysis include:

- Using mesoscale numerical modeling to study the threat of windborne chemical and biological agents.
- Mathematical modeling of tornado windfields.
- Parametric estimates of wind spectra from short time series.
- Identification of localized structures in direct wind field measurements.
- Correlation of localized damage patterns with Doppler radar and satellite measurements for real-time evacuation decision-making.

Economics and Risk Management

The magnitude of damage caused by an extreme wind event depends on: 1) the severity of the weather and 2) the human decisions that place persons and property at risk. This research thrust focuses on the interaction between weather and human decisions. Decisions by individual households and companies use a much different perspective than decisions made by public officials. Their objectives, at times, may even be at odds. Household decisions include residential location, insurance, mitigation and disaster response. Household decisions are based on risk perceptions and current incentive structures as they relate to the well-being of the family unit. The response of individual decision-makers to windstorm risk will depend on a number of socioeconomic factors which include household makeup (e.g. children, elderly, pets) wealth, ethnicity, and gender. Company decisions are made with the goal of maximizing the value of the company. Decisions are based on the available information concerning the risk, knowledge of mitigation technologies and the risk posture of management.

Public officials measure the success of their decisions in terms of the well-being of a community or region. Decisions by public officials must reflect a thorough understanding of the economic benefits and costs (including externalities) of an action as well as the probable response by individuals to the policy decision. Examples of public decisions that in turn affect business and household decisions include:

- Urban planning
- Evacuation planning
- Public shelter provision
- Building code creation and enforcement.
- Insurance regulation.
- Emergency response.
- Targeted taxes and subsidies.
- Compliance enforcement.

CONCLUDING REMARKS

This research volume is devoted to the third of the three research thrusts described above. If we look closely, the first two research thrusts are focused on creating an accurate and information-rich environment that supports the decision process. The economics/risk management area provides the last piece of the puzzle to support the decision process. It provides the "missing metric" described in the RAND Report, "Assessing Federal Research and Development for Hazard Loss Reduction" (Meade and Abbott, 2003). This metric is a monetary measure that allows for comparison across diverse alternative wind risk mitigation decisions that have both public and private consequences. The alternative strategies can be as diverse as choosing whether:

- to offer tax subsidies for residential wind mitigation measures versus placing the wind mitigation measure requirement in the local building code.
- to construct more highways, subsidize construction of saferooms, or invest in better weather forecasting technology to improve lead time to solve the problem of evacuation congestion in populated coastal areas.
- to allow the development of locations vulnerable to wind and flood with mitigation measures or set them aside as green space.

This third research thrust also gives a glimpse of the "human factor" that must be considered when assessing the probable impact of any public policy. Lessons learned in the past tell us that people do not always behave as described by model assumptions. Decision models that allow for diverse and sometimes seemingly perverse choices in their sensitivity analysis will lead to robust highly effective public policy.

REFERENCES

Meade, C. and M. Abbott. 2003. *Assessing Federal Research and Development for Hazard Loss Reduction. Prepared for the White House Office of Science Technology and Policy,* RAND, Santa Monica, CA.

INDEX

A

B

C

D

E

R

S

T

U

V

W